CJ Lim + Ed Liu

# smartcities
## + eco-warriors

Routledge

# Smartcities + Eco-warriors

**Dedicated to Matthew Wells, Andy Ford, and Colin Hayward**

First published 2010
by Routledge
2 Park Square, Milton Park, Abingdon, Oxfordshire, OX14 4RN

Simultaneously published in the USA and Canada by Routledge
270 Madison Ave, New York, NY 10016

Routledge is an imprint of the Taylor & Francis Group, an informa business

© 2010 CJ Lim / Studio 8 Architects

Printed and bound by Graphos SA, Barcelona, Spain

British Library Cataloguing in Publication Data
A catalogue record for this book is available from the British Library

Library of Congress Cataloging-in-Publication Data
Lim, C. J.
Smartcities and eco-warriors / C.J. Lim and Ed Liu.
p. cm.
Includes index.
1. Urbanization--Environmental aspects--Case studies. 2. Sustainable design--Case studies. I. Liu, Ed. II. Title.
HT361.L56 2010
307.76--dc22                                        2009049744

ISBN10: 0-415-57122-7 (hbk)        ISBN13: 978-0-415-57122-7 (hbk)
ISBN10: 0-415-57124-3 (pbk)        ISBN13: 978-0-415-57124-1 (pbk)
ISBN10: 0-203-85032-7 (ebk)        ISBN13: 978-0-203-85032-9 (ebk)

# Contents

# Preface

What is a Smartcity? 'Smartcity' is a vision. A vision of how the city of the 21st century might appear if we are serious about living sustainably and wish to leave any form of legacy to our descendants. Instead of a reactive approach to the manifold problems that contemporary life has thrown up, the Smartcity examines how we might live from first principles, taking the key component of any city – its people – as its starting point and raison d'être.

This book represents the culmination of CJ Lim and Studio 8 Architects' ongoing explorations into sustainable city design that began with a proposal to revitalize the community landscape of Chicago's DuSable Park in 2001 and matured with Guangming Smartcity, a new town in Southern China for 200 000 inhabitants. The Smartcity is a vision of an urban future from an architectural perspective as opposed to a planning, environmental engineering or socio-economic one. Current discourse on sustainability appears either to focus on the technical aspects of ecological design at the scale of individual buildings or establishes the general principles for planning urban environments: 'Smartcities + Eco-warriors' attempts to address what the spatial and phenomenological implications are when sustainable design is applied to a city, what new hybrid typologies of programme and landscape are birthed, and the role that we as citizens rather than designers will play in the production of a relevant social space.

This book is structured around a series of international case studies, some commissioned by government organizations, others speculative and polemic. What makes an architect's reading of urban design different from that of a planner is a human-scale design sensibility. A constant running through the projects is the application of a modular in the tradition of Vitruvius, da Vinci, Alberti and Le Corbusier, but one that pertains to social relations rather than the ratios of physical dimensions. Hence the frequent reference to domestic vernacular such as urban living rooms, garden cities and metropolitan carpets.

A central component of the Smartcity is urban agriculture and the establishment of an ecological symbiosis between nature and built form. Over human history, agrarian economies have been replaced by industrial economies that have in turn been supplanted by post-industrial economies. The Smartcity postulates that the next and final stage of evolution can only be a circular economy that subsumes agriculture, energy and industry into co-dependency and self-perpetuation.

Finally, the Smartcity is a manifesto and provocation. It should not be seen as an exercise in architectural monomania, but an invitation to planners, politicians, scientists and engineers to further a holistic dialogue and to stimulate activity. The book therefore concludes with a series of essays written by experts representing divergent positions including food urbanist Carolyn Steel, architectural historian (MIT) Mark Jarzombek and David Satterthwaite of the International Institute for Environment and Development (IIED).

# Urban Utopias and the Smartcity

**UTOPIA**

**noun**

**an imagined place or state of things in which everything is perfect. The word was first used in the book 'Utopia' (1516) by Sir Thomas More. The opposite of dystopia.**

**origin based on Greek ou 'not' + topos 'place'.** [1]

At the time of writing, more than half of mankind, some 3.3 billion people, are living in urban areas. By 2030, this is expected to swell to almost five billion.[2] We are simultaneously experiencing a global food crisis resulting from low productivity, government policies diverting food crops to the creation of biofuels, climate change, and intensifying demands from an exponentially expanding population. 'The world is heading for a drop in agricultural production of 20 to 40 percent, depending on the severity and length of the current global droughts. Food producing nations are imposing food export restrictions. Food prices will soar and, in poor countries with food deficits, millions will starve.[3]

In November 1992, 1700 of the world's leading scientists issued a warning to humanity, urging a response to the unsustainably high consumption levels of finite energy resources, the reckless creation of deleterious effluent, and the generation of greenhouse gases causing irreparable damage to vital planetary systems.[4] While the Kyoto Protocol came into force in February 2005 with the aim of preventing detrimental anthropogenic effects on the climate system, it appears unlikely that the protocol's signatories will deliver on their obligations. James Lovelock, author of 'The Revenge of Gaia' and 'The Vanishing Face of Gaia', foresees an unavoidable and radical climatic shift resulting in an environment less suitable for human habitation. In the absence of humanity mounting a massive 'sustainable retreat', he postulates 'a global decline into a chaotic world ruled by brutal warlords on a devastated earth'.[5]

At the same time, the world's economic order, premised on capital accumulation with scant regard to social well-being and employment, is leading inexorably to extreme socio-economic differentiation and a fractured society of the privileged and the dispossessed. The vast populations that make up modern cities result at best in weak social ties, at worst, mass control with concomitant violence and repression. As Lefebvre wrote in 'La Révolution Urbaine' in 1970, the big city sanctifies inequality, and is the most favourable milieu for the establishment of authoritarian power, pressing the countryside into servitude.[6] Long before the telematic assault of the virtual world, the Situationists described the alienating nature of the city as a strange hybrid of crowd and solitude. The advent of the internet and online transactions

facing page: NASA Earth observatory photograph of fields in Kansas: corn, sorghum and wheat crops using pivot irrigation

1. 'Oxford Pocket Dictionary of Current English', Oxford University Press, USA, 2009

2. J Moncrieffe et al., 'UNFPA State of world population 2008 Report', United Nations Population Fund, New York, 2008

3. E deCarbonnel, 'Catastrophic Fall in 2009 Global Food Production', Global Research, retrieved 3 September 2009, www.globalresearch.ca/index.php?context=va&aid=12252

4. 'World scientist's warning to humanity', authored by Henry Kendall, former chair of the Union of Concerned Scientists and endorsed by the majority of Nobel laureates in the sciences

5. J Lovelock, 'The Revenge of Gaia: Why the Earth is Fighting Back and How We Can Still Save Humanity,' Allen Lane, London, 2006, p.154

6. H Lefebvre, 'La Révolution Urbaine', Gallimard, Paris, 1970

has formed a society of now faceless, as well as nameless, strangers with an attendant diminution in social constraints motivated by anonymity.

Global famine. A poisoned earth. Societal collapse. Civilization, it appears, is leading us down a path of ruin and steering us towards dystopia rather than utopia. Lovelock, in particular, portends an apocalyptic future one might expect from a science fiction author or religious prophet rather than a respected environmental scientist. In actuality, the complexity of weather systems and the factors that affect climate are still not well understood, lending plausibility to climate change denial. Whether the case has been overstated or not, there is an overwhelming consensus of opinion amongst the worldwide scientific community that deforestation and the burning of fossil fuels have led to grave environmental problems. Evidence of the current and escalating global deficiency in food security is uncontested but has only recently received any media coverage or impetus to drive political action. With the inevitable exponential growth of the urban environment, future cities incorporating mechanisms for food production, responsible energy use and social unity must be reassessed along with our visions for utopia.

By definition an unreachable destination, broadsides on utopia have been launched since its very inception. The word 'utopian' is more often than not used in the pejorative, pertaining to proposals featuring alternate realities rather than dealing with society's real and pressing ills. Such criticism misses the point and dismisses the potency of the utopic vision. Plato's 'Republic' (400 BC), Thomas More's 'Utopia' (1516) and Francis Bacon's 'New Atlantis' (1627) were intended as neither fantasies nor blueprints for reification, but reflections on the societies in which they were written. More significantly, they provided a stalking horse for the development and evolution of new communities that would improve on the status quo. Ebenezer Howard's garden city, for example, was inspired by the utopian tract, 'Looking Backward: 2000–1887', by the American lawyer, Edward Bellamy. The third largest bestseller of its time when published in 1888, Bellamy's novel immediately spawned a political mass movement and several communities living according to its ideals. Letchworth Garden City and Welwyn Garden City in the UK are founded on Howard's concentric plan of open space, parkland and radial boulevards. Housing, agriculture and industry are carefully integrated, and the developments remain two of the few recognized realizations of utopia in existence. There are valid concerns, however, that the tradition of utopian town planning as advocated by the Congress for the new urbanism (CNU) and developments such as the Duchy of Cornwall-owned Poundbury, are elitist and non-inclusive. The cost of utopia is what lies outside utopia, the forgotten communities and infrastructure required to support it, a counterpoint that is sharply observed in the Peter Weir film, 'The Truman Show', depicting the New Urbanist town of Seaside in Florida.

The 21st century has witnessed a phenomenal escalation in urban construction; entire cities are emerging fully formed in India and China rather than slowly evolving and accreting, made possible by the availability of affordable yet skilled labour, land and an uncompromising autocratic vision. Without invoking the term utopia, the aspiration and inspiration of nascent cities such as Dongtan in China and Masdar in the United Arab Emirates, both heralded as the first model eco-city, are both clear and vital. A model for how we should be living with improved modes of transportation, hydrological control systems, streamlined energy and supply programmes, and agencies for societal cohesion must surely be planned, albeit in forms protean enough to deal with the vicissitudes of urban living.

Sustainable design of the built environment has largely focused on discrete buildings, and we have become relatively adept at incorporating insulation, cooling, natural ventilation, solar control, greywater recycling, green roofs and

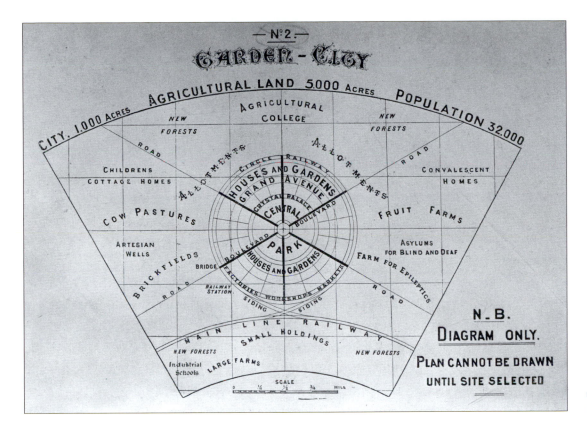

left: Plan of an Ideal Garden City,
1902; Sir Ebenezer Howard

renewable energy collection into architecture. Cities, though, are infinitely more complex than buildings, and the shift in scale to sustainable city design calls for a radically different approach to take advantage of the synergistic systems available. A conglomeration of buildings offers thermal efficiencies that are unachievable with smaller detached structures. The compact city, as championed by Richard Rogers, makes communal transport truly viable over the private car. During his address at the Reith Lectures of 1995, 'Cities for a Small Planet', Rogers presented a series of startling statistics demonstrating how the automobile has shaped the city. 'An efficient parking standard requires twenty square metres for a single car. Even supposing that only one in five inhabitants owns a car, then, a city of ten million (roughly that of London) needs an area about ten times the size of the City of London ('the square mile'), just to park cars.'[7] 'As transport by car becomes integral to city planning, the street corners and the shapes and surfaces of public spaces are all determined for the benefit of the motorist. Eventually the entire city, from its overall shape and spacing of new buildings to the design of its curbs, lamp posts and railings, is designed according to this one criterion.'[8] Now imagine a city with no cars – the possibilities are legion.

A high density mixed-use city also allows waste products to be shared and recycled, land-use to be zoned vertically as well as horizontally, and the implementation of urban agriculture and energy generation at a meaningful scale. In addition to environmental benefits, public and private space can be configured to promote social inclusion and economic growth. In short, the future of sustainable city design cannot be limited to sustainable buildings set within the outdated model of a European masterplan. Currently, the first phase of Masdar City, built by the Abu Dhabi Future Company and designed by Foster + Partners, is

7. R Rogers, 'Cities for A Small Planet: Reith Lectures,' Faber and Faber, London, 1997, p.36

8. ibid

nearing completion and will replace cars entirely with mass and personal rapid transit systems.[9] Significantly, the length of streets have been determined by wind fluid dynamics for urban cooling rather than vehicular traffic efficiency; whether Masdar will deliver a new urban paradigm wholly liberated from any vestigial legacies of car-based infrastructure remains to be seen.

Traditionally, there has been a division of disciplines between architectural and urban planning. City design, a more inclusive term than urban planning, needs to embrace a number of disciplines that extend beyond land-use zoning and plot ratios – we need to engage agronomists, hydrologists, economists, transportation engineers, social scientists and politicians in addition to urban planners and architects. An urban infrastructure freed from the hegemony of the motorcar could and should manifest in a spatial manner radically different from the contemporary metropolis. Furthermore, existing car-based infrastructure – parking lots, motorways, service stations, driveways and garages – will require imaginative overhaul and programmatic adaptation.

'The world is sick. A readjustment has become necessary. Readjustment? No, that is too tame. It is the possibility of a great adventure that lies before mankind: the building of a whole new world ... because there is no time to be lost. And we must not waste time on those who laugh or smile, on those who give us ironical little answers and treat us as mystic madmen. We have to look ahead, at what must be built.'[10]

Le Corbusier's commentary from 1967 might appear prescient, but could have been written at any time in the history of the city. The urban condition raises recurring as well as fresh challenges for every generation. In the past, architects have not been slow to offer their vision of utopia or ideal city, ranging from the polemic (Ron Herron's 'Walking City', 1964) to the serious (Le Corbusier's 'Radiant City', 1935), the futuristic (Paolo Soleri's arcologies) to the arcadian (Frank Lloyd Wright's 'Broadacre City', 1932). Tellingly, the architect's ideal city is frequently characterized by an immediately comprehensible visual order, whether as a grid or radial system. The meme of the concentric-ringed plan, for example, has been proposed by Filarete in the imaginary city of Sforzinda in 1465, John Claudius Loudoun whose 1829 plan for London predated Howard's Garden City green belts by 69 years, and Claude Nicolas Ledoux at the city of Chaux centred around his half-completed Royal Saltworks at Arc-et-Senans. Konstantinos Doxiadis, on the other hand, is a celebrated exponent of the grid city, establishing a flexible plan for Islamabad that allows for gradual low-cost expansion. Other recurring motifs of the ideal city include a coalition between the countryside and the city, the orientation of buildings to a heliothermic axis to maximize daylight, and the liberation of the ground plane for public occupation.

Henri Lefebvre, the French sociologist and author of the seminal neo-Marxist works 'Critique of Everyday Life' and 'The Production of Space', argued that every society produces it's own spatial practice and that without a distinctive space to mould it, a drive for societal change will never escape from its ideological beginnings. He ascribed the failure of the Soviet Constructivists of the 1920s and 1930s to the uncritical recycling of the modern urban masterplan rather than inventing an appropriate new space to shape and be shaped by new social relations. Planners and architects, then, have a crucial role as the agents of social change, and certainly the authors of the ideal city in their various incarnations saw themselves as such. At this critical juncture, the shape of the space that will help us contest climate change, social deprivation, and deficiencies in food, water and energy has to be re-imagined and re-produced.

As producers of space, architects represent a tiny minority of the rest of society who must in turn modify and refine

left: Royal Saltworks, Arc-et-Senans, 1779; Claude Nicolas Ledoux

the blueprint that has been mapped in front of them. They are well placed, however, to understand and design space that is of a human scale and more comprehensible to the general populace than large scale zoning development maps. What will a city draped in a productive landscape or an array of gasification plants look, feel, smell and sound like? As urban real estate becomes increasingly scarce, can we cross-programme public buildings and time-share streets instead of holiday homes? These are questions that require a synthesis of spatial design and a holistic understanding of social, political and economic practice to answer. Fortunately, advances in visualization graphics and computer rendering have made it far easier for designers to describe spatial propositions and as a consequence attract the necessary private and public sector investment to back them. Circumspection is necessary, however, to avoid the prevalence of visual information at the expense of less visceral information, and to ensure that the resulting built environment delivers more than a fleeting resemblance to its conceptual origins.

The central thesis of this book is the re-establishment of closed cyclical systems within urban and peri-urban areas and how they will manifest in the spaces of a notional 'Smartcity', The Smartcity differentiates itself from the 'Eco-city' by embracing new paradigms of programme, form and sociological interaction. It is neither a fixed place nor a singular approach but rather a manifesto for the production of a space relevant for the 21st century.

The Smartcity is not a creation from blank slate, but an evolution of long-standing sustainable principles that intertwine with contemporary desires for a healthier physical, mental and social existence in an increasingly alienating world. It aims to preserve and enhance natural and cultural resources, expand the range of eco-transportation, employment and housing choice and values long-term regional

9. Personal rapid transit (PRT) or podcar describes an on-demand network of small independent vehicles running on guideways. At Masdar, PRT pods will be battery-powered and computer-navigated

10. Le Corbusier, 'The Radiant City: Elements of a Doctrine of Urbanism to be used as the basis of our machine-age civilization', Faber and Faber, London, 1967

sustainability over short-term focus. The currency of an 'eco-' prefix has become devalued through overuse and abuse, and 'sustainability' is a blanket expression – clearly, some aspects of our lifestyle are worth sustaining and others are not. Deciding and acting on which category they fall into, however, is not as straightforward as it appears. Conservation of energy and the environment are key priorities, but so too is the conservation of heritage, tradition and human interaction. Each generation is the proprietor of its own values, and the current zeitgeist has reacted against the mass-produced and anodyne, whether in the guise of housing, jobs and clothing or fruit and vegetables. Without ignoring technological advances, the Smartcity embraces leanness and the low-tech by adopting an operating system that filters out excess and reboots our social space. Smartcity living does not ask for 'more' but determines how to use less in the creation of a healthier mental and physical existence.

At the forefront of the Smartcity manifesto is urban agriculture. The hybridization of agriculture and urban fabric can lead to an association that is symbiotic rather than parasitic, reducing carbon emissions and food shortages in addition to providing less tangible but equally significant environmental and social benefits. Food in most cultures is the glue that binds families and communities, and the restoration of the primal link between town-dwellers and their sustenance would constitute an important foundation to an increasingly ungrounded universe.

The notion that the efficiencies achieved through technology and good design result in increased unemployment is a fallacy – the logical corollary of improved efficiency is increased productivity. In this technologically advanced age we live in, there are shortages of food, shortages of basic living standards, shortages of education and literacy. There should be no shortages of jobs. The Smartcity programme comes with a host of fresh employment opportunities that are cross-sector and require a range of skills in the renewable energy, recycling, agriculture, construction and transportation industries. The business case for 'greening' the economy is robust. A UN report on green jobs indicates that with energy and commodity costs soaring and growing pressure to adopt greener practices, the global market for environmental products and services is projected to double from $1370 billion per year at present to $2740 billion by 2020. Half of this market is based in energy efficiency and the balance in sustainable transport, water supply, sanitation and waste management. The potential for improving labour markets is greatest in developing nations, where over 40% of the global workforce and their dependants are condemned to a life in poverty and insecurity.[11]

Smartcity strategies are inclusive, engaging all age groups, cultures and ethnicities. The Smartcity is an integrated holistic vision, not an appendix or a collection of unrelated ideas. The Smartcity calls for the renaissance of a manual universe in which we do things – grow food, play, travel, and design – from first principles again. It is a mindset questioning the way we live, driven by its inhabitants and prioritizing human sustainability above all else. The rest will follow.

**(i)** **manifesto**

# From Soil to Table

**'And the LORD God made all kinds of trees grow out of the ground – trees that were pleasing to the eye and good for food.'**        **- Genesis 2:9**

**'And the LORD God commanded the man, "You are free to eat from any tree in the garden …"'**
                              **- Genesis 2:16**

Prior to their fall from grace for eating from the tree of knowledge, the fruit from the Garden of Eden provided Adam and Eve with food aplenty without them having to toil for their sustenance. Since humanity's earliest days, we have yearned for immediate access to fresh healthy food. Refrigeration and rapid transport systems have, to a certain extent, made time and distance an irrelevance. In developed nations, however, processing, packaging, transportation and storage account for 80% of the energy used to place food on the kitchen table. Produce in the United States travels an average of 1300 to 2000 miles from farmer to consumer.

It is estimated that an acre of farmland is lost to urbanization and highway production for every added person. It has been projected that by 2025, all food grown in the US – the largest exporter of food worldwide – will be used for domestic purposes. Economically, this will result in an annual $40 billion loss of income. When compounded by the reality that verdant fertile industrialized nations such as the UK have abandoned the objective of self-sufficiency and are hugely dependent on imported food, and that food security is indefensibly lacking for two billion people, the need for increased food production and its equitable distribution is clear; a rapprochement needs to be reached between the praxis of urban living and food production.

The modern food industry epitomizes the Marxist theory of alienation[12] perhaps better than any other labour activity. Unlike other trades and crafts that have followed esoteric and non-essential vectors, procurement of basic sustenance has always been a universal and innate occupation – foraging, hunting, husbandry and harvesting are straightforward exchanges of human capital in the form of energy expended and nutritional recompense. The abstraction of food from its origins through processing, portioning and packaging constructs a disassociation between the food producer and product, and between urban consumer and rural supplier. The consequence of this disassociation is that we, as consumers, are not seeing the clear effects of climate change and energy shortage on food production. Food supplied through the supermarket monopolies is still highly affordable despite the rising prices of fuel essential for modern agriculture, but the cost of food we do not see takes into account the expense

11. M Renner, S Sweeney & J Kubit, 'United Nations Environment Programme Report: Green jobs – towards decent work in a sustainable, low-carbon world', Retrieved 7 August 2009, www.unep.org/civil_society/Publications/index.asp

12. As expounded in the 1844 'Paris Manuscripts'

of environmental damage. Excess nitrogen runoff from fertilizers causes eutrophication of our lakes and rivers, resulting in contaminated water and the destruction of aquatic ecosystems. Land-based ecologies are not spared either, despoiled by pesticides and herbicides. It is important to note that these are not simply costs to the environment, but fiscal costs to the general public in the form of subsidies, clean-up costs, and health treatment for poor nutrition, obesity, contaminated food and disease.

We, as city dwellers, need to re-engage with the roots of our sustenance in a way that does not involve abstract extruded vacuum-sealed meals if we are to alleviate the burdens of food production on the planet. The implementation of urban agriculture – the cultivation, processing and distribution of food within the city – would have the two-fold effect of making these processes transparent and offering a means for the re-establishment of food and its production as a social relationship rather than commodity. It would mean an end to a nonsensical boomerang trade that sees the UK importing 22 000 tonnes of potatoes from Egypt and exporting 27 000 tonnes in the other direction.[13] Urban agriculture would result in food immediacy within cities, providing nutrition and health benefits. It would create job opportunities, generate income for urban poverty groups and provide a social safety net. Urban organic waste would be turned into an agricultural resource. Social inclusion of disadvantaged groups and community development would be facilitated, and the city would benefit from urban greening and the maintenance of green open spaces. Bringing living food back to where we live would not re-establish the Garden of Eden, but there would be no second, third and fourth parties responsible for the commodification of produce, giving a new meaning to hand to mouth existence.

Urban agriculture is not a new phenomenon; its popularity and adoption has waxed and waned over the millennia, from the recycling of urban wastes and qanat tunnel irrigation networks in Ancient Persia for agriculture, to the stepped cities and farming terraces of Machu Picchu that can be considered as a precursor to hydroponics. In more recent times, victory

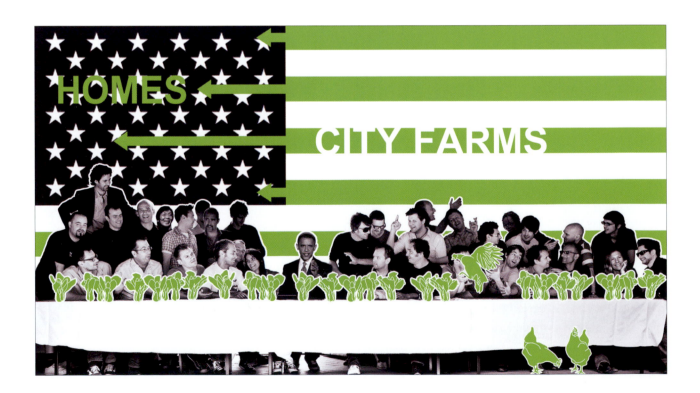

facing page: Imagining Recovery – Ready access to nutrition and reduction in food-miles

left: Berliners establish war gardens in front of the Reichstag, 1946

gardens during the two world wars were employed to alleviate food shortages with rooftops, balconies, pontoons and public parks appropriated for food production. In a remarkably ambitious programme, gardening classes, literature, seeds, fertilizer and committees were organized, yielding over half a billion dollars worth of war-garden crops at the end of the First World War in America alone.[14]

Today, the enduring arcadian dream of green space and growing food for oneself can be found in the allotment, a land reform system that has taken the form of the American community garden, the Russian dacha, the French jardin familial, the Dutch Volkstuin and the Danish Kolonihave. Growing one's own food in Russia is a long-established tradition, among the affluent and underprivileged alike. In Germany, according to the concept of granting, there is the kleingärten, the schrebergärten, kolonie, parzelle, armengärten, sozialgärten, arbeitergärten, rotkreuzgärten and eisenbahnergärten. Perhaps most noteworthy is the intercultural garden, a project of the German Association of International Gardens that aims to improve racial integration and promote intercultural interaction.

The positioning of farming within the city also addresses water management considerations. Conventional agriculture is hugely dependent on water resources, leading a UN world development report to declare water as mankind's most serious challenge of the 21st century. Environmental activist and author of 'Water Wars', Vandana Shiva, estimates that the food intake per person in the developed world uses approximately 3000 litres of foreign water every day. She pointedly describes this trade as the import of virtual water to the rich and the export of drought to food producing nations in the developing world.

Within our cities, the impermeability of urban fabric – roads, roofs, hard standing and concrete landscape

13. A Simms, V Johnson, J Smith & S Mitchell, 'The Consumption Explosion: the Third UK Interdependence Day Report', NEF, London, 2009, p.4

14. Charles Lathrop Pack, 'The War Garden Victorious', Press of J B Lippincott Co., Philadelphia, 2009

constitute flood risks due to their inability to attenuate surface water. Vegetation, edible or otherwise, is a ready-made natural sustainable drainage system, harvesting rainfall and mediating extremes of temperature as well as being the most efficient photovoltaic cell currently available to us by virtue of chlorophyll's photosynthetic properties.

While city farms go some way to redressing the disjunction of food production between the city and the countryside, farming practices outside urban areas also need to be reappraised and it is worth looking at how these have changed. The classic cyclical system of crop sequencing has been used since antiquity, with farmers rotating crops and introducing fallow periods so that nutrients in the soil can be replenished naturally by plants that have differing requirements, and which can release by-products that are beneficial to the crops that supplant them. The build-up of pathogens and pests is curbed and soil structure improved. Combined with moisture trapping and terracing, crop sequencing even renders agriculture in semi-arid environments possible, a process known as dryland farming. By the early 20th century, the practice of crop rotation had largely been discontinued, contributing to the dust bowl of the Great Plains that dramatically worsened the impact of the US depression of the 1930s. The resulting Soil Conservation and Domestic Allotment Act of 1935 corrected earlier government policy in the United States that had allowed agricultural land to become vulnerable to wind erosion. The mass planting of trees, reintroduction of native grass and an educational programme of non-destructive farming techniques paid rapid dividends.

The advent of synthetic fertilizers has meant that monocultures have become once again dominant, causing new problems relating to contamination of watercourses and immense energy expenditure. As Carolyn Steel, author of 'Hungry City', points out, there is no such thing as 'cheap food' – for every calorie of food modern agribusiness produces, it is burning an estimated 10 in the form of fossil fuels.[15] The cost of high yields from specifically chosen cultivars is borne by the soil, and monocultures have become so successful that worldwide surpluses have depressed the crop prices that farmers receive, threatening their livelihoods. Cash crops are currently plentiful enough to feed the planet's human population, but distribution to world markets is driven by economics leading to the paradox of wasted food and hungry millions.

Is there a way back? James Lovelock believes that we will need to resort to genetically modified crops on a global scale in order to stave off catastrophe and has advocated the synthesis of fermented food from air, water and trace chemicals as the future. If we are to avoid wholly synthetic foods that will definitively sever all connection between our sustenance and us, we may have to re-employ cyclical farming systems and self-sustaining permacultures.

The farming revolution in Cuba may be seen as a historic microcosm of the problems we are now facing and offers a model for adoption in appropriate environments. Following the collapse of the Soviet Bloc in 1989, from which it imported most of its food, Cuba developed the world's first and only state-supported urban agriculture infrastructure that has been well documented by Raquel Rivera Pinderhughes at San Francisco State University. The sudden loss of petroleum, machinery and fertilizers severely affected

19

facing page top to bottom: Imagining Recovery – Grocery shopping in New York's Central Park; Car boot allotments in Detroit

15. R Heinberg speaking at the 'Soil Association One Planet Agriculture Conference', January 2007, cited in C Steel, 'Hungry City', Vintage Books, London, 2009, p.50

local food production, distribution and even refrigeration, compounding the immediate food shortage. This sequence of events highlights the fragility of food dependence in many developed nations and is well summarized in the NEF report 'Nine Meals from Anarchy', describing the paralysis of Britain's supply infrastructure by farmers and truck drivers who blockaded fuel depots around the country in 2000. In response, the inhabitants of Havana, Cuba's capital city, took over every available surface in the city for growing food and rearing livestock in a collective effort redolent of the world war victory gardens. The Cuban government retrospectively sanctioned this impromptu occupation by declaring public land usufruct, granting free right to cultivate the land in perpetuity. Fears that the Cuban market would be flooded by low-cost imported food in an opening economy have been assuaged by planning policy ensuring the relocation of any garden displaced by new development while state incentives allow farmers to achieve parity of earning with white collar workers, although this may not be sustainable in a partially free market.

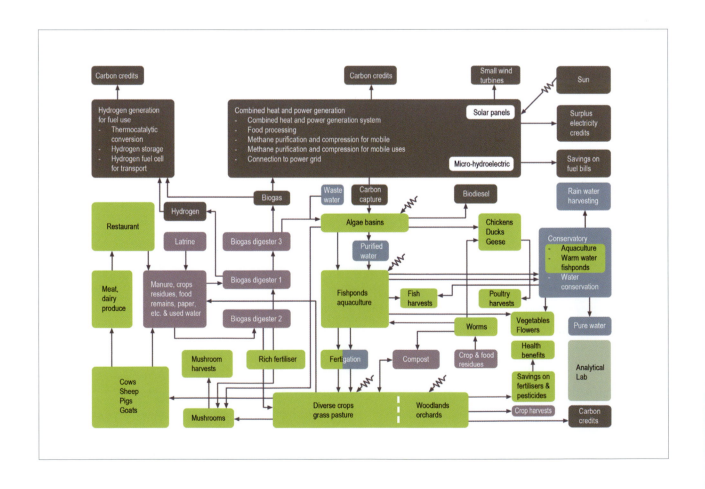

# The Perpetual Motion Machine

'Mulberry trees are grown to feed silkworms and the silkworm waste is fed to the fish in ponds. The fish also feed on waste from other animals, such as pigs, poultry, and buffalo. The animals in turn are given crops that have been fertilized by mud from the ponds. This is a sophisticated system as a continuous cycle of water, waste and food ... with man built into the picture.'[16]

The Chinese mulberry dyke fishpond system, first introduced during the dying days of the Ming dynasty (16th century) in the northern part of the Pearl River Delta, is a striking model of a closed sustainable ecosystem deployed by mankind to provide food and clothing. The benefits of each link in the system had been known to the farmers of the area for many years, as reflected in the folk saying that 'the more luxuriant the mulberry trees, the stronger the silkworms and the fatter the fish; the richer the pond, the more fertile the dyke and the more numerous the cocoons.'[17]

Elegant forms of such closed systems in farming have fallen victim to new technologies, in particular the Haber Bosch Process to synthesize ammonium nitrate. The Agricultural revolution enabled the evolution of an urban lifestyle, dramatically reducing the agricultural labour force and freeing the populace for other pursuits. Ironically, the unchecked growth of an urban lifestyle at the expense of agricultural land is now threatening the production of food that made the city's existence initially possible.

Urban agriculture provides an overdue mediation between the countryside and city, making possible a circular economy that has the same seductive clarity and well-tempered logic of the mulberry dyke fishpond system – the solid organic waste of city dwellers can be alchemically transformed via anaerobic digestion into gaseous energy and fertilizing digestate; greywater and blackwater from showers, sinks and gutters can be treated and rechannelled to irrigate our crops provided they are in close enough proximity. With the added ingredient of sunlight, we have food from a living grocery store to propel another cycle of the human perpetual motion machine.

Since the 1920s, when Chinese exports of raw silk were at their peak, the mulberry dyke fishpond system has seen a sad decline after having evolved for over two millennia, the Chinese orthodoxy of a circular economy implacably usurped by urbanization and industry. In recent years, however, cyclical systems founded on mulberry dyke farming have seen resurgence in academic circles as an alternative to unsustainable agriculture and have credible potential for real world application.

Dr Mae-Wan Ho, geneticist and director of the Institute of Science in Society (ISIS), has been developing

facing page: Dream Farm 2 Systems Diagram; Dr Mae-Wan Ho (ISIS)

16. Jennifer Pepall, 'New Challenges for China's Urban Farms', IDRC Report', International Research Development Centre, Ottawa, 1997, 21.3

17. Asia-Pacific Environmental Innovation Strategies (APEIS); Research on Innovative and Strategic Policy Options (RISPO)

the 'Dream Farm 2', a model of an integrated, zero-emission, zero-waste farm that maximizes the use of renewable energies and turns waste into food and energy resources. An implementation and extension of George Chan's Integrated Food and Waste Management System (IFWMS), Ho likens the farm to an organism, ready to grow and develop, to build up structures in a balanced way and perpetuate them. The closed cycle creates a stable, autonomous structure that is self-maintaining, self-renewing and self-sufficient.

Key to the process is a zero-entropy or zero-waste directive that must be adhered to as far as possible. The human body tends towards this ideal, explaining why we age relatively slowly and do not spontaneously decompose. The Dream Farm becomes more productive as more life cycles are incorporated, with increasing amounts of energy and standing biomass stored within the system. Echoing the lessons of crop rotation, academic researchers have rediscovered that productivity and biodiversity are happy bedfellows in a sustainable system, with different life cycles reciprocally retaining and circulating energy for the whole system.

Circular economies are not restricted to agriculture. The reduction of energy demand through inter-seasonal heat transfer (IHT) is the perfect example of a Smartcity cyclical system. Excess heat during the summer can be collected in a thermal store and retained until wintertime, when it is redistributed through pipework to provide thermal comfort (usually with the assistance of heat pump technology), all the while building up a store of chilled water or chilled ground stores which will be used for cooling during the summer. At the scale of a city, the potential for reduction in energy demand is immense, making our current scattering of energy-autarkic houses pale into insignificance. Coupled with waste recycling and renewable offsets, a citywide net zero carbon lifestyle could actually be possible.

Harvard-based sustainability expert Nader Ardalan estimates that a staggering 75% reduction in carbon emissions is possible purely by using energy more efficiently. The largest opportunity for cutting demand lies in the employment of holistic design and the configuration of buildings to passively heat and cool our environments for thermal comfort.

As in the case of agriculture, antiquity provides us with lessons in our age of technological marvels. We need to look back to the Ancient Greeks, who reorientated entire city grids to increase southern exposure for passive solar heating in the winter months. We need to recycle the wisdom of cavemen who somehow knew that annualized thermal stasis is achieved at a depth of 6m below ground level and took advantage of the land's ability to mediate extremes of temperature. We need to duplicate the extensive underground labyrinths of the ancient Persians that were used to cool their buildings over 5000 years ago.

Shifting scale from seasons to days, temperature changes of the diurnal cycle can also be manipulated by using exposed heavyweight construction materials that retain daytime heat in their thermal mass to be released during the night. Cooling strategies in tropical climates utilize the water cycle, reducing temperature by releasing latent heat of evaporation. Here we can refer to the baud geer wind towers and cisterns of traditional oriental architecture, or the fountains and reflection pools of Moroccan courtyard riads.

The vast majority of discourse on energy conservation focuses on the shift from fossil fuels to renewable energies in the form of wind turbines, hydro-electric plants, combined heat and power (CHP), photovoltaics and ground source heat pumps. With ongoing concerns regarding the safety of nuclear power, such technologies serve a vital purpose, and

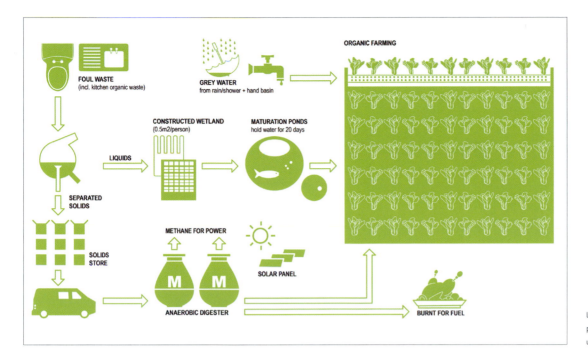

ORGANIC FARMING

FOUL WASTE
(incl. kitchen organic waste)

GREY WATER
from rain/shower + hand basin

CONSTRUCTED WETLAND
(0.5m2/person)

MATURATION PONDS
hold water for 20 days

LIQUIDS

SEPARATED
SOLIDS

METHANE FOR POWER

SOLIDS
STORE

SOLAR PANEL

M    M

ANAEROBIC DIGESTER

BURNT FOR FUEL

left: Imagining Recovery – The perpetual motion machine channels urban waste back into farming

in urban areas offer the only viable solutions. As an alternative to burning fossil fuels and releasing radioactive materials, heavy metals, volatile organic compounds, greenhouse gases and acids into the atmosphere, 'renewable' energy generation can only be welcomed. The idea that such energy is 'clean', however, is fundamentally flawed – biomass crops require food, water and energy for growth and transportation while photovoltaics and wind turbines require maintenance, replacement and significant energy resources in their production. In order to amplify the benefits of cleaner energy supplies, however, the reduction of energy consumption from the outset must be considered. Our first question should not be 'How do we generate more energy to feed our destructive lifestyles?' but rather 'How do we minimize our need?'

A second alternative to the generation of new energy is to share and recycle it. With hydro-electric, fossil fuel and wind plants situated in locations remote from cities, there are huge losses in efficiency and little potential for heat capture that could be used for district heating. Cogeneration fuel cells, now compact enough to be installed in an urban basement, provide one solution. The Industrial Symbiosis at Kalundborg in Denmark is a commercial-scale example of an energy-sharing cooperative often cited by industrial ecologists. Seventy-five miles west of Copenhagen on the coast of Denmark, this industrial complex is characterized by a network of companies that decided to generate new revenue streams by trading energy and byproducts with their neighbours.

In the early 1970s the Statoil refinery agreed to provide waste gas as a fuel source to Gyproc that the latter was able to use as a low-cost fuel source. Treated wastewater was and is still sold to the nearby Asnæs fossil fuel power station which, losing 60% of its energy through heat, began to temper thermal inefficiencies by providing heating to 4500 homes and selling process steam to the refinery and the pharmaceutical company, Novo Nordisk, for sterilization purposes. The cooling water is also passed on to a fish farm, resulting in improved breeding conditions and growth in the warmer water. The 30 tonnes of annual ash by-product are recycled in the cement industry, and sulphur dioxide from flue gases are sold to Gyproc for gypsum production. Wastes from all the symbiosis companies in the municipality are collected by Kara/Noveren I/S to produce electricity. Enzyme production at Novozymes A/S creates over 150 000 cubic metres of solid biomass as part of the fermentation process which is exported as fertilizer and yeast slurry from insulin production at Novo Nordisk and used in the pig-farming industry. This circular economy, mirroring the symbiotic farming systems of the Dream Farm 2, has resulted in a considerable reduction in water, air and ground pollution whilst conserving natural resources. It is noteworthy that these environmental benefits are themselves by-products of profit-making commercial decisions.

Urban growth can no longer continue through synthetic linear processes that are colossally wasteful, discharging contaminants into the air, ground and water. Circular organic systems are in comparison regenerative, and it makes sense to ride the wave of these natural systems, harvesting the fruits of a harnessed ecology and feeding the process as necessary to reap disproportionate benefits from minimal investment. Natural systems are self-perpetuating and symbiotic. And it is high time that mankind rejoined these systems as a constructive rather than destructive force.

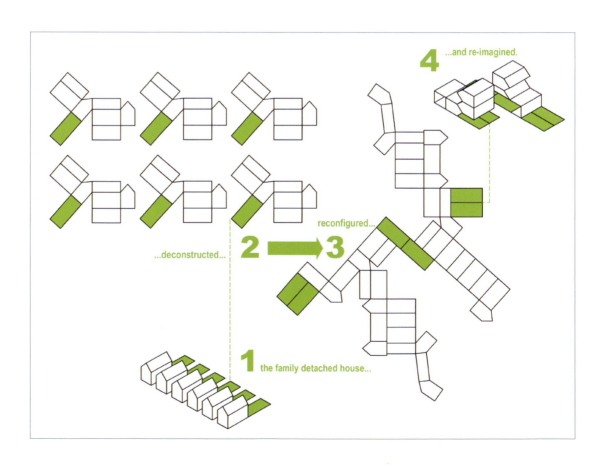

4 ...and re-imagined.

reconfigured...

...deconstructed...    2 ➡ 3

1 the family detached house...

24

# The American Dream Redux

**The American Dream is 'that dream of a land in which life should be better and richer and fuller for everyone, with opportunity for each according to ability or achievement. It is a difficult dream for the European upper classes to interpret adequately, and too many of us ourselves have grown weary and mistrustful of it. It is not a dream of motor cars and high wages merely, but a dream of social order in which each man and each woman shall be able to attain to the fullest stature of which they are innately capable, and be recognized by others for what they are, regardless of the fortuitous circumstances of birth or position.'**

**- 'The Epic of America', James Truslow Adams, 1931**

The dream that James Truslow Adams captured for the American people in 'The Epic of America' was one based on social and ethical principles, reflecting a country putatively unencumbered by religious, class and racial boundaries with life prospects based on talent and determination rather than wealth and political connections. Successive generations have seen recalibrations of the Dream and somewhere down the line, it became synonymous with home and automobile ownership as a symbol of affluence, precisely what Adams declared the Dream was not.

facing page: Imagining Recovery – The deep-rooted American ideal of the single-family detached house and automobile requires re-evaluation in order to effect change

Broadacre City, Frank Lloyd Wright's conception of the utopian city, reinforces this aspiration. A decentralized democracy, Broadacre City, or 'Free City' as Wright sometimes called it, was agrarian in nature, with a community built upon the transfer of a one-acre plot per citizen from federal land. In his own words, 'when every man, woman, and child may be born to put his feet on his own acres and every unborn child finds his acre waiting for him when he is born – then democracy will have been realized.' Every family would own their own home in the form of the 'Usonian House' that would come in different-sized variants depending on need. The sizeable distances between individual dwellings and educational, religious and leisure establishments would lend primacy to the motorcar, with the larger Usonian houses incorporating five-car garages and pedestrian safety guaranteed only within the one-acre plots.

As a model for new social space arising out of the Great Depression and advancing technologies in telecommunications and the automobile industry, Wright's vision was every bit as revolutionary as, but divergent from, Le Corbusier's Radiant City, revealed three years later in 1935 and extolling the virtues of stacked high-density mixed-use living.

In the light of today's world population growth and sustainability concerns, the Radiant City appears to be the more relevant model for city design. The ideal of the single-family detached house and automobile that has permeated the developing world is deep rooted but requires re-evaluation in order to effect change. The white picket-fenced suburban utopia of Wisteria Lane needs to be supplanted by a dream that is both leaner and more expansive, comforting but challenging.

The unattainable nature of utopia is less to do with an unreachable goal than the shifting of goalposts, what Greg Easterbrook terms the Progress Paradox in his book of the same name. We have never been wealthier, lived longer and amidst less crime. The environment has also, with notable exceptions, become cleaner. However, there has been no commensurate increase in happiness, a contradiction that Easterbrook attributes to choice anxiety and abundance denial. Similarly, the Easterlin paradox of 1974 posits that unlimited economic growth is not necessarily beneficial to contentment, correlating the 'happiness' index of countries at various levels of development; Easterlin showed that the inhabitants of low-income countries were not proportionally less happy than those of higher income nations.

Nevertheless, the influence of the American Dream as a driving force for individual improvement in the 20th century cannot be underestimated; studies have shown that it is only following the 'Great Recession' of 2008 to 2009 with its home foreclosures, burgeoning unemployment and increasing energy costs that national attitudes to the Dream have soured. The global recession may be seen, though, as an opportunity as well as a catastrophe, enabling society at large to realign itself with a grounded value system that eschews rampant consumerism and exploitation.

Similarly, it is time for designers to reassess the values of their profession. In order to regain public and political confidence, design needs to offer intelligent solutions that focus on need and demonstrate added value. Beauty will not be judged purely through the lens aesthetic but through the elegance of efficient arrangements and systems. Modesty rather than narcissm will be the acceptable face of sustainable design. On the one hand, the currency of architectural design is severely devalued when it comes to economic renewal, even in the spheres of housing and commercial developments that it is associated with. Spaces can be designed to be functional, flexible, to have green credentials and, even to be beautiful. Design can improve quality of life and contribute towards the wider society; on the other hand, the contribution of construction professionals is for the most part guided or stymied by government policy and developing agencies. The real influence of the designer, whether of food packaging or a city master plan, lies in the visualization of an alternative reality, a reality that is demonstrably better but conceivable only through the designer's shared vision. Too often, this alternate reality is seductive but bogus, used to market banal consumer products. As imagineers, however, designers are in a position to cajole the general public to embrace positive and profound change so that progress is not hampered by cultural bias and financial conservatism.

The compact city, which offers so many beneficial synergies, is at odds with the outdated American Dream. Change has to be gradual, and will be abetted by a modal shift in transportation such as that implemented in Curitiba, capital city of the Brazilian state Paraná, that will support physical interaction and societal cohesion. The space of the Smartcity needs to demonstrate that shared experience and pooled resources can offer an improved and viable model to individual advancement. The simple notion that public space in the shape of a favourite table at a café, a park bench or a painting hanging in the permanent collection of a gallery can be sequestered into a shared but personal ownership is nonetheless a powerful one.

There are also encouraging signs that America's love affair with the automobile is in decline. 'Walkability' has become a buzzword amongst American estate agents, who have reported that housing values have shown a significant increase where schools and public transport facilities are within walking distance compared to the past. The expense of maintaining an additional dependency that provides only sporadic benefit coupled with vehicular congestion, competition for parking spaces, increasing fuel costs and pollution are slowly making the car a convenience that does not always justify the expense. There is also a growing sense that the vibrancy of dense mixed-use neighbourhoods is more appealing than the bland suburbia of Levittown shaped by streets and cars.

Linked to the new American Dream must come a recalibration of the perception of beauty. The mowing of the front lawn in suburban America has become bizarrely ritualized, the beautiful manicured lawn a point of pride signalling conformity to a suburban code of conduct. The Canadian cultural critic and self-styled 'horticultural philosopher', Robert Fulford, sees the lawn as an instrument for public shaming and social control: 'As the death of a canary announces the presence of gas in a mine, so a dandelion's appearance on a lawn indicates that Sloth has taken up residence in paradise and is about to spread evil in every direction. Pretty as they might look to some, dandelions demonstrate a weakness of the soul. They announce that the owner of the house refuses to respect the neighbourhood's right to peace, order, good government.'[18] Hyperbole aside, the manicured lawn is an unfathomable oddity to countries where the front yard is not central to their culture, rendered all the more contentious in the wider context of sustainability and food security. Scaled up, the great American lawn covers over 50 million acres of the country – more land area than is used for the growth of wheat or corn – and consumes vast water and energy resources for its maintenance. Perversely, it offers no spatial function; it is effectively wasted space despite the 'beauty' it proffers. Corralling this land resource for the production of food would result in a different kind of beauty that is neither skin-deep nor associated with the vanity of status. Sustainable urbanism is characterized not only through the production of new social space, but also the creation of a new social aesthetic, and it is not inconceivable that this cultural anachronism, imported from England over a quarter of a millennium ago, will become a symbol of vulgar ostentation rather than good taste.

In addition to defining the American Dream, Adams is also remembered for his essay 'To "Be" or to "Do": A Note on American Education',[19] in which he declares 'There are obviously two educations. One should teach us how to make a living and the other how to live.' The relevance of his ideas remains undiminished.

18. Robert Fulford, 'The Lawn: North America's magnificent obsession', 1998, www.robertfulford.com/lawn.html

19. James Truslow Adams, 'To Be or to Do', 'Forum' magazine, Vol. LXXXI, No. 6, New York, 1929, p.321, H Goddard Leach (ed.)

# Rise of the Eco-warrior

**William Sweet • Fernando Pereira • Chico Mendes • Mike Hill • Tom Worby • Karel Van Noppen • Kenule Saro-Wiwa • Jill Phipps • David Chain • Bartolomeu Morais da Silva • Fernando Sarmiento • Celso Pojas • Roel Dotarot • Danny Qualbar • Rolando Antolihao • Vicente Paglinawan • Isabelino Celing • Dorothy Stang**

In the developed world, the eco-warrior is a figure of fun, bringing to mind tree-huggers, hippies and holier-than-thou evangelists. The roll call of names above comprises just a few of the environmental activists who have been killed defending habitats and causes counter to the interests of powerful economic groups, sometimes with governmental ties. Many of those habitats are also home to, or represent the livelihoods of, impoverished indigenous communities. One of the more celebrated environmental martyrs, Kenule Saro-Wiwa, dared to speak out against the environmental damage to his homeland, Ogoniland, following decades of oil waste dumping by multi-national corporations, and was summarily arrested, tried and executed by the Nigerian military in 1995. The term 'warrior' is neither hyperbole nor ironic.

Today's eco-warriors include scientists, politicians, entrepreneurs, financiers, celebrities and designers among their number. As the eco-warrior spirit has percolated down over the years from persecuted prophets to everyday members of society, there are two groups of unlikely players that have taken the stage in the war for humanity – storytellers and farmers.

Over the past decade, there has been a tidal shift in public awareness of unsustainable environmental practices, and this can be partly attributed to storytellers in the mass media. Science has provided us with the statistical proof that humanity is both perpetrator and victim of widespread environmental damage, but facts and figures are poor vehicles for galvanizing the electorate and grass roots action. At the end of this decade, the film world has seen a glut of movies with green agendas, most notably Davis Guggenheim's 'An Inconvenient Truth' and Robert Kenner's 'Food Inc.' The former documents Al Gore's commitment to exposing the 'planetary emergency' that global warming represents, the latter the detrimental effect the food industry is causing to health, farmers' livelihoods and the environment. Both documentaries were produced by Participant Productions, a company with a mission to raise awareness of world problems in the public consciousness through compelling narrative. They understand that statistical abstraction is unable to engage the public imagination in the way that story-shaped issues can. When even Bond movies tap into the zeitgeist – the villain in the 'Quantum of Solace', whose name is Greene, is not bent on world domination but the monopoly of water supplies in Bolivia under the guise

facing page: Imagining Recovery – greywater recycling and the experience of recovery of a bogus environmental organization – the critical mass necessary to effect change cannot be far away.

The second group of pivotal players are farmers, the individuals we have delegated to put food on our tables whilst we engage in more rarefied pursuits. In the Smartcity, with urban agriculture at the forefront, empowered farmers will take on a new instructional role, advising communities on how to best cultivate their crops. In a recent list of 50 people who could save the planet chosen by an expert panel assembled by the 'Guardian' newspaper,[20] five are farmers or have had farming experience, including Al Gore who worked on his family's smallholding as a boy. Also recognized is Bija Devi who has been a farmer in the foothills of the Himalayas since the age of seven. She now spearheads an international movement to conserve cereal, pulse, fruit and vegetable strains that are at risk of extinction from modern agricultural practices. Having established an extensive bank of indigenous seeds, Devi travels around India disseminating endangered crops and the ancestral knowledge to cultivate them, simultaneously insuring against climate change, soil infertility and disease, and preserving a rapidly disappearing cultural tradition.

Outside the Smartcity, the remit of farmers will become broader. Trained and reinstated as custodians of the land, a new breed of professional farmer will husband energy, natural ecosystems and forestry, arbitrating between the need for carbon sequestration, wildlife habitats, raw timber material and biomass. Provenance will enter the public lexicon in relation to energy and manufactured materials as well as food.

Sustainability must be accessible and applicable to the practice of everyday life. Consumers respond poorly to browbeating activism and need fiscal incentives to use less, and to be given greater control over the energy they use. Lower-carbon products and services need to become desirable, which is where the aesthetic aspects of design need to be employed. We are often told that we are the last generation able to make any effective change in the future of our planet. The day that the eco-warrior dies is a day to look forward to, for it will mean that there are no more unconverted to preach to, that sustainable living has become normative rather than alternative. That day has not yet arrived. There are still battles to be fought and won.

# Scenic Positions

'This whole mass of architecture which we had come upon so suddenly from amidst the pleasant fields was not only exquisitely beautiful in itself, but it bore upon it the expression of such generosity and abundance of life that I was exhilarated to a pitch that I had never yet reached.'

'"I don't understand," said he, "what kind of people you would expect to see; nor quite what you mean by 'country' people.  These are the neighbours, and that like they run in the Thames valley."'

- 'News from Nowhere', William Morris, 1890

The sites for Smartcity systems vary in scale, geography, culture and time, consequently requiring adaptation according to context. The concept of terroir – the climate, topography, soil conditions and aspect of a piece of land for the production of wine, is equally applicable to the cultivation of edible produce, renewable energy and communities, with the additional region-specific variables of politics, land ownership, extant infrastructure and cultural bias.

The Marseille Unité d'Habitation, the purest example of Le Corbusier's vision for communal living, was given the unflattering moniker 'La Maison du Fada', French-Provençal for 'House of the Mad', when it was built. The systems buildings that followed the wake of the Unité d'Habitation and corrupted its legacy are considered by many as the cause and symbol of deprivation and anti-social behaviour in the inner cities. On the other hand, while the very notion of the Unité would have been inconceivable in the United States, Le Corbusier's ideas would gain traction in South America and particularly Hong Kong, where the Parisian Plan Voisin of 1925 of giant cruciform towers has effectively been realized and is proliferating across Southern China. Acceptance of high-rise mixed-use living may be attributed to cultural factors as well as unusually high population densities.

At a macro level, the entire city becomes the site for a new urban land use – farming. Its location takes advantage of favourable adjacencies between agricultural processes and their raw materials, establishing a classic urban nutrient cycle.  Urban solid waste and greywater can be used as fertilizer and irrigation; food transport and associated carbon emissions are removed from the equation.

Due to the high premium of land in dense urban areas, urban agriculture is considered to be unfeasible within cities. The artist Agnes Denes eloquently articulated the disparity of land value in her installation 'Wheatfield: A Confrontation' in which she planted a golden field of wheat amongst the gleaming

facing page: A commentary on misplaced priorites: 'Wheatfield – A Confrontation', Dalston, London, 2009; Agnes Denes

20. J Vidal, D Adam, A Ghosh et al., '50 people who could save the planet', first published on guardian.co.uk, 5 January 2008

skyscrapers of downtown Manhattan. In the autumn of 1982, Denes harvested her crop that had a value of US$93 on land valued at US$4.5bn. The piece was intended to 'call attention to our misplaced priorities and deteriorating human values'.[21]

In the summer of 2009, the work was reproduced in the London borough of Hackney and the questions she raised regarding the true value of sustenance are more germane now than ever before.

The city farming model of Havana and the victory garden movement belie the assertion that the cost of land is prohibitive – brownfield sites, car parks, rooftops, window boxes, barges and riverbanks have all been appropriated to create a productive landscape in the past and can once again beautify our townscapes, all the while providing good nutrition and generating social capital. For overgrown sites and derelict rooftops, it is simply a case of replacing buddleia and nettles with berries, tomatoes and herbs.

William Morris' new world idyll in his utopian novel, 'News from Nowhere', and Denes' visceral commentary owe their potency to the striking juxtaposition of the pastoral and urban, demonstrating how scale and context can effect beauty. A cabbage or wheat patch is not as conventionally beautiful as daffodils or tulips, but when scaled up, replicated a thousand fold, reconfigured into vertical surfaces or arrayed into pattern – in short curated - they can achieve the elegance of multi-sensory art and expand the limited palette of urban textures. In the Smartcity, buildings and roofscapes will transform in colour, volume and scent through the seasons. Morris' answer to the critics of his socialist vision, who argue that individuals will lack the incentive to work in a world where private property is abolished, is that work should be creative and pleasurable. In European cities where waiting lists for allotments number up to 40 years, widespread cultivation of the metropolis offers a way to disintegrate orthodox distinctions between work, leisure and art.

Agricultural land in outlying areas for the growth of biofuels

City farming for food

Within dense urban areas, rooftops, windowsills, balconies and walls can be appropriated for the growth of edible crops, evoking the spirit of the Second World War victory garden. With the support of government policy, the public realm could be fully reclaimed – plazas, parks, waterfronts, boats, car parks and greyfield sites where appropriate sunlight levels are available are all viable locations. The metrics of progress will be clearly manifest, growing before our eyes while beautifying our environment.

A scattering of community growing programmes are already in action, and publicity surrounding Michelle Obama's White House Garden has helped raise public awareness of the potential productivity of our backyards. The 'Urban Farming Food Chain Project' birthed in Los Angeles has expanded its operations abroad to Jamaica, Canada and the UK. The vertical growing walls can be installed either as freestanding frameworks or cladding elements, which the architect, Robin Osler, logically argues do not consume valuable horizontal real estate. Their adoption therefore becomes more attractive to developers under economic pressures to maximize usable floor area. These initiatives may appear modest in scale but they play a vital role in stimulating the perceptual shift in how we think about and procure our meals. Walls of living food in the city can vitalize urban communities by bringing food provenance and human-scale interaction back to the table, consumer friendly but not pre-packaged. Edifices of spatial theatre, these verdant edible walls also raise the public's awareness of architectural possibilities in the city that are not limited to brick, concrete or glass.

Perhaps an even more intelligent use of space can be found in the Brick City urban farms of Newark in New Jersey, based on the Small Plot Intensive (SPIN) relay-farming model that was thought up by the Canadian farmers Wally Satzewich and Gail Vandersteen. Using the simple device of a plastic crate or 'earthbox', Brick City farmers are able to colonize disused sites. The limited size of the units allows operations to decamp and re-root in other transient spaces as they become available. The deployment of earthboxes in Newark came out of necessity due to contaminated ground, but the containers have the added benefit of minimizing water and fertilizer use.

Alternative materials in the city do not have to be organic. Renewable technologies in the form of photovoltaics and wind turbines are still inchoate and typically retrofitted to rooftops either as green marketing strategies or to satisfy government sustainability policy. There are, however, buildings in recent years that have broken from this mould such as Toyo Ito's World Games Stadium in Kaohsiung, Taiwan, and Hamilton Associates Strata building in London. The former, a sinuous river of blue that coils out to form a public plaza, is entirely covered in photovoltaic cells. A striking example of integrative interdisciplinary design, the stadium is classified as an independent power plant (IPP), potentially generating 1.14 gigawatt hours per year with surplus energy fed into the grid when the arena is not in use.

Wind energy is more problematic, requiring strong laminar (unidirectional) wind and large swept areas to be efficient. The notion of buildings integrating turbines at their apex to power them is a seductive synergy of function and form. However, cities are typically situated in areas of low wind speed and the flow is turbulent by virtue of the buildings that constitute them. The top 20 metres of the Strata building

facing page: Imagining Recovery – Farming within the city takes advantage of programmatic and functional synergies

21. B. Oakes, B. 'Sculpting with the Environment – A Natural Dialogue', Van Nostrand Reinhold, New York, 1995, p.168

is a wind farm comprising three nine-metre diameter wind turbines. The angled elliptical concave surfaces into which the turbines are mounted create a venturi effect that channels the wind while minimizing vibration and wind noise. The projected energy returns are unremarkable, but the building does illustrate how energy farms and buildings can holistically coalesce.

The Smartcity thinks more in terms of inhabitable wind farms and photovoltaic parks rather than tower blocks with token micro-turbines and solar cells. The willful formalism of amorphous icon buildings favoured by marquee-name architects has shown that complex geometric forms are realizable using generative tooling software. There is no compelling reason why prodigious design skills and cutting-edge technology could not be channelled into developing clean energy morphology.

Shifting scale from innovative surfacing materials and interstitial spaces to buildings, the vertical farms championed by Dickson Despommier take the compact city argument for increasing plot ratio in advantageous areas to preserve remaining threatened ecosystems and apply it to agriculture. Despommier, professor of public health in environmental health sciences and microbiology at Colombia University, reasons that the success or failure of current crop production is wholly contingent on the vicissitudes of weather and disease, and any significant sustained deviation from an optimal range has catastrophic effects on yield. His solution lies in three-dimensional hermetic farms that ensure year-round high-yield crop production with minimal risk of infection from agents without the use of pesticides. The tower model also reduces the use of fossil fuels and takes advantage of energy-waste trades with other urban activities. He estimates that one vertical farm with a footprint of one square city block rising 30 stories would provide enough nutrition (2000 calories / day / person) to accommodate the needs of 10 000 people employing technologies currently available.[22] The controlled conditions of the farms will permit analysis of the chemical composition of each plant, with gas chromatography employed to test flavenoid concentration guaranteeing flavoursome and ripe produce. Increased levels of artificial lighting necessary could be obtained by generating biogas from inedible plant waste on site.

In the case of the new city, the scope for more comprehensive Smartcity intervention is possible. New housing developments can be planned to integrate farming at the scale of landscape; buildings can be used to terraform the natural topography, be surfaced in growing media, orientated to receive or protect from sunlight, and integrate water conservation, inter-seasonal heat transfer and waste recycling mechanisms. As illustrated at the industrial symbiosis at Kalundborg and the theoretical Dream Farm, remarkable economies of scale are achievable at the magnitude of a city when symbiotic self-perpetuating cyclical systems are adopted. Morris' dream of an agrarian society is not compatible with contemporary urban existence or even universally desirable in today's age, but his insistence that 'the material surroundings of life should be pleasant, generous, and beautiful'[23] remains unassailable.

34

# Cultivating Community

**CULTIVATE**

verb [ trans. ]

1 prepare and use (land) for crops or gardening.

• break up (soil) in preparation for sowing or planting.

• raise or grow (plants), esp. on a large scale for commercial purposes.

• grow or maintain (living cells or tissue) in culture.

2 try to acquire or develop (a quality, sentiment, or skill) : he cultivated an air of indifference.

• [usu. as adj.] ( cultivated) apply oneself to improving or developing (one's mind or manners) : he was a remarkably cultivated and educated man.

                    - 'The Oxford Pocket Dictionary of Current English', 2009

As evolving organic entities, communities grow, germinating from unlikely seeds and requiring careful nurture. They flourish when conditions are favourable, and when faced with a changing climate, they adapt to new environments or make way for better-suited alternatives; when faced with new arrivals, they are either crowded out or cross-pollinate, sharing resources and blending traits. Communities share much in common with agriculture, and one can show the way forward for the other.

Skid Row, in Los Angeles, home to one of the largest homeless populations in the United States, is one of the recent beneficiaries of Urban Farming, a Detroit-based non-profit organization dedicated to eradicating hunger founded by the singer, Taja Sevelle. Together with the architects Elmslie Osler and Green Living Technologies, Urban Farming have installed a series of 30-foot long walls, each containing 4000 plants to supply the area's dispossessed with tomatoes, spinach, peppers, lettuce, leeks and herbs. Just as significantly, the programme has drawn together diverse and disadvantaged members of the community of all ages and ethnicities as well as providing an opportunity to learn new skills and reducing local crime.

Food is a universal. It is cross-cultural, cross-gender, cross-class and cross-generational. As a key prerequisite for survival, food is the great democratizer that defines our society and is an essential element of Smartcity living. Claude Lévi-Strauss, the French anthropologist, makes the point that culinary rites are not innate but learned;[24] the human digestive system is able to process almost any organic material, and the distinction of what is edible and what is not is a cultural convention. Food, as a social medium, communicates a veritable smorgasbord of meaning, from Eucharistic sacrament in the Christian church and religious separation in kosher law to etiquette in the formal dining room,

22. D Despommier, 'Vertical Farm Essay II: Reducing the impact of agriculture on ecosystem functions and services', 2008. Retrieved 14 January 2007, www.verticalfarm.com/essay2_print.htm

23. From Morris' lecture 'How We Live and How We Might Live' delivered to the Hammersmith Branch of the Socialist Democratic Federation (SDF) at Kelmscott House, on 30 November 1884. N Salmon, 'The William Morris Internet Archive: Works', Marxist Internet Archive, www.marxists.org

24. C Levi-Strauss, 'Le Cru et le cuit' (1964), Mythologiques I-IV (trans. John Weightman and Doreen Weightman), Harper & Row, New York, 1969

celebration on feast days, societal responsibility in soup kitchens and protest in hunger strikes. Living food in the city fulfills a yearning for the haptic and tangible as well as the digital, presenting a city framework that engages people rather than automata. The vegetable walls of the Urban Farming Project are an example of spatial phenomenology in the city, stimulating our eyes, ears, noses, minds and tongues – imagination made real, architecture that you can taste.

The deployment of agricultural and energy generation systems within urban environments is only part of the story. Much criticism has been levelled at planned communities, from Levittown in the United States to the three waves of post-war New Towns in the UK and the ongoing Thames Gateway project. The Thames Gateway is Europe's largest regeneration programme, and there are recurring concerns that the result will be a concentration of 'Stepford Suburbias' and 'Noddy Towns'.

Many of the perceived failures of Levittown and Milton Keynes can be attributed to the hegemony of the motorcar and the lack of opportunities for unskilled and lower income workers. These new towns were self-financing and whilst this rendered the large-scale development programme possible, any pioneering visions for an urban future were of necessity watered down to pander to the public's demand for private transportation. Vehicular–pedestrian separation remains vastly unpopular amongst Britons and Americans, stymieing the reification of truly sustainable urban environments.

The transcription of a new city from paper to lived reality usually ignores the genius loci, the distinctive atmosphere of a location. Established European metropolises such as London, with their rich, variegated histories have become richly textured palimpsests, as extensively described by the urban chroniclers Peter Ackroyd and Ian Sinclair. Planned communities, however, do not have the luxury of having identities developed and nurtured over the passage of time. The same problems are faced by urban localities that suffer from social and economic deprivation, usually as a consequence of an anachronistic industrial heritage. In essence a mega-community, the city is a network of living systems that mutates or atrophies and dies.

Whether formed tabula rasa on an undeveloped site or integrated within an established metropolis, the Smartcity seeks to preserve the identity and the heritage of a place, ascribing as much importance to the past as the future. Traditionally, the character and industry of a settlement arose from the geographical uniqueness of the earth under and around it, whether it be from the geothermal springs of England's Bath Spa and onsen all over the volcanic region of Japan or the mining towns of Central Illinois, South western Pennsylvania, and West Virginia in the United States that resulted in railroad development across the continent. Similarly, viticulture in the Wine Country of Northern California that includes Sonoma County and Napa Valley came about from the unique variety of climate and soil conditions of the region, generating a form of employment, tourism and culture starkly different from, say, the Middle Eastern banking capital of Bahrain.

Financial institutions and agricultural terroir may appear unlikely partners, but in the wake of the 2009 global financial collapse, region-specific gourmet food has operated as a viable, if unlikely, form of currency. Credito Emiliano, a regional bank in Montecavolo, Italy, has been accepting Parmesan cheese as loan collateral since 1953. The bank owns two climate-controlled warehouses in which US$187.5 million worth of parmigiano-reggiano are stored. The loans may account for less than one per cent of the bank's revenue, but are vital in preserving Montecavolo's culinary heritage and local economy, given that the cheese needs to age for five years. Other artisan food products such as prosciutto in

San Daniele and brunello in Tuscany, have also been considered as unconventional collateral; these commodities are all highly site-specific, both in terms of raw material and local knowledge, and lend credence to Marx's labour theory of value: a commodity should be worth the amount of time and human labour invested in it.

The quest for urban identity must go beyond the current vogue for place-branding, an increasingly common exercise amongst municipal authorities in an attempt to regenerate inner city areas by attracting new residents and stimulating business investment. Places need to be made rather than hawked.  Too often, the features that are marketed are generic, such as good transport links and green space. Too often, there is little coincidence between expectation and reality. Cities are not products. They are more complex and are not in direct competition with one another, operating in multiple sectors and at different scales. Environmentally too, there are compelling reasons for exploiting the genius loci. Certain social and environmental conditions are inherently better suited for certain processes. Food miles notwithstanding, it is still appropriate, for example, to rear and export lamb from New Zealand. Due to the abundance of land and moderate climate, the livestock are able to remain in the pastures all year round, without any food additives or growth hormones.

The arguments for localism as an answer to globalization-linked identity loss extend beyond food to skills and construction materials. Built in the 16th century, the Mughal city of Fatehpur Sikri in the Indian state of Uttar Pradesh is almost entirely constructed in richly ornamented red sandstone, quarried from the same rocky landscape on which it stands. The 'Red City' is a world heritage site, as is the town of Bath, whose warm honeyed appearance comes from the extensive use of Bath stone. The use of aluminium in Reykjavik is a more contemporary instance of localism – as a by-product of Iceland's burgeoning aluminium industry that makes use of the country's natural geothermal resources, the city is characterized by brightly coloured corrugated aluminium facades, that, like growing vegetative walls, are recyclable.

Successful place-making and the fostering of community pride rely on differentiating one place from others and highlighting the character and activities of an area. Barcelona has used a combination of international events and architecture as the stimuli to reinvent itself since the Universal Exhibition of 1888 at Ciutadella, now the city's largest park. The Olympic legacy from the 1992 Games, including the creation of new beaches for public use, remains the standard for future Olympic cities. Significantly, the reconstruction of Barcelona in the wake of the Franco regime concentrated on improving the common urban fabric – schools, squares, museums, sewage treatment plants and community centres embellished by a relatively modest scattering of icon buildings by regional architects of international renown such as Santiago Calatrava, Enric Miralles and Carme Pinos. Taking a leaf out of the book of its Iberian neighbour, the port city of Bilbao has seen its fortunes completely transformed by Frank Gehry's Guggenheim Museum. Surveys have shown that 82% of tourists visit the city exclusively to see the museum.  More than a building, the Guggenheim effectively recentred the city, spearheading the economic reconstruction of the newly autonomous Basque country as a post-industrial service-based nation.

The cultivation of communities involves the generation of what Robert Putnam, author of 'Bowling Alone – The Collapse and Revival of American Community',[25] describes as social capital, the 'connections among individuals – social networks and the norms of reciprocity and trustworthiness that arise from them'. Putnam emphasizes the importance of bridging capital, the cross-connections between communities as crucial for the formation of a peaceful and multi-ethnic nation, and explores how public policy can facilitate or destroy social capital. The clearance of American slums in the 1950s and 1960s, for example, regenerated physical capital at the expense of arguably more valuable existing social bonding capital; similarly the consolidation of local post offices and small school districts in the name of efficiency has had unforeseen social costs. Gentrification, the influx of the affluent into inner city areas has resulted in physical proximity with deprived neighbours but also as much hostile as positive social interaction; ethnic enclaves such as Chinatown and Little Italy are not ghettos and demonstrate the distinction between accommodating diversity and pushing for assimilation.

Where regeneration frameworks and environmental protocols must be global in scope, communities emerge at grass roots level, and crucial to the growth of Smartcities is a devolution of power to local representatives at the front line who are better placed to allocate resources and evaluate need than profligate high-level quangos. Social capital is formed at a human scale between individuals, and local structures need to be in place to enfranchise the disenfranchised and affect the disaffected.

Food is but one common ground between disparate communities. Housing, transport, water, heating, electricity, sewerage, waste treatment and data services are all or are all becoming basic necessities of urban existence, making them ideal sites for the creation of new social capital. Legislation requiring mixed housing tenures and a minimum provision of affordable housing in new developments is a step forward. The Smartcity takes this idea further through the banishment of the private motorcar and the widespread use of community-tailored and community-owned multi-utility service companies (MUSCOs). Where the provision of energy, water and waste treatment are not solely state controlled, MUSCO arrangements operating entirely transparently can return excess profits to the city in the form of lower consumer bills or capital injection into other community projects.

The panacea to a deleterious food industry is to replace damaging large-scale monoculture with larger numbers of smaller mutually supporting diverse permacultures. Communities share much in common with agriculture, and one can show the way forward for the other.

left: Imagining Recovery – Communal creation of a productive landscape in disused and neglected sites offers a means to cultivate employment and social responsibility

25. R D Putnam, 'Bowling Alone – The Collapse and Revival of American Community', Simon & Schuster, New York, 2000

# Excavating the Concrete Jungle

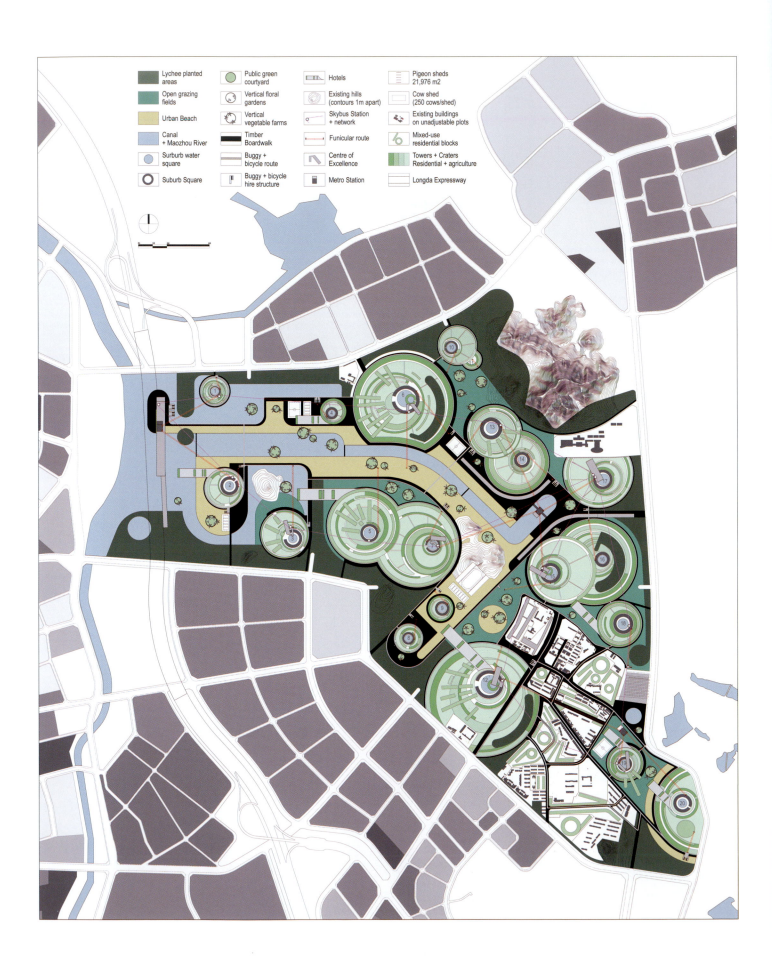

| | | | | |
|---|---|---|---|---|
| Lychee planted areas | Public green courtyard | Hotels | Pigeon sheds 21,976 m2 | |
| Open grazing fields | Vertical floral gardens | Existing hills (contours 1m apart) | Cow shed (250 cows/shed) | |
| Urban Beach | Vertical vegetable farms | Skybus Station + network | Existing buildings on unadjustable plots | |
| Canal + Maozhou River | Timber Boardwalk | Funicular route | Mixed-use residential blocks | |
| Surburb water square | Buggy + bicycle route | Centre of Excellence | Towers + Craters Residential + agriculture | |
| Suburb Square | Buggy + bicycle hire structure | Metro Station | Longda Expressway | |

# Guangming Smartcity China

Along the roadside, groups of men hunker down, waiting. Some of them idle away the hours gambling with small counters; others smoke out of boredom. Their trade is farming, but they no longer have farms on which to ply this trade. After the initial novelty of being moved from traditional rural houses to modern 'aspirational' high-rise developments, some of China's new urban residents have found a living running small businesses or hiring themselves out as construction labourers. Many others are surviving off a sudden windfall in cash compensation that is as double-edged as it is finite.

In order to fast-track China's economic development, over 200 million farmers have been divested of their livelihoods in the last 30 years to make way for industrialization and urbanization. All land in China is state-owned with plots granted to farmers on long leases, which has smoothed the way for land expropriation. Despite growing concerns regarding food self-sufficiency and a rural reform plan designed to secure farming land rights, local authorities have largely been able to ignore directives from the central government.

Legislation to preserve farmland is growing increasingly critical as China supports 22% of the world's population with only 10% of the world's cultivated land. Positively, more land has reverted to farming than appropriated for construction in the past few years, and the relocation of rural dwellers into urban environments has freed up land for cultivation. At the same time, the rural migration has displaced important social bonds in the form of native-place networks; villagers retain a strong allegiance to their place of origin that is reflected in their attitudes to upbringing, life rituals and employment.

Over the past three decades, China's cities have been developing at an overwhelming rate; some of them are even bigger than in many industrial nations. By 2010 it is anticipated that half of China's population will have moved from the countryside to the cities, triggered by the desire of rural inhabitants to take part in China's economic boom. The nation has eclipsed the US in the consumption of basic agricultural and industrial goods, and is now the world's largest consumer of grain, meat, coal and steel. With such huge industrial, agricultural and economic shifts come major demands on resources as well as environmental issues.

A new town centre for the 200 000 residents of Guangming in Shenzhen presents the opportunity to develop a city paradigm reconciling the contrasting needs of urban growth and rural preservation – in essence a Smartcity. China has a history of having built the largest and most spectacular cities before the modern era, with Beijing reaching some two million people as long ago as the 17th century AD. However, it has also continued to be a land of villages and farmers. Guangming will continue this agricultural

facing page: Guangming Smartcity masterplan

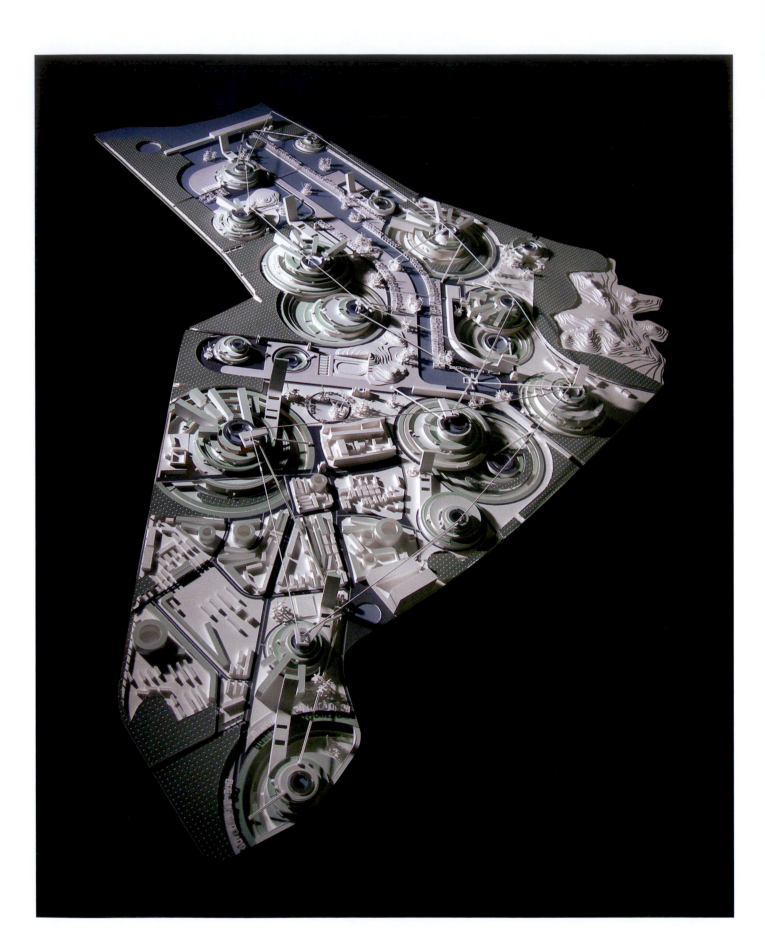

heritage, creating a hybrid city at the vanguard of eco-sustainability and pioneering a new way of urban living for Shenzhen.

Guangming Smartcity covers an area of 7.97km2 of Guangming New Town, northwest of Shenzhen in Guangdong Province. The site is surrounded by the region's agricultural land, with the Longda Expressway, Maozhou River and Gongming Village Industrial Cluster to the west, and Guangming Innovation and Hi-tech Industrial Park to the south. It is adjacent to Dongguan City, 18km to Shenzhen International Airport, 40km to Hong Kong and an hour's drive from the city centre of Shenzhen.

53

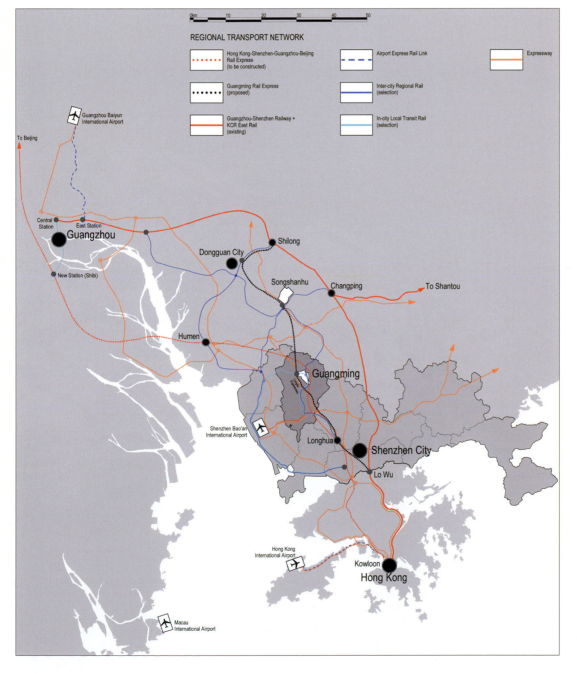

facing + following page: Model of Guangming Smartcity

left: Location plan of Guangming Smartcity and the regional transport network

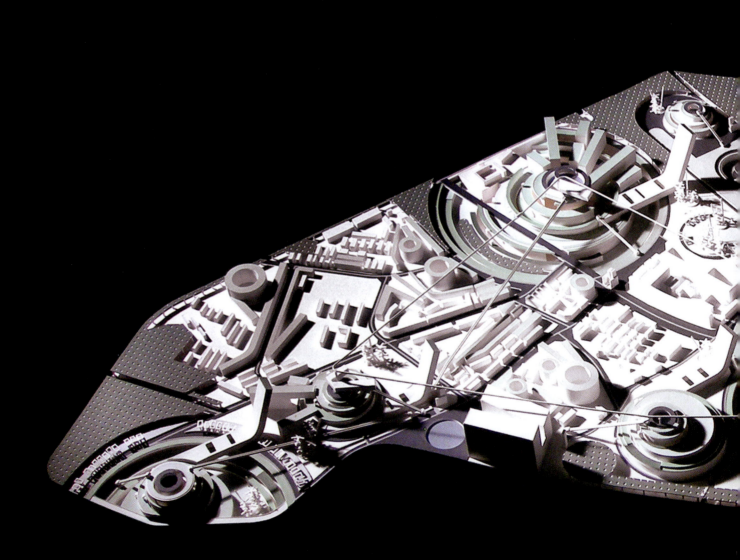

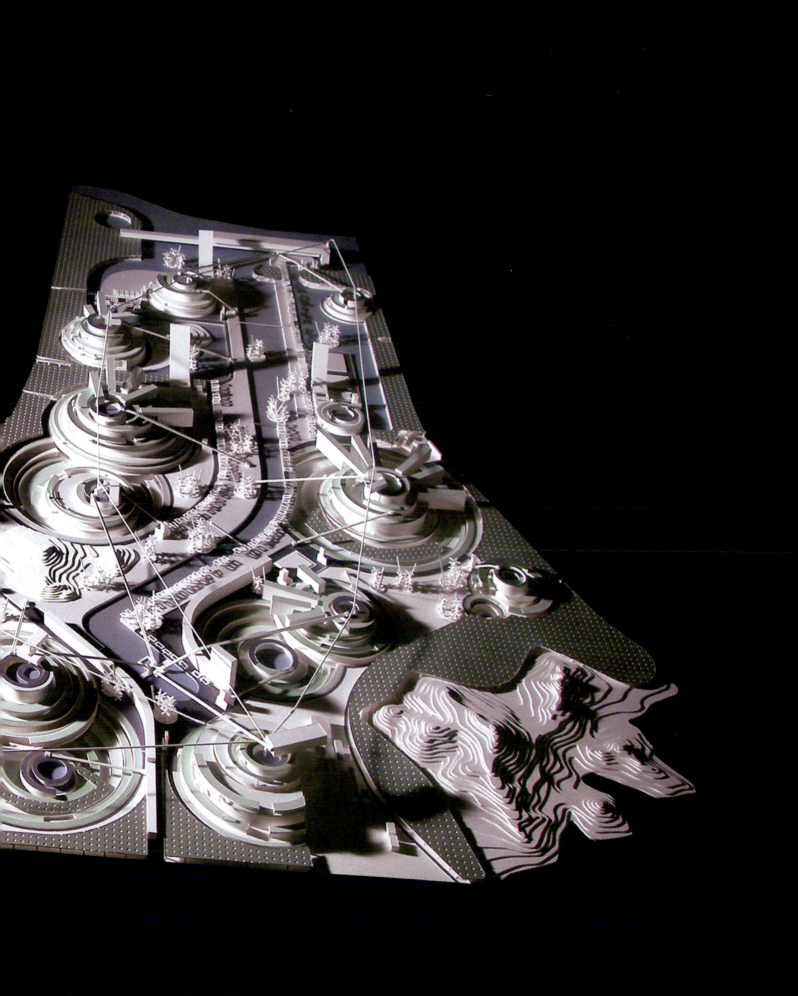

### Regional Development + New Programmes for the Smartcity

The programmes for Guangming Smartcity have been established with the development of the region clearly in mind. Fundamentally, the site cannot become an isolated island city – it must support, complement and act as a generative seed for the region and beyond. The proposals for Guangming Smartcity, fully supported by an effective transport infrastructure, integrate with the surrounding BaoAn district at various levels, providing civic, commercial, recreational, agricultural, cultural and tourist facilities. Overlaid onto this basic function of a town centre, the programmatic backbone of the Smartcity will comprise organic urban agriculture, agritourism and eco-gastronomy.

As well as servicing its own residents, Guangming Smartcity will act as a civic and commercial centre for Gongming and Songshanhu. Besides providing the usual services and necessities of daily life, the commercial centre will specifically promote eco-products, organic foodstuffs and holistic living in keeping with the sustainable ethos of the development. In this way, the Smartcity will not duplicate the retail and service industries in Shenzhen City or Dongguan whilst simultaneously reinforcing the brand image of Guangming as a model of sustainable living.

### Agricultural Context

China is currently struggling with the problem of increasing the efficiency of its agricultural production whilst finding employment for a vast number of rural migrants in cities already suffering from high unemployment rates. Within the next three decades, it intends to reduce its farm employment to 10% of the labour force. In the long term, the influx of new urban dwellers will create a new market for goods and services in the city, boosting employment and the country's GDP. In the short term, the erstwhile farmers lack the skills required for working in an urban environment, have been cut off from their social infrastructure, and are discriminated against by established city dwellers. The hybridization of city and arable land in Guangming Smartcity offers an interim solution by allowing farmers to retain their land, and by extension their social insurance that they do not receive if they work in cities, whilst offering opportunities to train in new employment sectors. Part-time farming becomes viable, and the city's diversification into high-end and high-yield agriculture presents an alternative career route, maintaining both a connection with the soil and financial parity with other vocations.

The local practice of dairy, vegetable, fruit and pigeon farming will be retained and modernized with advanced farming techniques. Guangming Smartcity will continue to be the principal supplier of milk and vegetables to Hong Kong, but will use aquaculture and hydroponics to increase crop yields. Disease prevention will be improved, and urban nutrient waste recycling introduced to establish a circular economy. Together with the innovative vertical farms and floral gardens, arable laboratories and institutions specializing in nutrition and food science, the Smartcity will be ideally placed to be a testing ground and partner for the South China Agricultural University in Guangzhou. Traditionally, education amongst villagers is seen as a means to migrate to urban employment; graduate level rural education could reverse this trend, allowing farmers to adopt new techniques and correct age-old urban prejudices.

The existing farming community, together with new agricultural schools, will play an important role in sustaining a skilled workforce in the local area that are able to run farms as viable businesses. Local food production will establish a strong sense of community and substantially help reduce energy and fuel consumption from food transportation. Guangming Smartcity locates people where the food grows instead of moving food to the people.

Livestock and crops will be allowed to grow at their natural pace without pesticides or preservatives and animals will be reared without the use of growth hormones. Livestock manure and human organic waste will be recycled for nutrients in anaerobic digesters, exemplifying the efficiencies of permaculture.

At present, most organic food in China is grown for the export market. However, with the standard of living and purchasing power of discerning Chinese consumers on the rise, greater demand is expected from the domestic market.

57

### Ecogastronomy and Agritourism

Ecogastronomy promotes healthy eating along with protecting the environment. With its accessibility to the finest local produce and livestock and commitment to organic farming techniques, visitors from the region and abroad will be able to enjoy first-rate cuisine and understand the provenance of their food. The Smartcity is well placed to become an international venue for symposia concerning the production, understanding, development and sharing of food.

Despite the high population density of Guangming Smartcity, layered planning leaves generous areas for public relaxation and leisure in the form of an urban beach and canal. The grazing fields and aquaculture terraces will also offer scenic beauty and green space in stark contrast with the urban fabric of industrial parks outside the city. The beach will be a closer and more convenient leisure destination than the coastline with luxury hotel and villa accommodation facilities, making the city centre an ideal weekend resort for Gongming and Shenzhen. Consequently, the Smartcity can act as a tourist base for other recreational locales such as Songshanhu that offer complementary leisure pursuits such as fishing and boating.

left: Local organic produce

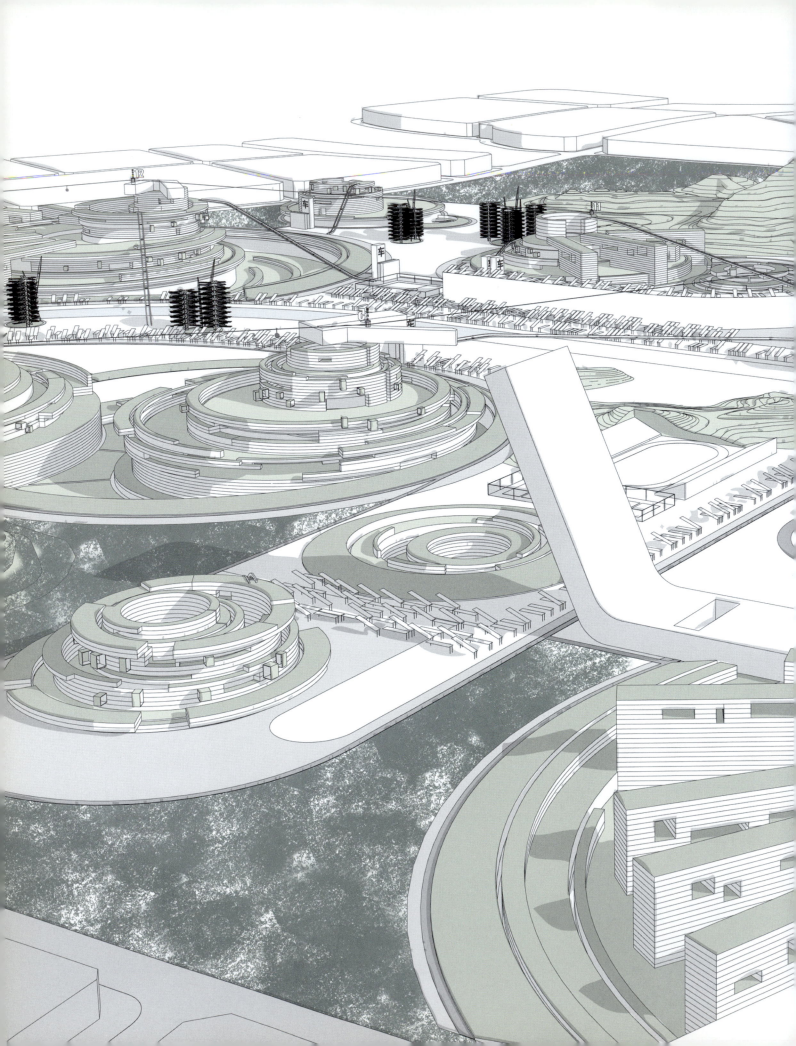

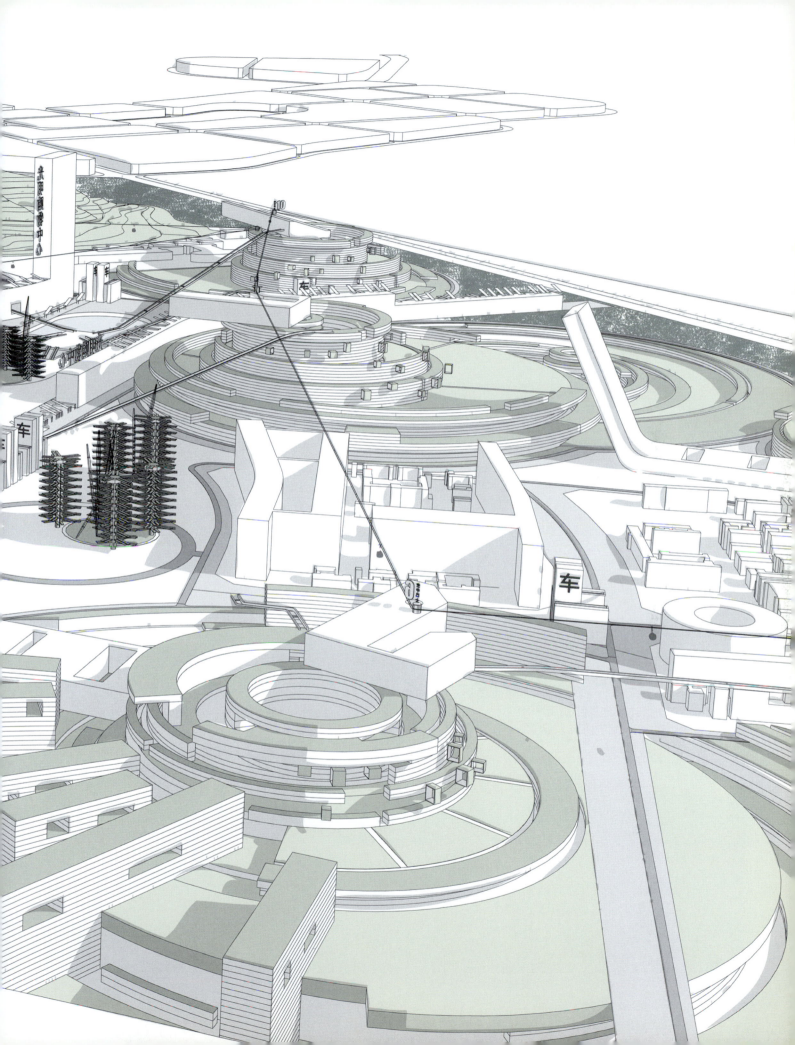

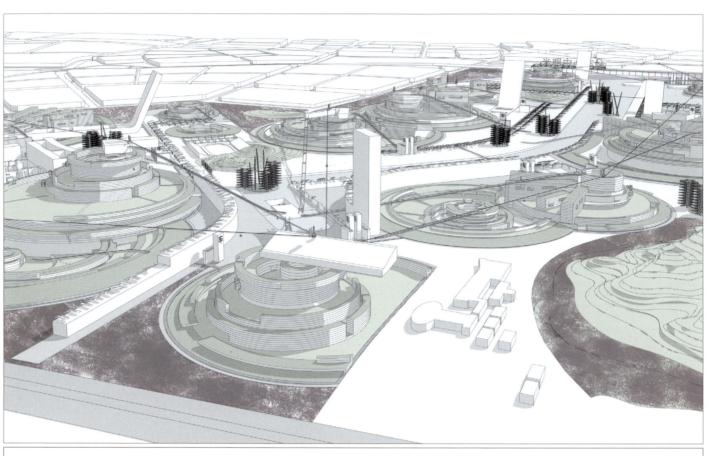

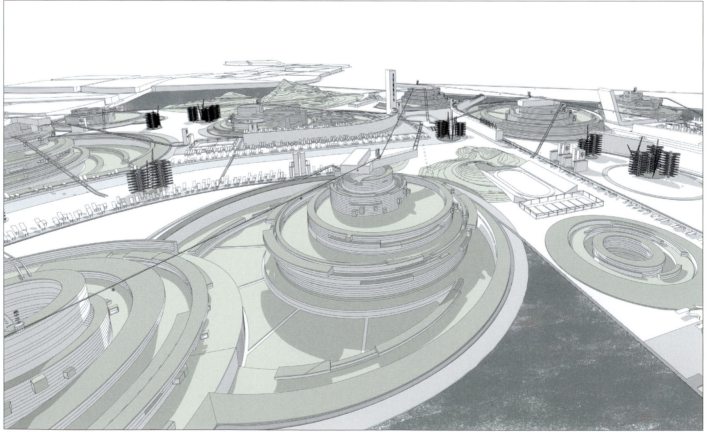

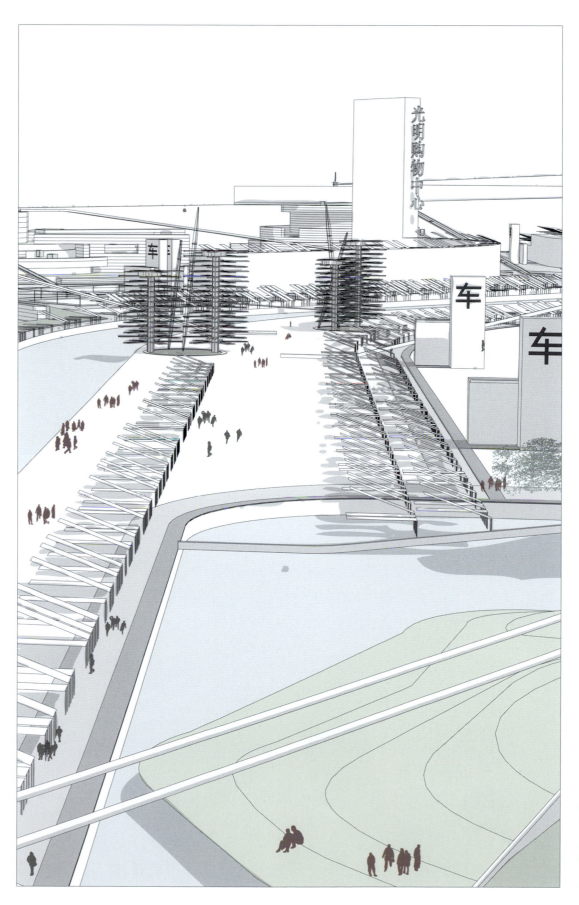

光明购物中心

车

车

车

previous page: View towards the commercial centre

facing top + bottom: View from the north; View from the east

left: View from the train station

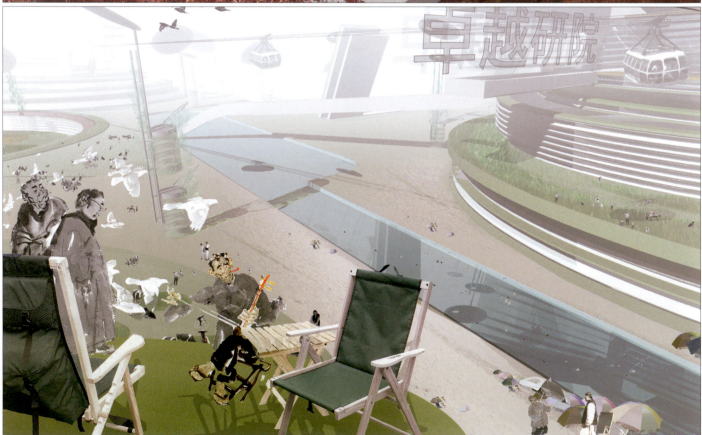

facing page top: Lychee orchards as natural pollution filters

facing page bottom: Social and cultural activities on the suburb terrace

top: Suburb plaza water reservoir

bottom: Farmers' market on the reservoir

## City Framework

Guangming enjoys rich mountainous and river resources that are exploited in the city's morphology. The Smartcity is arranged into optimally sized clusters of housing and farming suburbs that manifest as towers and craters, shaped by and augmenting the existing undulating topography. The towers and craters borrow from the technocratic formalism of the Japanese Metabolists and the utopian trope of concentric ringed streets and buildings, but introduce a third vertical dimension calibrated to storey-height terraces. This stepped arrangement improves the solar angle for natural lighting within the apartment buildings and offices; natural cross ventilation is possible and the distances between buildings can be reduced to increase housing density without adverse overshadowing. Most significantly, the terracing creates level rooftop surfaces that can be used for farming without fear of erosion and slippage. The result is an unprecedented spatial connection between mass housing and arable land. Where necessary, the terrain is reshaped by redistributing excavated material from the craters to the towers and the addition of inert but non-biodegradable landfill that has been accumulating around China's cities at an alarming rate.

The density of the tower and crater suburbs prevents urban sprawl and advocates compact land use patterns that assist in limiting the carbon footprint of the town centre's residents. Each tower or crater is self-sufficient with its own high street, suburb square and individual community identity.

In the centre of the development area is an artificial beach and canal leading into the revitalized Maozhou River where a reed bed water filtration system is introduced. The beach is a recreational oasis that contrasts with the ubiquitous open space that, although scenic, is fully productive. A boardwalk encircles the beach and connects the tower and crater communities providing a place to meet and socialize. Traversed by bicycle or electric buggy, the boardwalk also plays host to the practice of tai chi, jogging and constitutional walks.

Over 80 vertical kitchen garden farms can be found scattered throughout the central city, and collectively they form the city's arable research institute. The city's vertical floral gardens sit alongside the vertical kitchen garden farms around which people can sit, mingle and enjoy the scent of local flora. The interstitial landscape is used to graze livestock.

The Smartcity is a car-free zone and individual suburbs are designed with their own local municipal facilities to ensure day-to-day activities are within walkable distances. The primary transport system between neighbourhoods will be via light rail (MTR). Electric or biogas sky-buses run between the urban plazas at the top of each tower and crater community that are individually accessed by funiculars, lifts and escalators. The City Hall lies on an axis along the Maozhou River with the Central Train Station and overlooks the entire city from the top of the largest suburb tower. Six other Centres of Excellence sitting astride the remaining suburb towers complete an urban sky court in a reinterpretation of the traditional city square.

Lychee and longan orchards, the fruit of which are renowned in the region, border the site and act as a filter for the clean inner heart of the city. The orchard belt is periodically interrupted by peripheral car parks and recycling centres serving the community as well as incoming visitors who can also deposit waste for local energy generation. The bank of trees extends along the embankments of the Maozhou River, metaphorically reaching out and embracing the Smartcity's neighbouring towns. Guangming's new centre is self-sufficient but not inward looking, its environmental programme offering a resource for the region to the mutual benefit of both parties.

# urban agriculture: Guangming Smartcity

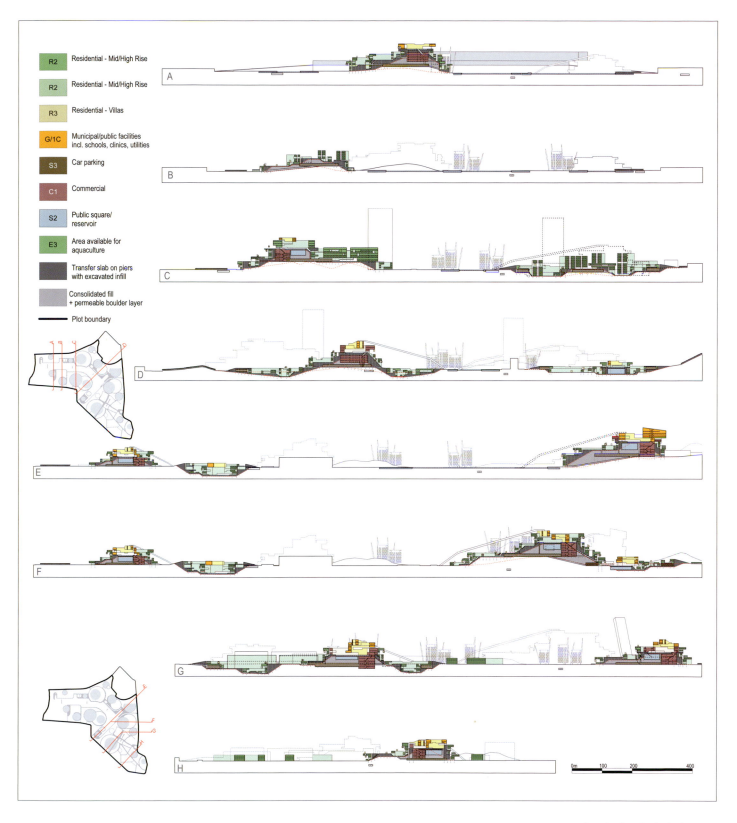

**Legend:**

- **R2** — Residential - Mid/High Rise
- **R2** — Residential - Mid/High Rise
- **R3** — Residential - Villas
- **G/1C** — Municipal/public facilities incl. schools, clinics, utilities
- **S3** — Car parking
- **C1** — Commercial
- **S2** — Public square/reservoir
- **E3** — Area available for aquaculture
- Transfer slab on piers with excavated infill
- Consolidated fill + permeable boulder layer
- Plot boundary

Sections: A, B, C, D, E, F, G, H

0m  100  200  400

above: Sections showing land use distribution in the Smartcity

following page: Infrastructure plans of Guangming Smartcity

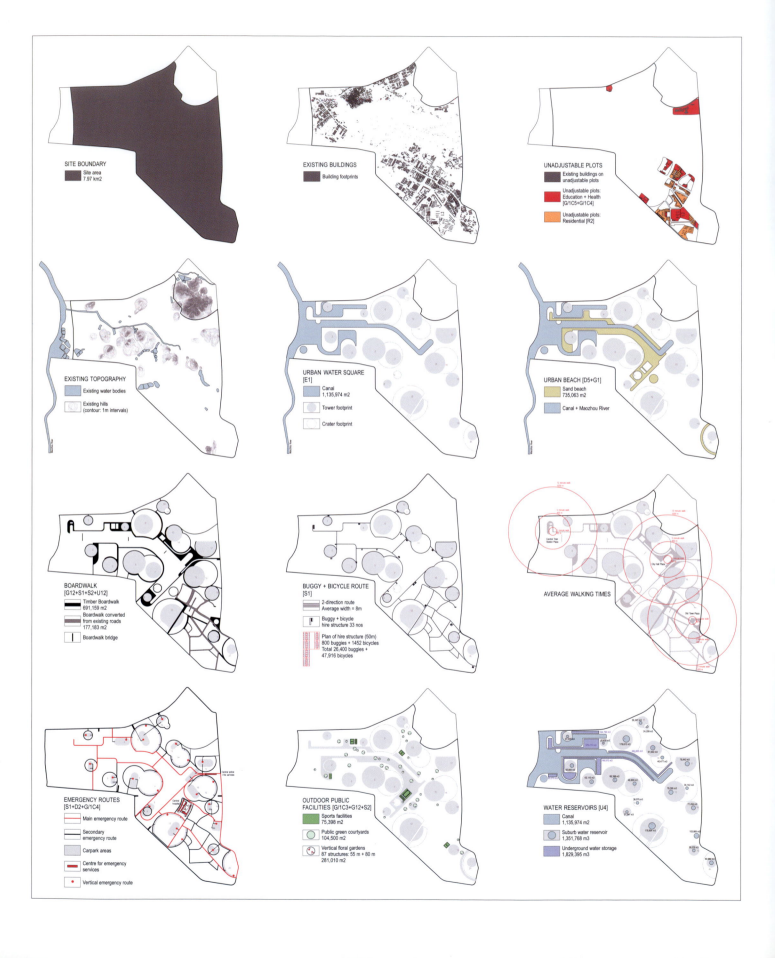

**SITE BOUNDARY**
- Site area
  7.97 km2

**EXISTING BUILDINGS**
- Building footprints

**UNADJUSTABLE PLOTS**
- Existing buildings on unadjustable plots
- Unadjustable plots: Education + Health [G/1C5+G/1C4]
- Unadjustable plots: Residential [R2]

**EXISTING TOPOGRAPHY**
- Existing water bodies
- Existing hills (contour: 1m intervals)

**URBAN WATER SQUARE [E1]**
- Canal 1,135,974 m2
- Tower footprint
- Crater footprint

**URBAN BEACH [D5+G1]**
- Sand beach 735,063 m2
- Canal + Maozhou River

**BOARDWALK [G12+S1+S2+U12]**
- Timber Boardwalk 691,159 m2
- Boardwalk converted from existing roads 177,183 m2
- Boardwalk bridge

**BUGGY + BICYCLE ROUTE [S1]**
- 2-direction route Average width = 8m
- Buggy + bicycle hire structure 33 nos
- Plan of hire structure (50m) 800 buggies + 1452 bicycles Total 26,400 buggies + 47,916 bicycles

**AVERAGE WALKING TIMES**

**EMERGENCY ROUTES [S1+D2+G/1C4]**
- Main emergency route
- Secondary emergency route
- Carpark areas
- Centre for emergency services
- Vertical emergency route

**OUTDOOR PUBLIC FACILITIES [G/1C3+G12+S2]**
- Sports facilities 75,398 m2
- Public green courtyards 104,500 m2
- Vertical floral gardens 87 structures: 55 m + 80 m 281,010 m2

**WATER RESERVOIRS [U4]**
- Canal 1,135,974 m2
- Suburb water reservoir 1,351,768 m3
- Underground water storage 1,829,395 m3

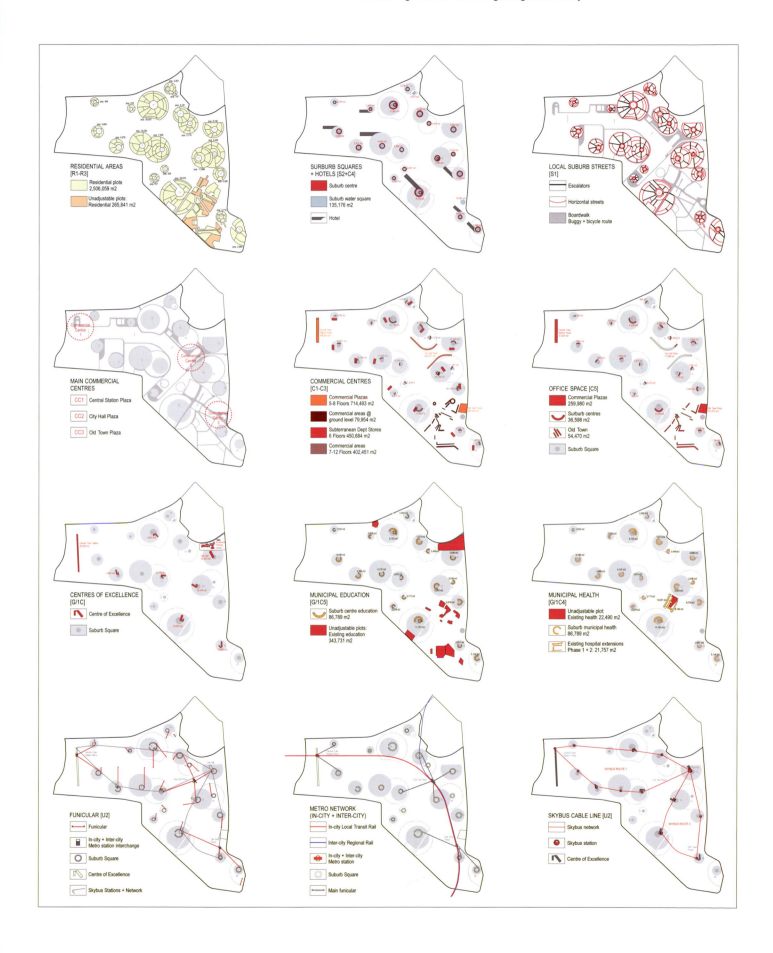

RESIDENTIAL AREAS
[R1–R3]

Residential plots
2,506,059 m2

Unadjustable plots:
Residential 265,841 m2

SURBURB SQUARES
+ HOTELS [S2+C4]

Suburb centre

Suburb water square
135,176 m2

Hotel

LOCAL SUBURB STREETS
[S1]

Escalators

Horizontal streets

Boardwalk
Buggy + bicycle route

MAIN COMMERCIAL
CENTRES

CC1  Central Station Plaza

CC2  City Hall Plaza

CC3  Old Town Plaza

COMMERCIAL CENTRES
[C1–C3]

Commercial Plazas
5-8 Floors 714,493 m2

Commercial areas @
ground level 79,954 m2

Subterranean Dept Stores
6 Floors 450,684 m2

Commercial areas
7-12 Floors 402,451 m2

OFFICE SPACE [C5]

Commercial Plazas
259,980 m2

Surburb centres
36,598 m2

Old Town
54,470 m2

Suburb Square

CENTRES OF EXCELLENCE
[G/1C]

Centre of Excellence

Suburb Square

MUNICIPAL EDUCATION
[G/1C5]

Suburb centre education
86,789 m2

Unadjustable plots:
Existing education
343,731 m2

MUNICIPAL HEALTH
[G/1C4]

Unadjustable plot:
Existing health 22,490 m2

Suburb municipal health
86,789 m2

Existing hospital extensions
Phase 1 + 2: 21,757 m2

FUNICULAR [U2]

Funicular

In-city + Inter-city
Metro station interchange

Suburb Square

Centre of Excellence

Skybus Stations + Network

METRO NETWORK
(IN-CITY + INTER-CITY)

In-city Local Transit Rail

Inter-city Regional Rail

In-city + Inter-city
Metro station

Suburb Square

Main funicular

SKYBUS CABLE LINE [U2]

Skybus network

Skybus station

Centre of Excellence

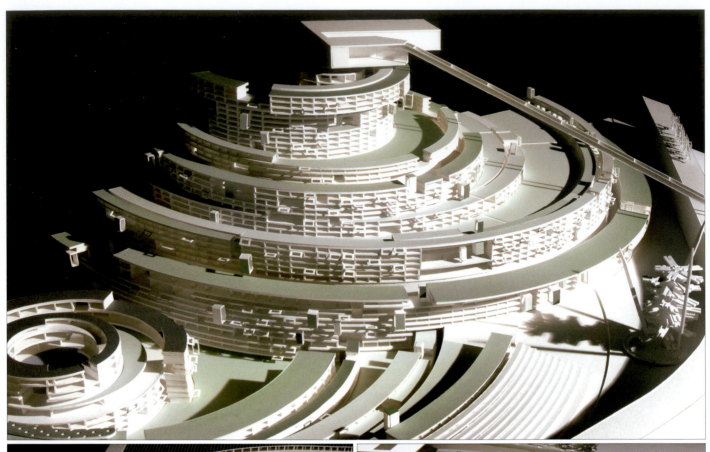

## Tower + Crater Suburbs

The sizes of the tower and crater communities are carefully designed both to provide a variety of environments and to take advantage of shared resources. Environmentally, there are synergistic benefits of common walls, reduced energy consumption and improved structural integrity. Socially, the planned populations of each community are optimized to be autarkic in terms of education, health, commerce and recreation, catering for residents of all ages and from every stratum of society. A significant proportion of its housing stock will be affordable units, and all buildings will meet the accessibility needs of an increasingly ageing population. The radially stacked arrangement of the housing addresses the generational domestic politics of the family, especially those households comprising of more than two generations. A broad range of typologies including houses, apartments, villas, studios and care homes cater for the community spectrum, all within a stunning agrarian landscape.

Each suburb has a main street at its apex with local shops and services to meet quotidian needs: a tailor, a grocer, a health clinic with medics, dentists, opticians and a natural healing centre, a cinema, a post office, banks, schools, religious centres and office buildings. The suburb square operates as a farmers' market, community gathering space and outdoor arena for concerts and festivals. A reservoir is located in the centre of the square that stores rainwater, contributes to the summer cooling strategy, and provides an attractive backdrop for community events. Although the tower and crater suburbs possess similar basic amenities each has its own individual character and specialization in the eight Centres of Excellence which comprise a mediatheque, the International Food Festival convention centre, the Museum of Eco-Gastronomy, the Agricultural University, the International Food Forum, the International Culinary and Catering College, Guangming Smartcity Central Station and Guangming City Hall. This urban arrangement encourages social communication between the different tower and crater communities.

## Tower Formation

The proposal amplifies the natural topology of the area by excavating and filling certain areas. Existing hills are built up with material taken from adjacent earth cuttings. The base of each tower is naturally formed. Onto this, large boulders taken from nearby bedrock are piled. Stone columns, local compactions of the rock, are installed using standard methods. A car parking basement in reinforced concrete, base slab, columns and cover slab is placed as the building-up work proceeds. Over the final hill profile, geo-textile layer and sand is applied. This seals the boulder layer through which cooling air is to pass towards the buildings above.

Reinforced concrete pad foundations are set on the stone column locations and an under-croft built up. Suspended slabs support the public spaces at their chosen level. Areas of solid build-up support roadways and agricultural areas. Piers for the large annular accommodation structures bear on the stone columns and pass up through the ground plane to support pre-stressed in-situ placed reinforced concrete transfer slabs. These slabs are stiffened by concrete cross-walls. Simple plates of concrete support a variety of accommodation completed in reinforced concrete, block-work, timber and lightweight steel framing.

facing page: A suburb tower and crater

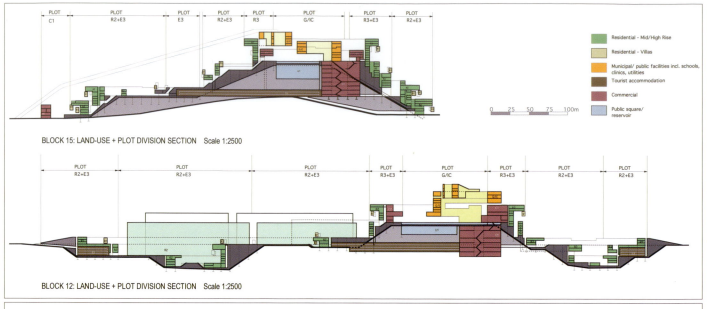

PLOT C1 | PLOT R2+E3 | PLOT E3 | PLOT R2+E3 | PLOT R3 | PLOT G/IC | PLOT R3+E3 | PLOT R2+E3

**Residential - Mid/High Rise**
**Residential - Villas**
**Municipal/ public facilities incl. schools, clinics, utilities**
**Tourist accommodation**
**Commercial**
**Public square/ reservoir**

0  25  50  75  100m

BLOCK 15: LAND-USE + PLOT DIVISION SECTION   Scale 1:2500

PLOT R2+E3 | PLOT R2+E3 | PLOT R2+E3 | PLOT R3+E3 | PLOT G/IC | PLOT R3+E3 | PLOT R2+E3 | PLOT R2+E3

BLOCK 12: LAND-USE + PLOT DIVISION SECTION   Scale 1:2500

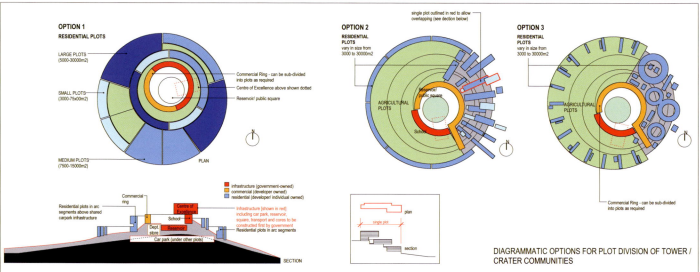

**OPTION 1**
RESIDENTIAL PLOTS

LARGE PLOTS (5000-30000m2)

SMALL PLOTS (3000-75x00m2)

MEDIUM PLOTS (7500-15000m2)

PLAN

Commercial Ring - can be sub-divided into plots as required
Centre of Excellence above shown dotted
Reservoir/ public square

Commercial ring
Residential plots in arc segments above shared carpark infrastructure

Centre of Excellence
School
Dept. store
Reservoir
Car park (under other plots)

infrastructure (government-owned)
commercial (developer owned)
residential (developer/ individual owned)

Infrastructure [shown in red] including car park, reservoir, square, transport and cores to be constructed first by government
Residential plots in arc segments

SECTION

**OPTION 2**
RESIDENTIAL PLOTS
vary in size from 3000 to 30000m2

single plot outlined in red to allow overlapping (see section below)

AGRICULTURAL PLOTS

Reservoir/ public square
School

plan
single plot
section

**OPTION 3**
RESIDENTIAL PLOTS
vary in size from 3000 to 30000m2

AGRICULTURAL PLOTS

Commercial Ring - can be sub-divided into plots as required

DIAGRAMMATIC OPTIONS FOR PLOT DIVISION OF TOWER / CRATER COMMUNITIES

## A Day in the Life in Guangming Smartcity

### Mrs Lam – Elder

1. Mrs Lam wakes up early and sweeps the apartment.
2. She then ascends to the suburban sky square
3. Where she practises tai chi on the reservoir.
4. Mrs Lam meets several of her friends for dim sum at the food court and picks up some groceries from the market a short walk away.
5. She then goes to see the herbal doctor at the health clinic in the municipal quarter of the square.
6. Mrs Lam returns home and has some rice and steamed vegetables for lunch.
7. Mrs Lam has an afternoon nap.
8. In the early afternoon, she goes to visit her friend who lives on the outer residential ring.
9. Mrs Lam returns home to prepare dinner for herself and her son who will soon return from working in the lychee groves.

### Zhang Siu Ming – Teenager

1. After breakfast, Siu Ming meets his schoolmate Siu Fun who lives a few doors away.
2. Siu Ming + Siu Fun walk to school which is in the municipal district above the kindergarten.
3. Siu Ming spends the day at school. For lunch he can eat in the school dining room, on the rooftop playground or go to a café in the nearby suburb square.
4. After school, Siu Ming ascends to the Skybus platform outside the Centre of Excellence.
5. He takes the cable car to the local stadium where he plays football.
6. After the game, he takes the Skybus back to the tower community where he lives.
7. Siu Ming returns home via the suburb square.
8. After having a quick meal, Siu Ming finishes his homework and goes to bed.

### Mr Jiang – Farmer

1. Mr Jiang lives at the base of the main inner ring with his elderly mother, Mrs Lam. He rises early.
2. Mr Jiang spends most of the morning tending his vegetables in the aquaculture field outside his home.
3. He is able to return home for lunch as the farmland is so close.
4. In the afternoon, Mr Jiang takes the escalator down to the base of the tower and makes his way to his lychee orchard.
5. He spends several hours pruning his trees.
6. Mr Jiang returns home via the escalator.
7. At home, he has dinner with his mother.

### Mr Zhang – Industrial Park Worker

1. Mr Zhang lives on an inner ring with his wife, son and baby daughter.
2. After breakfast, he descends to the underground car park by lift.
3. He leaves Guangming Smartcity by car via one of the two peripheral link roads and drives to the Innovation + Hi-tech Industrial Park where he works.
4. Mr Zhang returns to the tower community after work.
5. He enters the department store from car park level and picks up a few household items.
6. He then ascends to the food court in the commercial ring at the top of the tower and meets his wife and daughter for dinner.
7. After enjoying a leisurely meal, they take a short walk around the shops before taking the lift down to their floor.
8. Mr Zhang and his family return home and retire for the evening.

The new structures are arranged so that movement joints fall on radial divisions of the site. This allows for the segmental development of each area. The central square and reservoir of the tower rests on the built up fill on a flexible pre-stressed concrete base. Vertical ducts in the perimeter walls bring cooling air upwards from the rock layer.

## Plot division + flexibility

Despite the strong form of the circular towers and craters, there is inherent flexibility in the design proposal at a range of scales. Each tower and crater can be considered to be a series of linear streets, wrapped into concentric rings. Each ring is subdivided into plot segments separated by radial circulation paths, ensuring that each plot is easily accessible. Plot sizes range from 3000m2 to 350 000m2. The ratio and sizes of these plots can be easily redistributed to suit land conveyance demands.

Additionally, the master plan incorporates hybrid tower and crater communities in which the circular forms are opened up to incorporate more conventional orthogonal urban typologies that radiate from the same centre. This has the benefit of introducing a wider range of places and characteristics, integrating with the existing settlement, and allowing for complexities of land attornment.

At a community scale, the spatial and structural design of the towers and craters also invite future change. Based on standard depths of six or eight metres for natural ventilation and lighting, apartments are arranged in 40m2 modules. Residences can be 40m2, 60m2, 80m2, 120m2 or 200m2 in size; the ratio will again depend on the mix of tenure and demand, but a column and beam system will allow walls to be reconfigured so that smaller apartments can be expanded into larger ones, or vice versa should the need arise.

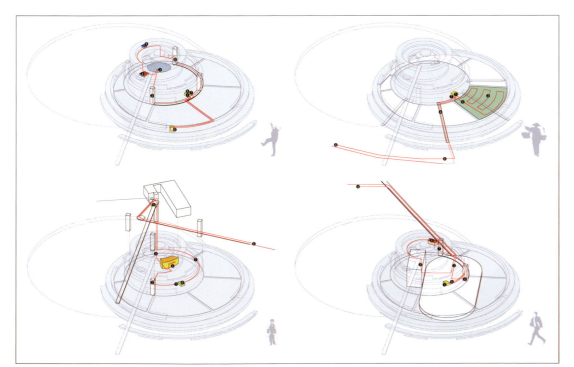

facing page top: Section showing land-use and plot division

facing page bottom: Diagrammatic options for plot division in the tower/crater communities

left (clockwise from top left): A day in the life of Guangming Smartcity: Mrs Lam – elder; Mr Jiang – farmer; Mr Zhang – industrial park worker; Zhang Siu Ming – teenager

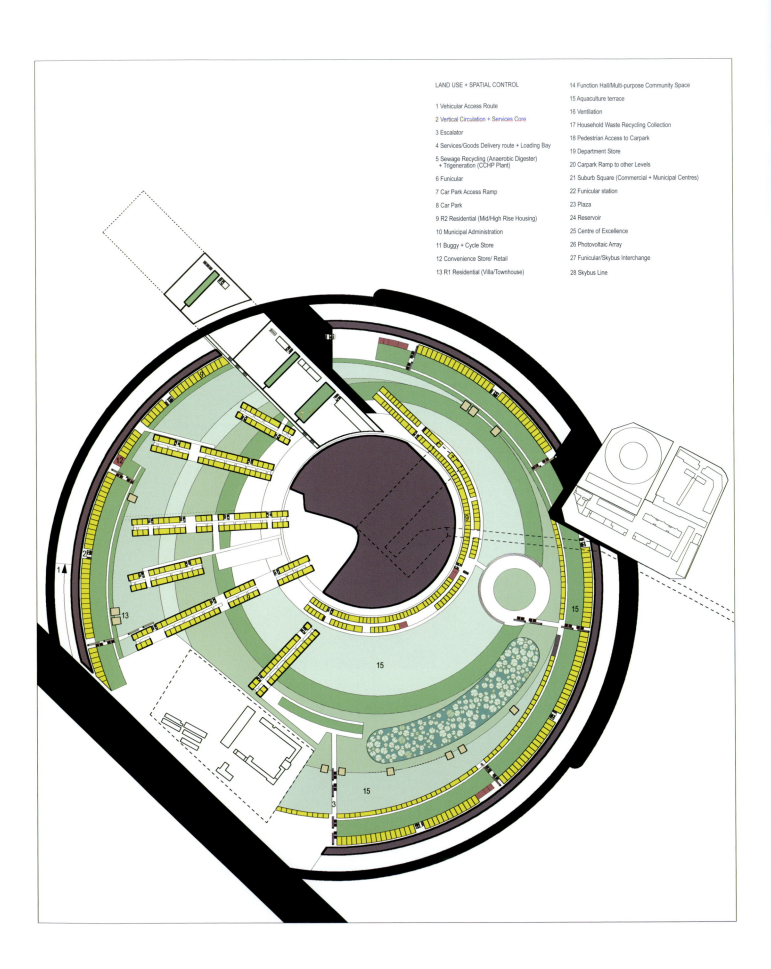

LAND USE + SPATIAL CONTROL

1 Vehicular Access Route
2 Vertical Circulation + Services Core
3 Escalator
4 Services/Goods Delivery route + Loading Bay
5 Sewage Recycling (Anaerobic Digester)
  + Trigeneration (CCHP Plant)
6 Funicular
7 Car Park Access Ramp
8 Car Park
9 R2 Residential (Mid/High Rise Housing)
10 Municipal Administration
11 Buggy + Cycle Store
12 Convenience Store/ Retail
13 R1 Residential (Villa/Townhouse)

14 Function Hall/Multi-purpose Community Space
15 Aquaculture terrace
16 Ventilation
17 Household Waste Recycling Collection
18 Pedestrian Access to Carpark
19 Department Store
20 Carpark Ramp to other Levels
21 Suburb Square (Commercial + Municipal Centres)
22 Funicular station
23 Plaza
24 Reservoir
25 Centre of Excellence
26 Photovoltaic Array
27 Funicular/Skybus Interchange
28 Skybus Line

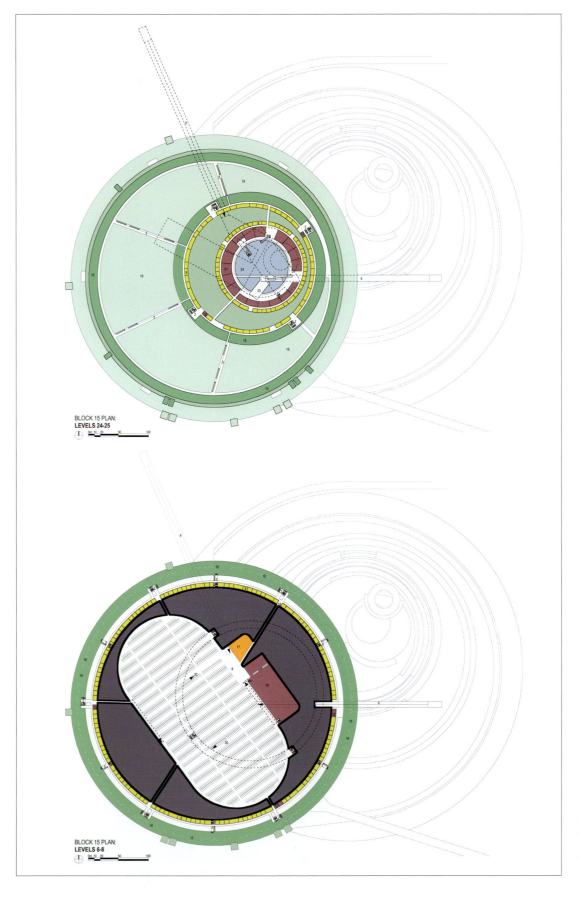

**BLOCK 15 PLAN:**
**LEVELS 24-25**

**BLOCK 15 PLAN:**
**LEVELS 6-8**

facing page + left top + bottom:
Generic plans of suburb tower

following page: Country living in the
Smartcity

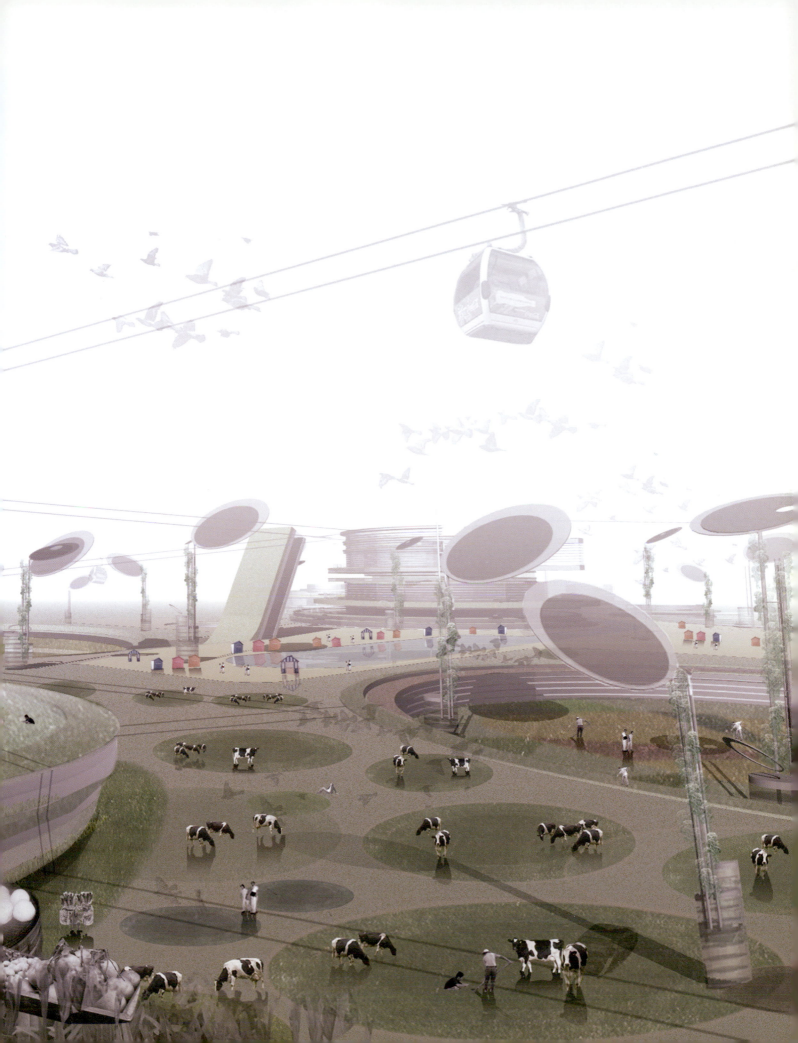

Table 1 Technical and Economic Index Table for the Main Urban Construction Land

| 序号 No. | 用地性质 Land Use | 用地面积(公顷) Area [Ha] | 建筑面积(万平米) Floor Area [10 000m2] | 建筑密度 Building Density | 建筑密度 Plot Ratio | 绿化率 Green Ratio | 人口容量 Population Carrying Capacity |
|---|---|---|---|---|---|---|---|
| 1 | 居住用地 Residential Land | 277.80 | 495.80 | 42.79% | 1.78 | 0.57 | 189 831 |
| 2 | 商业+服务设施用地 Commercial + Service Facility Land | 42.80 | 276.79 | 85.42% | 6.47 | 0.15 | 18 072 |
| 3 | 政府和社团用地 Government + Community Land | 66.70 | 149.72 | 36.69% | 2.24 | 0.63 | N/A |
| 4 | 绿地 Green Space (incl. beach + agricultural) | 296.11 | 0.00 | 0.00% | 0.00 | 1.00 | N/A |
| 5 | 其它用地 Miscellaneous (incl. Roads + Transport) | 113.69 | 6.64 | 5.84% | 0.06 | 0.00 | N/A |
| | 合计 Total/ Mean | 797.10 | 928.95 | 23.40% | 1.17 | 0.77 | N/A |

Table 2 Technical and Economic Index for Block 15 (Typical)

| 地块编号 Block No. | 用地性质 Land Use | 用地面积(公顷) Area [Ha] | 面积(万平米) Floor Area [10 000m2] | 建筑密度 Building Density | 容积率 Plot Ratio | 绿化率 Green Ratio | 人口容量 Popuation Carrying |
|---|---|---|---|---|---|---|---|
| 15 | 居住用地 Residential Land | 14.17 | 31.17 | 54.74% | 2.20 | 0.45 | 11 568 |
| | 商业+服务设施用地 Commercial + Service Facility Land | 1.04 | 4.33 | 94.96% | 4.17 | 0.05 | N/A |
| | 政府和社团用地 Government + Community Land | 0.35 | 1.93 | 76.72% | 5.52 | 0.23 | N/A |
| | 绿地(包括农业用地) Green Space (incl. Agricultural Land) | 1.10 | 0.00 | 0.00% | 0.00 | 100.00 | N/A |
| | 其它用地 Miscellaneous | 0.00 | N/A | N/A | N/A | N/A | N/A |
| | 合计 Total | 16.66 | 37.43 | 54.09% | 2.25 | 0.46 | 11 568 |

Table 3 Technical and Economic Index Table for Residential Land

| 类别 Item | 编号 No. | 名称 Name | | 单位 Unit | 数量 Quantity | 百分比 % | 平方米/人 m2/ Person | 备注 Remarks |
|---|---|---|---|---|---|---|---|---|
| 用地规模 Land-use Scale | 1 | 居住用地 Residential Land | | ha | 152.15 | 19.09% | 8.06 | % is residential building footprint area to site area. Floor area per person is 26.26m2 |
| | 2 | 其中 Including | 二类居住用地 R2 Land | ha | 150.90 | 18.90% | 8.03 | |
| | | | 二类居住用地+商业用地 R2 + C1 (commercial) land | ha | 193.70 | 24.30% | N/A | % is R@ + C1 building footprint area to site area. Floor area per person is 40.97m2 |
| | 3 | 居住户数 Number of Households | | Households | 56 591 | N/A | N/A | |
| | 4 | 平均每户人数 Average no. of Persons per Household | | Persons | 3.34 | N/A | N/A | |
| | 5 | 居住人口 Resident Population | | In 10 000 persons | 18.88 | N/A | N/A | |
| | 6 | 居住用地总建筑面积 Total Building Area in theResidential Land | | m2 (in 10 000) | 922.31 | N/A | 48.84 | % figure to total floor area on site |
| | 7 | 其中 Including | 住宅建筑面积 Residential Floor Area | m2 (in 10 000) | 495.72 | 53.75% | 26.25 | |
| | | | 商住建筑商业面积 Commercial Area in the R2/C1 Complex | m2 (in 10 000) | 276.79 | 30.01% | 14.66 | |
| | | | 配套公建面积 Public Service Area | m2 (in 10 000) | 149.72 | 16.23% | 7.93 | Area includes education, health + government admin facilities |
| | 8 | 平居户居住建筑面积 Average Floor Area/ Household | | m2 | 162.98 | N/A | N/A | Figures for residential, commercial and public service area per household. |
| | 9 | 人口毛密度 Residential Density | | persons/ha | 236.90 | N/A | N/A | |
| | 10 | 居住用地总建筑密度 Total Building Density of the Residential Land | | % | N/A | 44.39% | N/A | Figures for building density of all land excluding lychee groves, beach, canal + broadwalk + grazing fields. |
| | 11 | 居住区容积率 Plot Ratio for the Residential District | | | N/A | 2.28 | N/A | Figures for building density of all land excluding lychee groves, beach, canal + broadwalk + grazing fields. |

Table 4 Main Public Service Facilities Planning List

| 序号 No. | 类别 Category | 项目 Item | 现状 Current Status Reservation | 规划增加 Planned Increase | 合计 Total | 备注 Remarks |
|---|---|---|---|---|---|---|
| 1 | 教育设施 Educational Facility | 幼儿园 Kindergarten | 5 406 | 43 855 | 49 261 | Existing figures estimated |
| | | 小学 Primary | 22 084 | 142 295 | 164 379 | Existing figures estimated |
| | | 初中 Middle | 25 266 | 85 377 | 110 643 | Existing figures estimated |
| | | 高中 High | 21 516 | 94 864 | 116 380 | Existing figures estimated |
| | | 职业训练 Vocational Training | 101 286 | 12 744 | 114 030 | Existing figures estimated |
| 2 | 医疗卫生设施 Medical + Healthcare Facilities | 医院 Hospitals | 15 560 | 174 056 | 189 616 | Existing figures estimated |
| | | 诊所 Clinics | 0 | 28 050 | 28 050 | |
| 3 | 文娱体育设施 Sports + Recreational Facilities | 海滩 Beach | 0 | 693 123 | 693 123 | |
| | | 体育馆 Stadium | 0 | 60 295 | 60 295 | Sports playing fields currently on site, area unknown. |
| | | 网球/ 篮球 Tennis/ Basketball | 0 | 19 320 | 19 320 | Existing figures unknown |
| 4 | 行政管理与社区服务设施 Admin + Community Service Facilities | 市政厅 City Hall | 0 | 24 903 | 24 903 | |
| | | 地方行政单位 Local Municipal Admin | 31 536 | 540 965 | 572 501 | Figures include police, fire + postal services. |
| 5 | 对外交通设施 Intercity Transport Facilities | 火车站 Railway Station | 0 | 26 659 | 26 659 | |
| | | 巴士站(包括长程) Bus Station (incl. long distance) | 30 202 | 35 202 | 65 404 | |
| 6 | 道路交通设施 Urban Traffic Facilities | 塔堡/环山进入道路 Residential Access Roads | 0 | 131 956 | 131 956 | Existing access roads uncalculated |
| | | 步道 Boardwalk | 0 | 868 342 | 868 342 | |
| | | 轻轨车站 Light Rail (MTR) Stations | 0 | 8 325 | 8 325 | Figures for above ground entrances only |

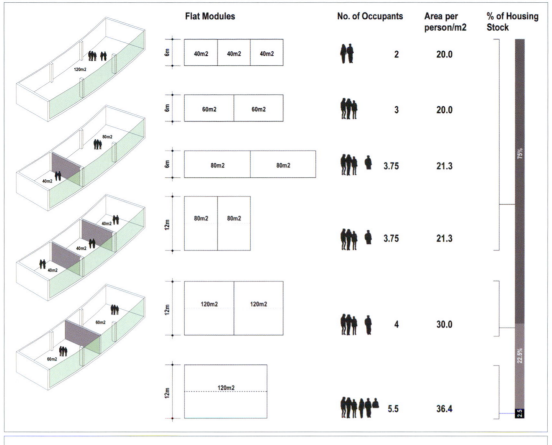

| Flat Modules | No. of Occupants | Area per person/m2 | % of Housing Stock |
|---|---|---|---|
| 40m2 / 40m2 / 40m2 (6m) | 2 | 20.0 | 75% |
| 60m2 / 60m2 (6m) | 3 | 20.0 | |
| 80m2 / 80m2 (6m) | 3.75 | 21.3 | |
| 80m2 / 80m2 (12m) | 3.75 | 21.3 | |
| 120m2 / 120m2 (12m) | 4 | 30.0 | 22.5% |
| 120m2 (12m) | 5.5 | 36.4 | 2.5 |

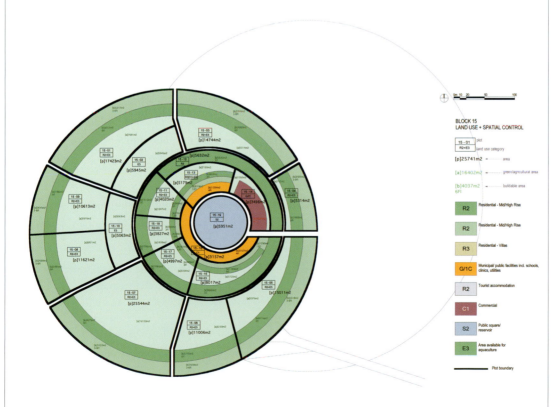

BLOCK 15
LAND USE + SPATIAL CONTROL

| 15 - 01 | plot |
| R2+E3 | land use category |
| [p]25741m2 | area |
| [a]16402m2 | green/agricultural area |
| [b]4037m2 6Fl | buildable area |

| R2 | Residential - Mid/High Rise |
| R2 | Residential - Mid/High Rise |
| R3 | Residential - Villas |
| G/1C | Municipal public facilities incl. schools, clinics, utilities |
| R2 | Tourist accommodation |
| C1 | Commercial |
| S2 | Public square/ reservoir |
| E3 | Area available for aquaculture |
| — | Plot boundary |

facing page: Executive recommendations and measures

top: Housing modules

bottom: Land-use and spatial control

### Environmental Sustainability of the Smartcity

The environmental implications traditionally associated with accommodating 200 000 people in a new high-density urban environment are substantial. An orthodox approach to waste and water processing, energy consumption and transport would be neither appropriate nor desirable when a holistic approach can be adopted that integrates architectural, landscape, services, agricultural and civic systems.

In Western industrialized countries, lighting and comfort heating or cooling within buildings can be responsible for over half of greenhouse gas (GHG) emissions. Many of the cities in these countries were designed and built in a time of perceived infinite resources, but even as we have come to the realization that resources are severely depleted and that our actions have caused profound detrimental effects on the planet, change has been slow. The response has generally been characterized by ineffective approaches relying on 'end of pipe' solutions – buildings are designed and built to poor standards and greenhouse gas emissions are 'offset' or negated through green technologies such as wind turbines, solar thermal heating or solar PV panels. This methodology does not address environmental sustainability in the long term, and energy production quantities and performance standards often fall short of demand. Reluctance to adopt different, and often low-tech, approaches to construction has ironically left industrialized nations relying on emerging science; a fear of change leading to faith in ever more alien solutions.

It has been calculated that the earth has around 11.3 billion hectares of productive land and sea space and 6.1 billion people, equating to 1.85 hectares per person if shared equitably and ignoring other species. This figure has been used to calculate the 'ecological footprint' of different countries; the average citizen in the United States uses over nine hectares to sustain their way of life, meaning five planets would be required to support the world's population were this lifestyle to be adopted as a benchmark. In 2004, Chinese citizens used on average under one global hectare per person according to a WWF Living Planet Report, a figure that had increased to 2.1 hectares by 2008 due to China's rapid transition from rural landscape to cityscape. The relationship between rural and urban ecological footprints, however, is not a straightforward one and varies according to territory. In wealthy countries, the lifestyles of rural dwellers can be effectively urban in nature with consumption exacerbated by distance, resulting in increased per capita emissions compared to their city counterparts. Moreover, modern agricultural practice and deforestation contribute heavily to carbon emissions while compact city arrangements can minimize consumption through shared public transport and efficient space heating.

The city framework for Guangming Smartcity takes a hybrid approach that capitalizes on rural and urban advantages to help China maintain economic growth and increase the well-being of its people without exerting undue pressure on the rest of the world's natural resources. The scale of the Smartcity means that almost all sustainable technologies are economically viable, allowing the design process to focus on the relative merits of different approaches in terms of social and environmental impact; equally, the opportunity for integration is almost unprecedented as 'waste' metamorphoses from material to be disposed of to a potential resource, as demonstrated in the industrial symbiosis at Kalundborg.

As well as reusing traditional 'waste' on site for energy generation and fertilizer, Guangming Smartcity demonstrates a positive influence on its neighbours by incorporating waste streams from neighbouring areas, exemplifying how the Smartcity can turn the traditional pitfalls of western development. Where Santa Monica (8.3 square miles), has an ecological footprint 350 times its size (2914 square miles), Guangming Smartcity will become a net importer of 'waste' and a net exporter of energy while promoting tourism, education and food production to the benefit of the wider region.

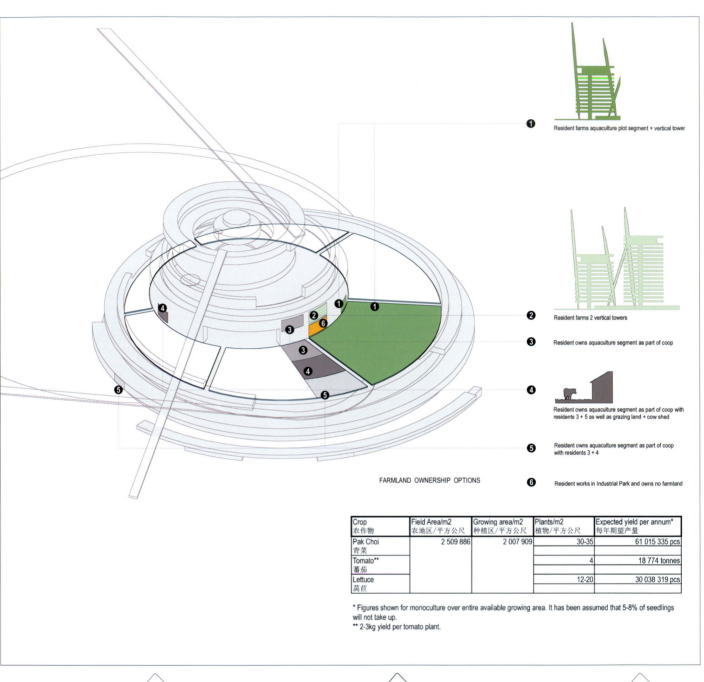

○1 Resident farms aquaculture plot segment + vertical tower

○2 Resident farms 2 vertical towers

○3 Resident owns aquaculture segment as part of coop

○4 Resident owns aquaculture segment as part of coop with residents 3 + 5 as well as grazing land + cow shed

○5 Resident owns aquaculture segment as part of coop with residents 3 + 4

FARMLAND OWNERSHIP OPTIONS

○6 Resident works in Industrial Park and owns no farmland

| Crop 农作物 | Field Area/m2 农地区/平方公尺 | Growing area/m2 种植区/平方公尺 | Plants/m2 植物/平方公尺 | Expected yield per annum* 每年期望产量 |
|---|---|---|---|---|
| Pak Choi 青菜 | 2 509 886 | 2 007 909 | 30-35 | 61 015 335 pcs |
| Tomato** 蕃茄 | | | 4 | 18 774 tonnes |
| Lettuce 莴苣 | | | 12-20 | 30 038 319 pcs |

\* Figures shown for monoculture over entire available growing area. It has been assumed that 5-8% of seedlings will not take up.

\*\* 2-3kg yield per tomato plant.

AGRICULTURE [E3]
- Terrace vegetable farms 2,124,376 m2
- Vertical vegetable farms 45m + 65m 281,010 m2

LIVESTOCK [E6]
- Open grazing fields 472,242 m2
- Grazing fields in lychee orchards 1,396,003 m2
- Reedbed filtration system
- Pigeon sheds 21,976 m2
- Cow shed 250 cows Total capacity 2,000 cows

LYCHEE ORCHARDS [E4]
- Lychee planted areas 1,396,003 m2

## Organic Food Production

Roofs in most cities serve only one function – to shelter – often creating bleak, uninspiring surfaces. In keeping with the philosophy of 'nothing is waste', every square metre of Guangming Smartcity is used, in this case as a hydroponic membrane capable of growing significant amounts of food. Beneath the growing surface, a gravel substrate is used to clean household water. The city consequently integrates the three functions of shelter, water purification and crop cultivation into the same space in addition to improving thermal insulation and surface water retention.

The hydroponic system uses an absorbent medium such as vermiculite or mineral wool instead of soil; a nutrient-rich solution is passed through the medium allowing plant roots to absorb the required minerals. Hydroponic farming is one of the most efficient cultivation methods in terms of crop spacing and access to sunlight, providing crops with more nutrients and using less energy in the process. Furthermore, hydroponic crops stay fresh for longer once harvested as they can be harvested without killing the plant; there is no need for soil disposal and sterilization, and soil-borne diseases are virtually eliminated.

Conservative estimates suggest that the available roof space in Guangming Smartcity can produce a substantial quantity of produce. A combined growing area of 450ha over the site could produce either 18 800 tonnes of tomatoes or 61 million pak choi annually.

Vertical kitchen garden farms and laboratories can be found scattered throughout the central city with accompanying vertical floral gardens. The facilities located in each vertical farm contribute to research projects, forming a major centre for agronomic and nutritional science. Each tower is constructed as an array of growing trays projecting from a cylindrical circulation spine. The trays are configured in pairs with a central gantry and staggered to maximize photosynthetic reaction. The preservation of endangered crop species is encouraged through research in arable laboratories located at the top of each tower.

As part of the city's urban agricultural programme, livestock is farmed as well as vegetables, fruit and flowers. The flat pockets of land in-between the craters and towers are used as grazing fields for livestock.

Located in each suburb is a farm shop run by the city's utilities management organization where produce is marketed at a price specified by the farmer. Unsold vegetables will be broken down in the anaerobic digesters, contributing to methane production used in electricity generation. The system will reach a natural equilibrium as the shop cannot exert pressure on the farmer to sell crops at a reduced profit, but if prices are set too high, produce is recycled. The outlets will act as a hub to connect everyone within the community. It is by such interconnections on a local scale that effective sustainable urban master plans can be implemented.

previous page: Farmers – the new eco-warriors

facing page top: Farmland ownership options; Expected crop yield

facing page bottom: Plan diagrams of terrace + vertical farms (left), and open grazing fields

## Waste treatment

Traditional sewage treatment is very energy intensive, using 65 000 gigajoules a day in the UK. At Guangming, waste is dealt with as efficiently as possible through a combination of natural low energy processes, but is also used to produce methane powering the city, and fertilizer for the city's farms and flower gardens.

Traditional methods of sewage treatment deal with all waste flows together, which includes vast quantities of relatively clean greywater from showers, baths and washing machines; moreover, the water used to flush toilets is often fully treated to drinking quality. This has the effect of diluting the actual sewage and making it much harder to remove and process. In the Smartcity, blackwater is kept separate, enabling the city's sewage to produce rather than consume energy. Greywater will be cleaned in gravel-bed hydroponics (GBH) systems in the roof farms, dramatically reducing the quantity of water requiring full treatment. Once processed, the water is clean enough to discharge into local watercourses, or is 'polished' and recycled to potable standards.

Kitchen sinks will be installed with waste macerators so that organic waste can be combined with foul drainage from toilets. This blackwater passes through an aquatron device that separates liquid from the solids. The former continues to natural reed beds or further GBH systems for purification while the latter are transported to an anaerobic digester. Here, the solids are broken down naturally into methane, which is captured and used to generate electricity, a nutrient-rich liquor called digestate that can be used as fertilizer once pasteurized, and fibrous mass which can be applied to soil to improve retention capacity or be incinerated for electricity.

## Internal Climate Control

Air conditioning is generally regarded as a necessity in the region, but the landscape and component infrastructure of the Smartcity allow natural low energy design to counter this convention. Calculations suggest that no mechanical space cooling will be required in residential dwellings and commercial buildings will require only 50% of their usual demand. This is achieved through reducing direct solar access during the summer, the thermal mass of exposed heavyweight construction materials, and a labyrinth cooling system located in the base of the tower structures that transfers inter-seasonal heat. By drawing air underground where temperature is a constant 22°C throughout the year, hot summer air is cooled using the labyrinth walls as a heat sink; in winter, cold air is preheated by the warmer conditions underground. To reduce the embodied energy required for its construction, the labyrinth is built from excavated rock rather than concrete. The interstitial space between the crushed rocks creates a convoluted path to increase the contact period for heat exchange, functionally replicating a conventional concrete labyrinth.

The Smartcity is a car-free zone but provides underground parking for residents who require personal vehicles for travelling beyond Guangming's centre. The car parks will be ventilated through 'solar chimneys' at the top of the towers. Air in the chimney rises as it is warmed by the sun, drawing fresh air through the car park while phase change material (PCM) is used to store the excess heat effectively so the system can continue to run through the night. In the same way that labyrinth cooling uses constant underground temperatures to cool the air, the air being drawn through the car park is cooled as it spends time in contact with the thermally massive walls underground. This cool air is not suitable for ventilation, but is made use of by circulating it around the external envelope of a subterranean shopping mall to reduce cooling loads.

82

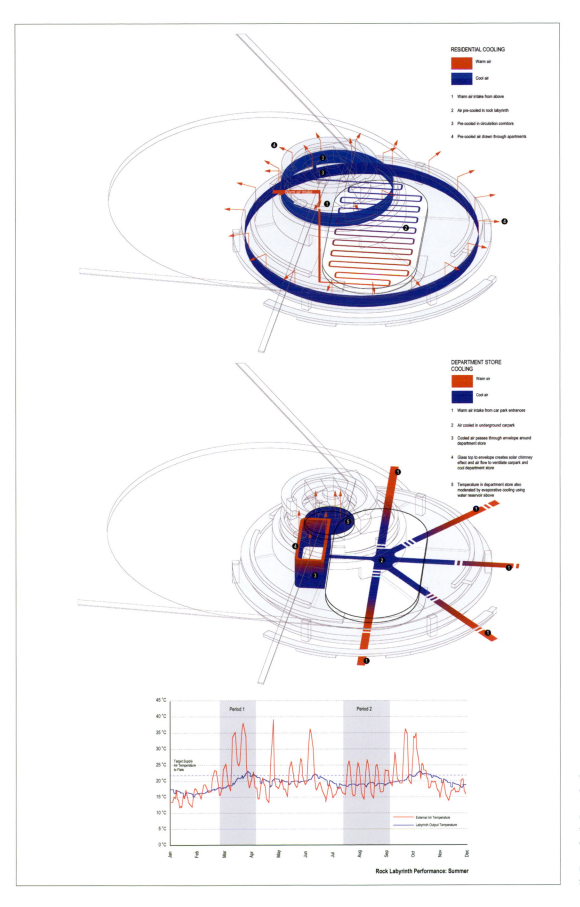

**RESIDENTIAL COOLING**

Warm air
Cool air

1 Warm air intake from above
2 Air pre-cooled in rock labyrinth
3 Pre-cooled in circulation corridors
4 Pre-cooled air drawn through apartments

**DEPARTMENT STORE COOLING**

Warm air
Cool air

1 Warm air intake from car park entrances
2 Air cooled in underground carpark
3 Cooled air passes through envelope around department store
4 Glass top to envelope creates solar chimney effect and air flow to ventilate carpark and cool department store
5 Temperature in department store also moderated by evaporative cooling using water reservoir above

Rock Labyrinth Performance: Summer

top: Cooling strategy for residential units

middle: Cooling strategy for the underground commercial development

bottom: Rock Labyrinth Cooling System – seasonal performance

Low energy displacement cooling is employed in all the larger internal city spaces. Fresh air is supplied at low level from wall or floor mounted diffusers at around three degrees Celsius below the desired room temperature, forming a reservoir of cool air across the floor. On contact with a source of heat gain, the air warms and rises through natural buoyancy to settle in a ceiling reservoir leaving the occupied zone fresh and cool. The depth of the stale air reservoir is controlled by the careful distribution of high level extracts.

### Energy Demand + Generation

Every strategy employed at Guangming has been chosen for the benefits they confer in terms of energy demand reduction, efficient resource use, and improved well-being. Often the benefits of a strategy are multi-faceted, offering gains in more than one area. This means that the energy demand for the new city is the lowest it can be, requiring less energy to be produced, no matter which route is taken. Using benchmarks for developments in the surrounding region, a development of this size using standard construction methods to meet modern living standards would require 321 750MWh/year; Guangming's demand is estimated at 127 110MWh/year, while still achieving the highest standards of modern living.

To complement the most effective methods of reducing energy demand, the Smartcity's energy supply strategy adopts the same fundamental principles of economy, practicality, synergy and anti-wastefulness.

Anaerobic digestion has been used with great success throughout China, generating biogas energy equivalent to 280 million tonnes of coal every year and meeting almost 14% of the nation's energy demand. The quota generated at Guangming will depend on which waste streams are harnessed. If limited to human and domestic organic waste, the methane produced could constitute around half the city's energy supply; with the addition of organic matter from farms, shops and restaurants, the city would become a net energy exporter, generating a new revenue stream.

The Smartcity will also employ waste-to-energy plants (WtE) where incinerators will burn non-recyclable municipal solid waste (MSW) in high-efficiency furnaces to produce steam or electricity. Modern air pollution control systems will be fitted and emissions continuously monitored. The intention is to expand the scale of operations to assimilate waste from neighbouring Gongming, increasing electricity production and reducing waste build-up in the region. Waste heat from electricity generation, normally lost to the atmosphere, will be used to provide 'free' hot water for the city and channelled into absorption chillers for additional cooling.

China is already a major supplier of photovoltaic panels with future demand both in China and abroad expected to increase dramatically in the coming decade. Integrated PV panels along the riverside boardwalk will provide shading as well as contributing to the Smartcity's electricity output. The scale of Guangming would permit the sanctioning of an entire PV factory, benefiting the local and national economy, and driving down unit costs. Guangming's PV farm represents a guaranteed investment, confirming a colossal order of panels years in advance and enabling manufacturers to bypass 'start-up' and 'growth' phases to full-scale production, furthering China's standing as a world leader in PV production.

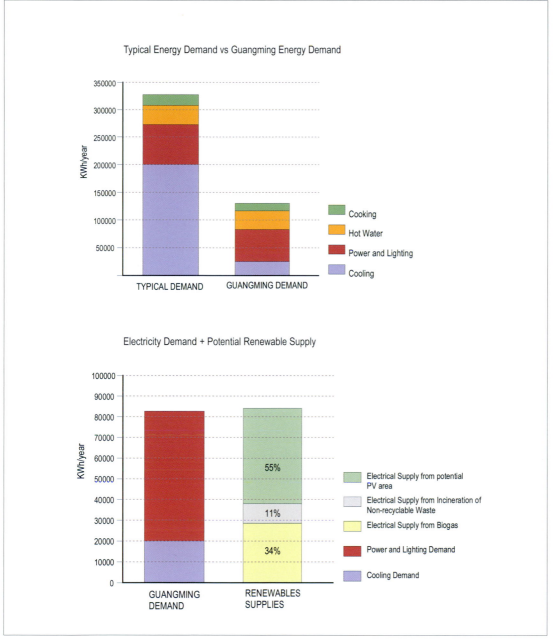

Typical Energy Demand vs Guangming Energy Demand

KWh/year

- Cooking
- Hot Water
- Power and Lighting
- Cooling

TYPICAL DEMAND    GUANGMING DEMAND

Electricity Demand + Potential Renewable Supply

KWh/year

55%

11%

34%

- Electrical Supply from potential PV area
- Electrical Supply from Incineration of Non-recyclable Waste
- Electrical Supply from Biogas
- Power and Lighting Demand
- Cooling Demand

GUANGMING DEMAND    RENEWABLES SUPPLIES

top: Guangming Smartcity's energy demand

middle: Renewable supply potential

bottom: Plan diagrams showing distribution of anaerobic digestors + reedbeds (left), photovoltaic fields (middle), and recycling centres

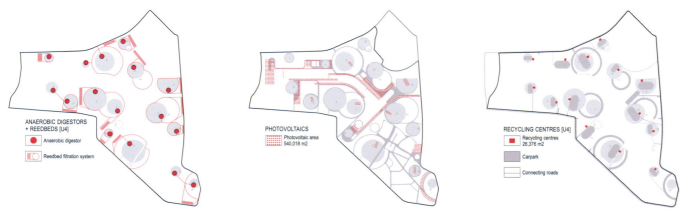

ANAEROBIC DIGESTORS + REEDBEDS [U4]
- Anaerobic digestor
- Reedbed filtration system

PHOTOVOLTAICS
- Photovoltaic area 540,018 m2

RECYCLING CENTRES [U4]
- Recycling centres 26,376 m2
- Carpark
- Connecting roads

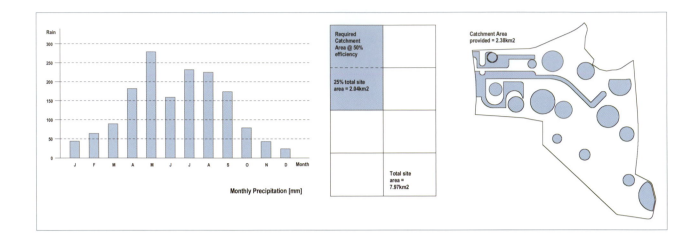

## Hydrology

The varying topography of the land with its hills and valleys is naturally suited to the formation of large water bodies that benefits a multitude of uses. Working with the existing surface water network, the natural tributary that eventually merges with the Maozhou River to the east of the site is sculpted to form a central canal. The disposition of form in the amplified towers and craters results in a cascade of water bodies, stepping down from one to the next in the circular aquaculture terraces.

The water bodies will act as a medium for transport, agriculture and recreation with all uses mutually reinforcing. They will provide the main water storage for the whole development and be linked to the reservoirs at the apex of each tower. In addition to the rainfall directly collected, the water storage bodies adjacent to the canal will gather surface runoff and water drained from the hills, increasing the catchment area. There is approximately 1575mm of rainfall in Shenzhen per year, peaking between May and September; relatively little water is available between October and March. Storage will be required during this dry period, although greywater and blackwater recycling will mitigate the shortage.

## Transport

Guangming Smartcity is a car-free city designed to ensure that every resident is able to carry out all their needs within their local area – to live, to play, to learn and to work – while still having the freedom for inter-local and regional mobility if they wish. The transport infrastructure will provide the foundation for a dense diverse urban community with an environment that encourages the use of public space. Walking and cycling in a humane environment will be given the highest priority leading to a human scale urban community that places high value on personal contact.

The public transport system has a clearly defined hierarchy fundamental to the design of an efficient infrastructure that interfaces well with private modes of transport. This is especially important at Guangming where public transport systems must deal with vertical as well as horizontal movement.

Residents of the Smartcity are served at regional inter-city scale by car, rail and bus. The Longda Expressway on the west boundary of the site provides the main regional road traffic connection with Guangming. The expressway is elevated to accommodate the extension of the city boundary to the edge of the Maozhou River, removing the physical barrier to

Gongming village and its Industrial cluster whilst forming a striking gateway to the development and offering an elevated panorama over the Shenzhen's green haven. The gateway incorporates Guangming Central Train Station, enabling easy access and interchange with road traffic and a visitor car park. At the base of the structure, the underground mass transit rail can be accessed, together with buggy and cycle hire stations for local travel. To put Guangming on the map as a vanguard city and tourist hub, and to create an attractive and viable commuter settlement, a new railway network linking Guangming Smartcity to Hong Kong, Lo Wu and Guangzhou is proposed. Noise from the high-speed trains will be attenuated by the groves of lychee trees.

Three mass transit rail stations at strategically located positions serve the Intercity fast line (linking Shenzhen, Shiyan, Guangming, Huangjiang, Songshanhu and Guancheng), Incity fast line (serving Shenzhen, Longhua, Shiyan, Guangming and Gongming), and Local Area line (linking Shanjing and Guangming). These are integrated into the residential and commercial growth centres located at the Central Train Station Gateway, City Hall Plaza at the opposite end of the east–west town axis, and the Old Town settlement.

Guangming Central Bus Station is located to the east of the old town and caters for long-distance inter-city coach journeys including a shuttle service to Shenzhen International Airport 18km away. Three new local bus routes covering the perimeter of the site are proposed, linking into the existing network of Bao An district by making full use of the proposed new underpasses.

At inter-local scale, Guangming Centre is provided with three new light rail (MTR) stations spaced approximately 2km apart that connect to the wider regional system. The Skybus, a cable car service, provides a quick hop service between principal tower-crater communities linking the Centres of Excellence. Intended for low cost everyday use as well as for recreational purposes, the elevated network allows the Smartcity's hybrid landscape and rooftop occupation to be fully appreciated.

The boardwalk that lines the urban beach and canal, with its interconnected network of pathways, is traversed by buggies and cycles that operate as a shared resource similar to the bike rental Product Service System (PSS) that have proved so successful in Lyon, Copenhagen and Barcelona. Buggy and cycle storage towers on a lowerator system are positioned at transport nodes and at the base of each tower community. The boardwalk will also be used for emergency vehicle access.

The communities are planned such that a commercial hub and inter-local scale transport hub are never more than 400m from a residence, the largest crater being 800m in diameter. Walking and cycling can therefore easily cover local scale transport. A funicular railway serves each tower and crater community, travelling directly from the base station to the public reservoir and suburb square at the summit. Radially distributed around the rings, escalators provide a secondary means of vertical transport within the towers and craters.

facing page: Hydrology – rainwater catchment area

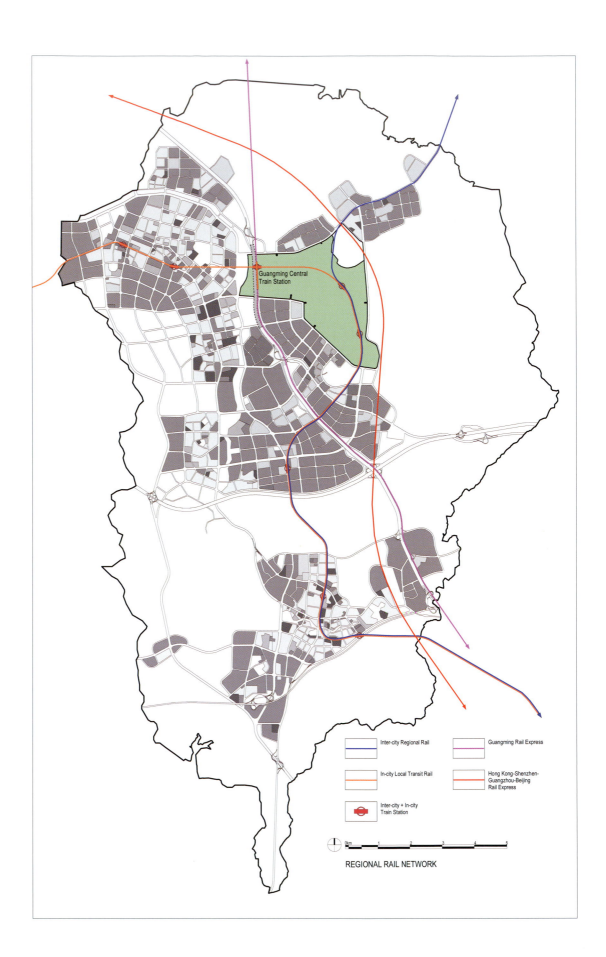

Guangming Central
Train Station

|  | Inter-city Regional Rail |  | Guangming Rail Express |
|--|--------------------------|--|------------------------|
|  | In-city Local Transit Rail |  | Hong Kong-Shenzhen-Guangzhou-Beijing Rail Express |
|  | Inter-city + In-city Train Station | | |

0km 1 2 3 4 5

REGIONAL RAIL NETWORK

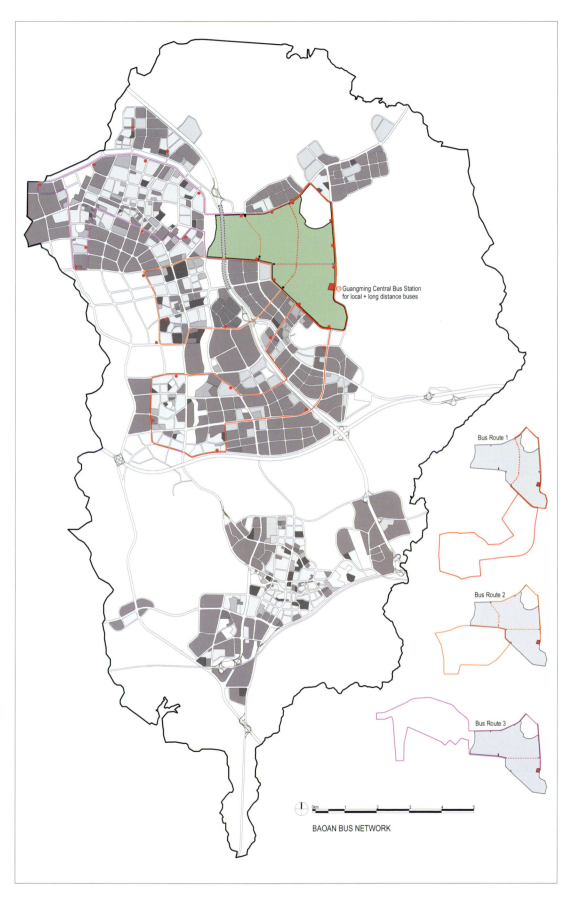

Guangming Central Bus Station
for local + long distance buses

Bus Route 1

Bus Route 2

Bus Route 3

BAOAN BUS NETWORK

facing page: Regional rail network

left: BaoAn bus network

following pages: Circulation diagrams

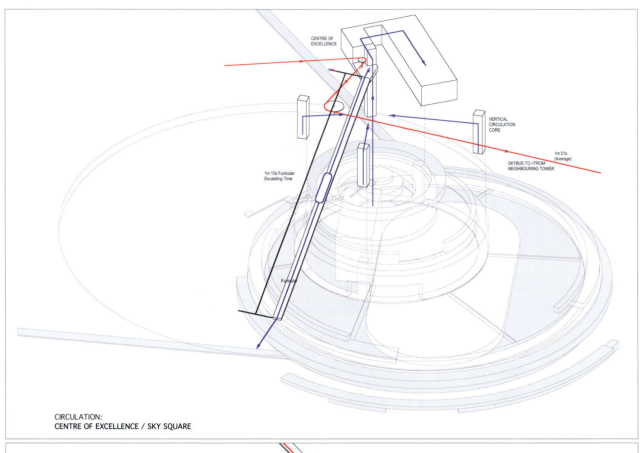

CENTRE OF
EXCELLENCE

VERTICAL
CIRCULATION
CORE

1m 51s
(Average)

SKYBUS TO / FROM
NEIGHBOURING TOWER

1m 10s Funicular
Escalating Time

Funicular

CIRCULATION:
**CENTRE OF EXCELLENCE / SKY SQUARE**

VEHICULAR
ACCESS ROUTE

Delivery Route +
Loading Bays

MULTI-STOREY
CARPARK

VEHICULAR
ACCESS ROUTE

CIRCULATION:
**VEHICULAR**

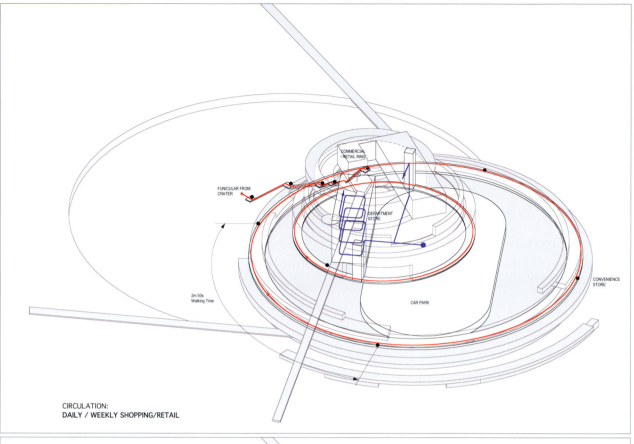

CIRCULATION:
DAILY / WEEKLY SHOPPING/RETAIL

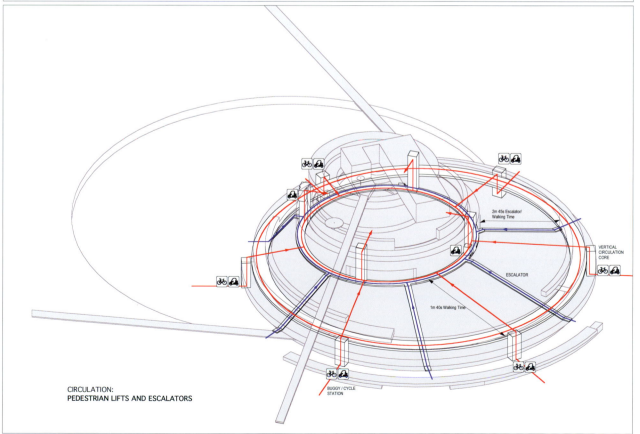

CIRCULATION:
PEDESTRIAN LIFTS AND ESCALATORS

## Construction Phasing

The city is to be built over a 13-year period. Four major construction phases are envisaged, each of which when complete will be a stable stage of development.

**Phase 1:** Three growth centres are established around Guangming Old Town, City Hall Plaza and the Central Train Station. Over the first four years, the major infrastructure elements are completed, and the first tower and crater communities built. Existing residential settlements are left undisturbed with minimal loss of agricultural land on the previously unconstructed zone. The Central Train and Bus stations, City Hall and their respective commercial centres are developed together with the new Fire, Police and Postal services. The existing schools and hospital will temporarily accommodate the increased demand.

After a year of detailed planning, work commences with the elevated Longda Expressway and main central station along the riverside. The urban light rail link (MTR) is constructed below ground level using 'cut and cover' technology. Construction roads are established from the existing ring road towards the city hall area of town as well as the three main underpasses, permitting the implementation of the new bus routes that will connect to Gongming and the Hi-tech Industrial Park.

The depressions and hills for the first two craters and three towers around the City Hall, and new Central Bus Station, are excavated and built up using a fixed system of mining excavation. Earth movement will be limited as far as possible with the 'fill' of the towers balanced by the 'cut' of the adjacent craters.

Photovoltaic structures, designed to be relocated as necessary, are erected at inception to provide energy for the construction work and to contribute to the national grid. The surface watercourses are redirected to feed into the central section of the canal and the balance tanks and water storage along the bank-sides installed. Main drainage and water treatment areas are established. Fresh water mains and hilltop reservoirs are built over the new topography. Buggy and cycle routes and their parking structures will be operational.

Communication within each area initially comprises local distributor roads constructed as circumferentially flexible pavements with diagonal ramps rising between each layer. Towards the completion of each ring segment, escalators will be installed. The first two Skybus links between the city hall growth centre and Guangming Central Train Station, and the southernmost tower and crater communities will be quickly placed once the hilltop public plazas are finished. The filled areas of the new towns are consolidated with ground improvement techniques and segmental development sites are then let to individual developers, introducing variation, character and local identity. A diversity of building types and public areas are set on the new ground level with shallow foundations or raised above simple reinforced concrete under-crofts.

**Phase 2:** Inhabitants of Gongming village and Loucun village are decanted into the newly completed Phase 1 housing that have a combined population capacity of 30 000. The communities between the city hall area and riverside are completed with additional Skybus lines serving them. The beach area of the town is built up, and lychee orchards established around the site boundary. The Phase 1 extension of the old hospital is underway.

The canal works are completed throughout the site. With full provisions for the Smartcity's water treatment and storage complete, the beach district is made using selected fill brought by river and deposited by water jet. Further excavation of towers and craters will take place.

The radial development of the first towers and craters is finished and the local routes pedestrianized allowing decanting of the village settlements to occur. The smaller tower and crater communities contain simple buildings bearing on existing ground, set alongside rings of elevated housing. As densities reach their intended level, prefabricated steel towers supporting vertical farms will be erected. These installations are coordinated with further photovoltaic arrays.

**Phase 3:** The area south of the central canal is developed. The internal vehicular circulation network (boardwalk) and recreational areas are completed. Residents of Guangming Old Town are decanted to completed housing. Phase 2 of the Hospital Extension is complete.

The longer runs of supply and drainage are now installed to open the entire site to urban development. Further blocks are developed together with extensions to the cable car network. Urban zones are created linking the city hall area to the riverside. Housing, agriculture, vertical farms and photovoltaic arrays are fully developed in this area of the site.

**Phase 4:** A final phase of community development in and around Guangming Old Town is implemented. There is a densification of all communities and renewable resource systems are fully deployed. Existing health and emergency service buildings are renovated and enlarged to service the increased population. Ground forming is complete and new development to plots in and around the old town is built. The segmental development of all urban areas is completed. Vertical farms distribution and energy collection reach their optimum level.

93

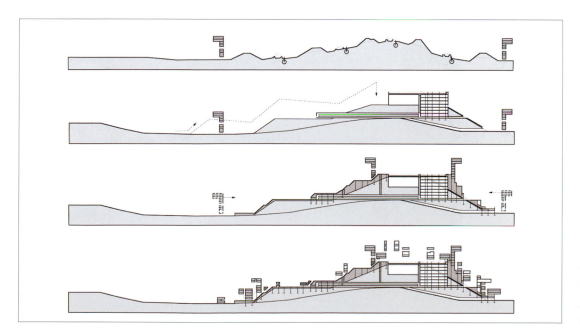

left: Construction phasing of a tower community

following page left: Construction phasing of the Smartcity

following page right: Views of a suburb tower (top), and crater

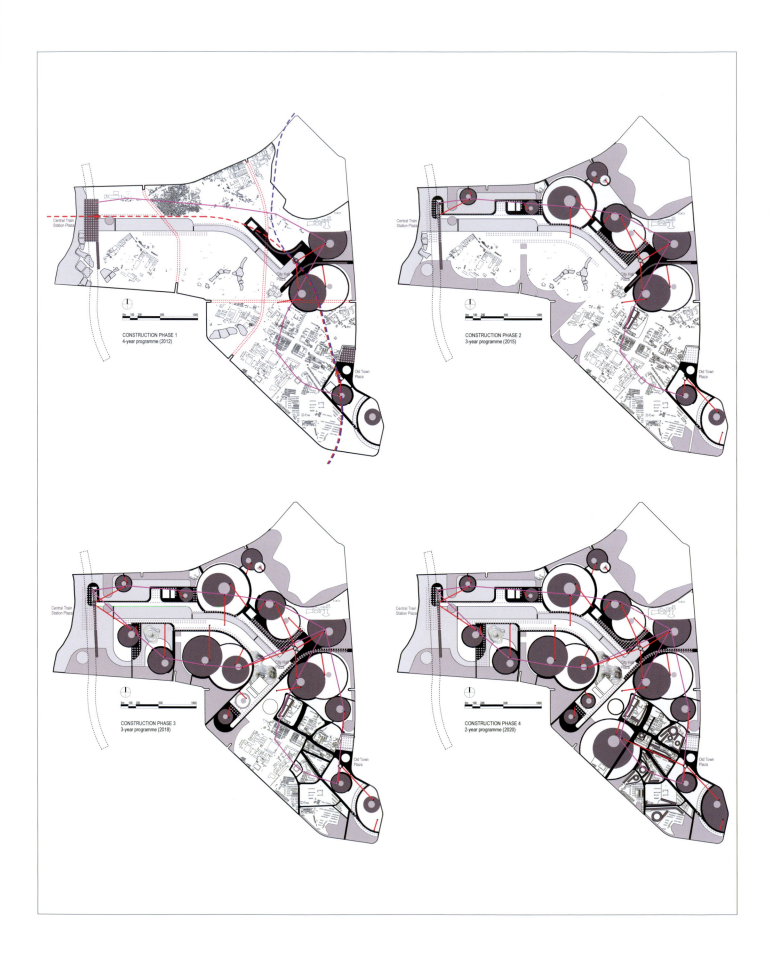

CONSTRUCTION PHASE 1
4-year programme (2012)

CONSTRUCTION PHASE 2
3-year programme (2015)

CONSTRUCTION PHASE 3
3-year programme (2018)

CONSTRUCTION PHASE 4
2-year programme (2020)

Central Train
Station Plaza

City Hall
Plaza

Old Town
Plaza

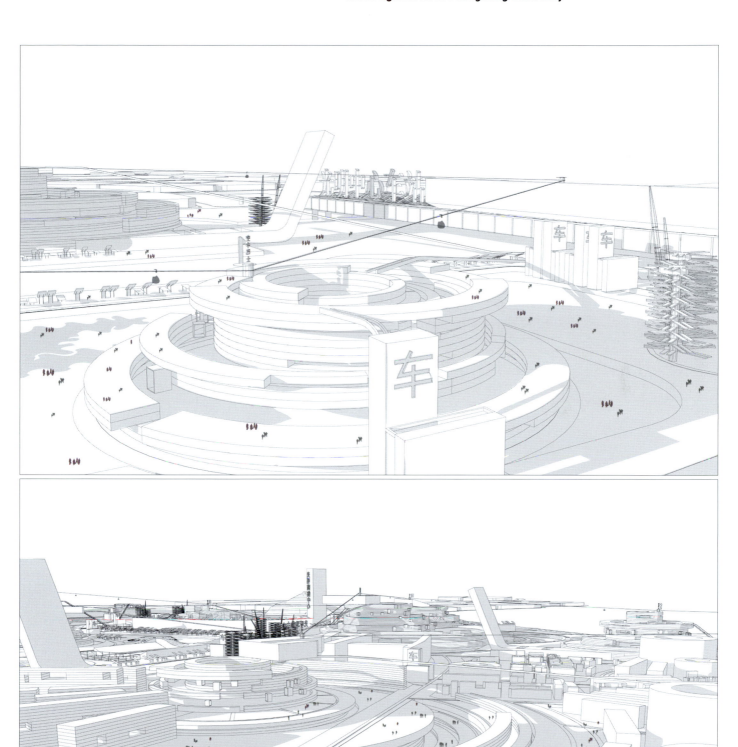

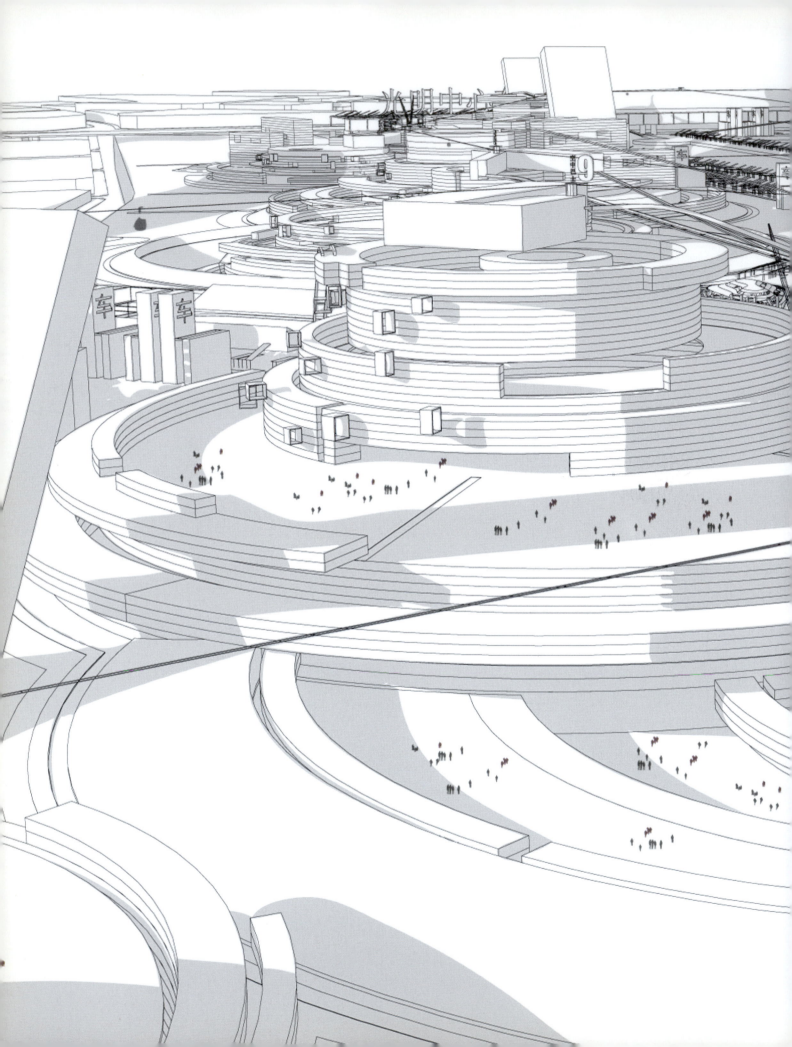

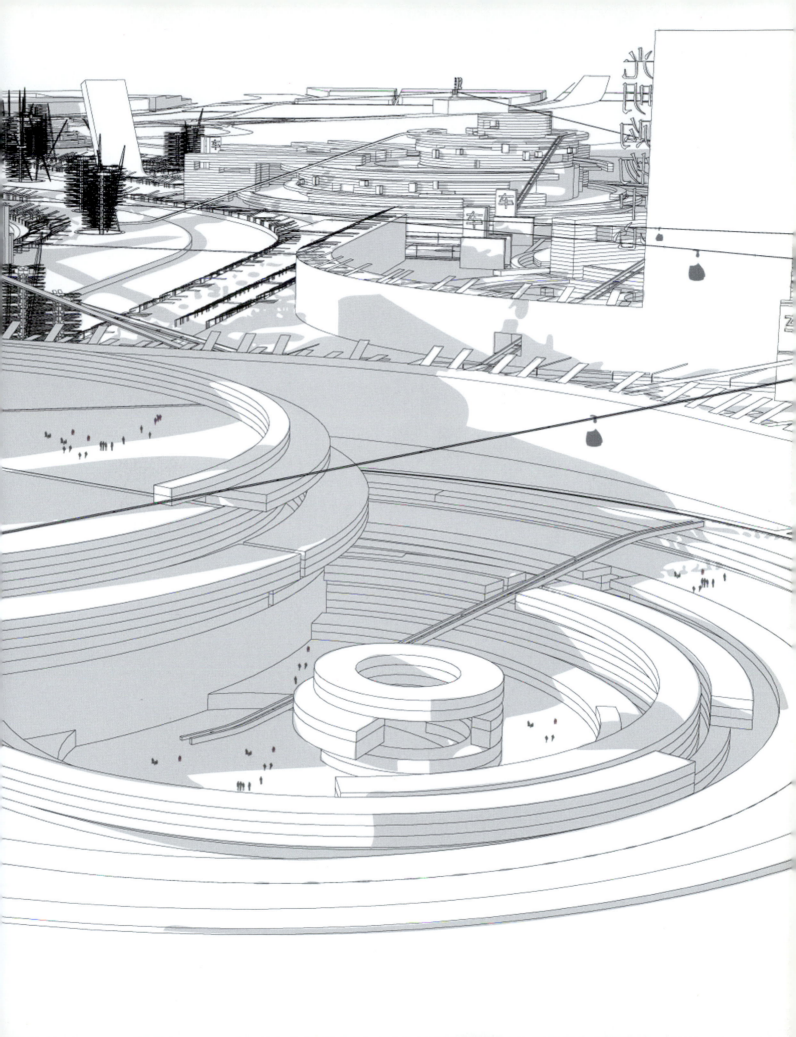

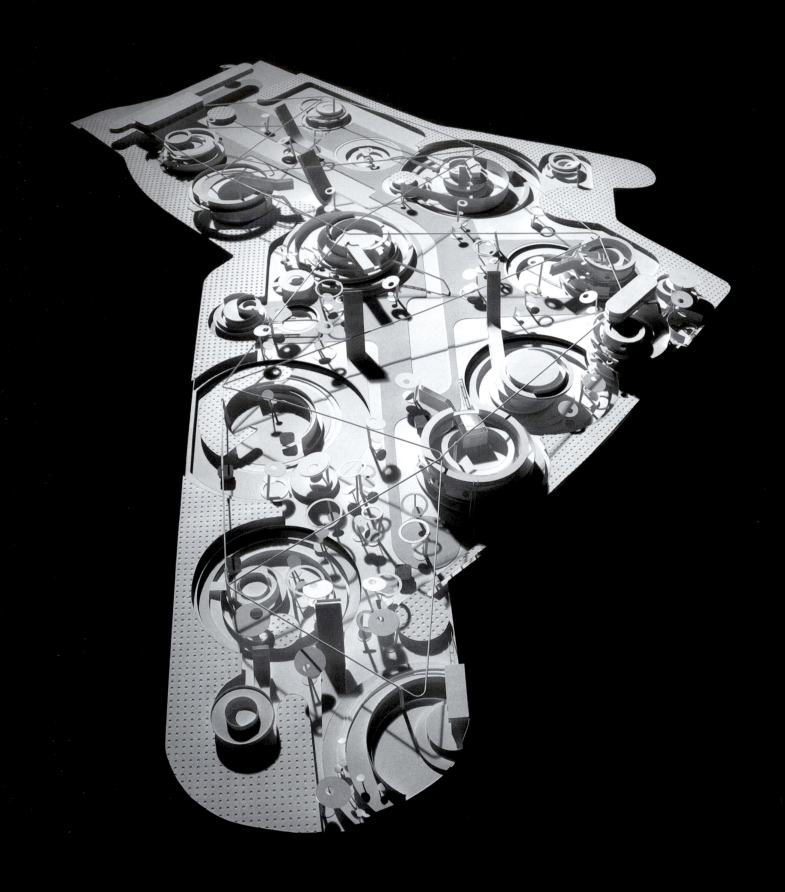

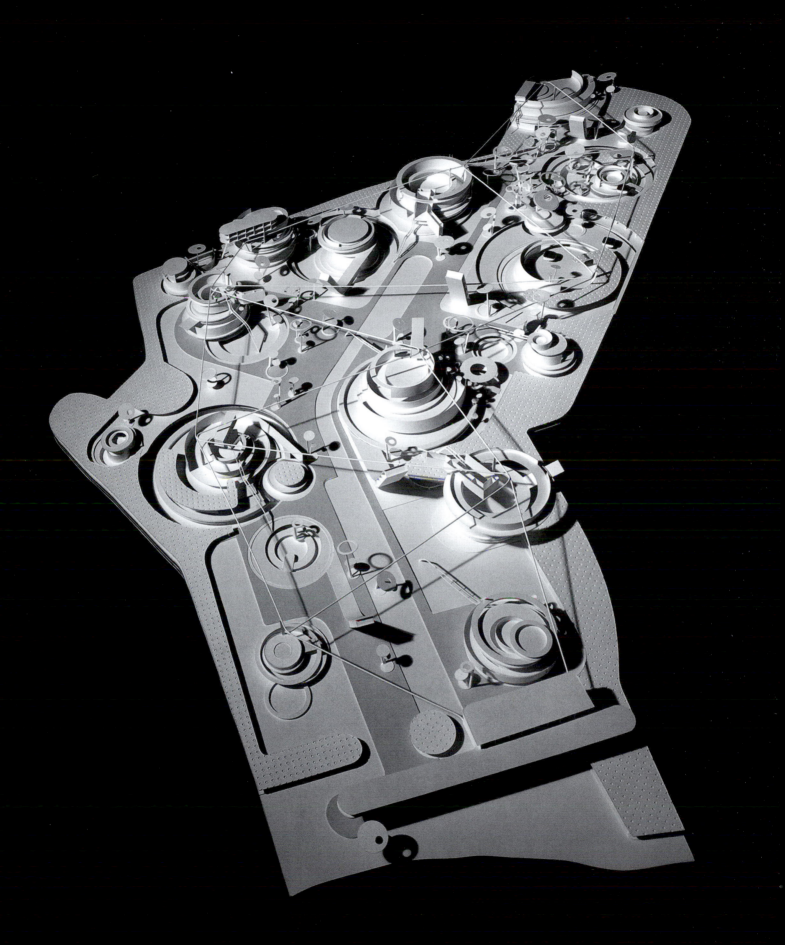

# A Lexicon for the Smartcity

**agritourism:** The act of visiting an agricultural or horticultural operation for leisure, educational or active involvement purposes. Agritourism offers an alternative revenue stream for rural communities and an insight into food production for the general public.

**agroforestry:** A land use system in which the growth of herbaceous crops is combined with trees and shrubs to preserve and improve productivity. Trees draw water and nutrients from deeper soil and provide temperature moderation and mulch whilst herbaceous plants prevent soil erosion and the proliferation of weeds.

**amoeba:** A free-form environmental trellis occupying interstitial urban spaces to provide shading for communal activities. The planar lattice additionally provides a framework for the incorporation of photovoltaic cells and vegetation.

**anaerobic digestion:** The breakdown of biodegradable material into biogas and nutrient-rich digestate using microorganisms in an oxygen-free environment. Widely used in the treatment of organic wastewater, the biogas produced is used as a renewable energy fuel and the digestate pasteurized for use as fertilizer. Fibrous mass, a third product of anaerobic digestion, is either pasteurized and used to improve the structure and water retention capacity of soil or incinerated for electricity generation.

**appropriate technology:** Technological solutions that take into account environmental, social and cultural considerations and are sustainable within the communities in which they are employed. The term is usually used in reference to manual-based solutions in developing countries or socially and environmentally sensitive technologies in industrialized nations.

**aquifer thermal energy storage (ATES):** A type of low-temperature geothermal energy storage system using open loops in aquifers to store seasonal heat and cold when it is available and to retrieve it when required for space heating and cooling. ATES uses substantial quantities of water as a heat storage medium, although this water is constantly recycled.

**artificial photosynthesis:** The conversion of carbon dioxide and photon energy into carbon-based fuel molecules with minimal energy expenditure, mimicking natural photosynthetic processes. While the technology is still in its infancy, the use of solar energy to convert carbon dioxide released from burning fuels back into usable energy would establish a closed sustainable fuel cycle.

**assimilative capacity:** The capacity of an environment, usually aquatic-based, to receive waste or toxic material and convert it into harmless or useful material.

**biochar:** Charcoal produced from animal waste or plant residue biomass through pyrolysis.

**biofuel:** Fuel produced from renewable organic resources such as plant biomass in contrast with fossil fuels that derive from long-dead biological material. The most common forms are bioethanol and biodiesel, which can be used either as additives or directly as transport fuel. Biofuel production is paradoxically energy intensive, and the appropriation of farmland for the growth of biofuels has led to significant increases in food prices as well as the destruction of natural habitats. However, agricultural waste can be used as a raw material, fast-growing crops such as switchgrass and hemp would minimize the impact on food production, and new technologies using cellulosic biomass conversion could reduce energy expenditure.

**biogeochemical cycles:** Natural cycles of the earth's atmosphere, hydrosphere, biosphere and lithosphere that involve biological, geological and chemical processes. Human activities can disrupt biogeochemical cycles by extracting material from reservoirs or depositing them into sinks, notably in the carbon cycle through the mining and combustion of hydrocarbons.

**biomass:** A renewable energy source derived from plant residue, vegetation or agricultural waste that is used in the production of heat or electricity. Fossil fuels are not considered to be biomass due to their long-established separation from the carbon cycle. Biomass crops tend to sequester more carbon than arable crops, but contribute in the same way as fossil fuels to greenhouse gas emissions when burnt.

**bioregionalism:** The establishment of social and environmental policies based on the ecological, geographical and cultural contexts of a region rather than political or economic boundaries. [Coined by Peter Berg in the early 1970s.]

**blackwater:** Water containing the waste of humans, animals or food. Separation from greywater permits the efficient processing of solid nutrient-rich waste into fertilizer or fuel and treatment of wastewater for reuse.

**boardwalk:** The main interconnected transport pathway of the Smartcity, modelled on the timber walkways found along beaches and wetlands. Although often located along an urban beach, the boardwalk combines the recreational qualities of a traditional boardwalk with urban functions. Capable of supporting emergency vehicles, the pathway is shared by pedestrians, cyclists and electric vehicles, expanding at key nodes into public plazas and transport hubs.

**borehole thermal energy storage (BTES):** An underground thermal storage system that uses closed loop boreholes to store solar heat collected in the summer for use in the winter. Boreholes are filled with a high thermal conductivity grouting material to ensure good thermal contact with the surrounding soil.

**carbon capture + storage [CCS]:** The capture of carbon dioxide emissions from industrial sources and their injection into deep geological formations or ocean masses for permanent storage as a form of greenhouse gas remediation. The dehydration, compression and transportation of $CO_2$ require considerable energy and storage depends on the availability of empty spaces in the earth's crust with potential problems of leakage. Alternatives to storage include the use of the $CO_2$ to feed algae for biofuel production and artificial photosynthesis.

**carbon offset deals:** A trading mechanism designed to reduce greenhouse gas (GHG) emissions by funding renewable energy technologies in compensation for GHG-emitting transportation or electricity use. A single carbon offset or credit is equivalent to one metric tonne of greenhouse gases.

**carbon sequestration:** The removal of atmospheric carbon and its storage in carbon sinks through biochemical or physical processes. Sequestration includes absorption into biomass such as crops, trees, soil and microorganisms as well as CCS permanent storage.

**cash cropping:** The cultivation of crops such as coffee, tobacco and flowers for sale, often specifically for export markets. The price of staple cash crops is set by global commodity markets leading to vulnerability in times of excess supply. Intensive farming practices have also been responsible for soil depletion.

**centre of excellence:** A building or collection of buildings with a specialized programme offering resources in a specific focus area. Smartcity districts are sized and designed to be self-sufficient; they are provided with an identity in the form of a Centre of Excellence (CoE) that generates new avenues of communication between neighbouring communities.

**circular economy:** The optimization of resource management and environmental efficiency by following the principles of reducing, reusing and recycling. Resource consumption and waste production is reduced, products are reused through repair and renovation, and waste products are recycled into resources to the fullest extent. 'Circular economy' is also the Chinese term for sustainability, a critical component of China's 18-year development plan for economic growth whilst mitigating negative ecological impacts.

**closed system:** A physical system that obeys the laws of conservation and does not interact with its external environment. In reality, no system can be completely closed. The Earth is a closed system with respect to matter, but an open system with respect to energy, receiving radiant solar energy that is for all intents and purposes, inexhaustible.

**cloud seeding:** The dispersal of silver iodide particles into the atmosphere to act as nuclei for cloud formation. Marine stratocumulus clouds reflect sunlight back into space, reducing the amount of heat received by the earth's surface. The use of seeding to expand and distribute clouds to reflect solar radiation offers an alternative geoengineering approach to counteract global warming.

**combined heat and power (CHP) + CCHP:** A system that simultaneously recovers waste heat from power generation to form useful energy such as steam or district heating. Combined cooling, heat and power (CCHP) additionally converts heat by-product into cooling energy by using absorption chillers and is also known as trigeneration. Multi-generation power plants are most efficient when waste heat or cooling can be used in close proximity to its source.

**Common Agricultural Policy (CAP):** An agricultural programme enshrined in EU legislation designed to increase productivity, stabilize consumer prices, ensure a fair income to farmers, and preserve rural heritage. Due to the capacity of other nations to produce food at significantly lower prices, the EU has had little option but to heavily subsidize agriculture in its member nations while keeping prices high. In its initial formulation, the CAP paid scant regard to the environment, leading to intensive and detrimental farming practices that have

been partially addressed by subsequent reforms.

**concentrating solar power (CSP):** The use of parabolic mirror arrays to focus large amounts of sunlight onto a small area for the generation of heat and/or electricity. Energy can be stored in phase-change materials to enable electricity supply through the night and during overcast conditions. CSP plants in desert environments have the potential for generating vast amounts of energy, whilst waste heat can be used for desalinating water for crop irrigation. The crops would also benefit from shade beneath the mirror arrays, facilitating horticulture in an otherwise hostile environment. Transport of the energy to population centres still proves problematic, but CSP could pave the way for the development of urban centres in arid regions.

**cool roof:** A roofing system that reflects and emits solar energy, reducing the transfer of undesirable heat into a building. Cool roofs reduce cooling loads, reduce urban heat island effects and smog, and mitigate global warming. In addition to reflecting sunlight, cool roofs can emit infrared radiation, presenting a viable geoengineering technique.

**cultivar:** A plant species cultivated for its unique characteristics that are uniform, distinct, stable and retain those characteristics on reproduction.

**cultural resources:** Components of social capital including physical assets such as architecture and sculpture, but also more abstract and less quantifiable assets such as history, language, folklore and heritage.

**cycle station:** A vertical storage tower for rentable bicycles located at transport nodes to encourage a car-free environment in the Smartcity. Bicycles are stored via a lowerator mechanism to occupy a smaller footprint. Illuminated at night, the towers also act as navigational beacons.

**domestic fuel cell:** A small-scale electricity generator using replenishable fuel sources that can be located in urban environments and consequently at the point of consumption. Domestic fuel cells can be as small in size as a washing machine, and generate electricity from gas more efficiently than modern power stations. Using solid oxide technology, the $CO_2$ released is combined with water vapour, facilitating capture and storage.

**Earthbox:** A patented planting system comprising a recycled plastic container that houses a water reservoir and growing substrate. The Earthbox's self-contained nature allows plants to survive without constant tending, the cultivation of a productive landscape above contaminated ground and ease of transportation.

**eco-warrior:** An alternative term to environmental activist that also encompasses educationalists, farmers and businessmen.

**ecotourism:** Environmentally responsible travel to natural areas in order to enjoy and appreciate nature (and accompanying cultural features, both past and present). Ecotourism must promote conservation, have a low visitor impact and provide for beneficially active socio-economic involvement of local peoples [definition adopted by the World Conservation Union].

**energy bonds:** Also known as Clean Renewable Energy Bonds (CREBs), energy bonds are long-term secure investments in renewable energy projects. Significant investment is required to finance the conversion from a fossil fuel-based economy; necessary capital can be raised by governments, electric companies and clean renewable energy bond lenders who issue tax credit bonds on which interest is paid in tax credits rather than interest.

**Engel's Law:** A law in economics correlating the proportion of national income spent on food with welfare level. As income rises, proportional expenditure on food tends to fall. The Engel coefficient is often used as a metric for national living standards.

**enhanced geothermal systems (EGS):** A geothermal power technology that does not rely on natural rock porosity. Also known as hot dry rock geothermal, EGS involves the high-pressure injection of water into boreholes drilled several kilometres into the earth's crust to fracture and increase the surface area of hot rock. The water emerges as steam that can be used to generate electricity and heat, offering a viable clean energy source irrespective of geographical or geological location.

**environmental remediation:** The chemical, biological or physical removal of pollutants or contaminants from the environment. Remediation is usually monitored and based on regulatory controls.

**eutrophication:** A proliferation in plant growth, especially algae, stimulated by excess mineral and organic nutrients. Eutrophication occurs naturally but is usually triggered or accelerated by human sewage and the leaching of chemical fertilizers from arable land. The sudden increase in vegetation has a detrimental impact on the aquatic ecosystem, depriving fish and other aerobic organisms of oxygen. Eutrophic conditions additionally affect drinking water treatment and the use of water bodies for recreation and leisure.

**farming carpet:** An expanse of land within the Smartcity used for the cultivation of arable crops. Colour, pattern and texture are considerations in plant selection.

**food species:** Plant and animal species consumed in the human diet. Despite the great number of edible plant species, the vast majority of the world's food is limited to only 20. [Swanson, 1994]

**Gaia hypothesis:** the theory formulated by James Lovelock in the mid 1960s that the planet functions as a single self-equilibrating organism with the capacity for self-regulation.

103

**gathering wells:** Public spaces recessed into the landscape and used for a variety of recreational purposes from floral and sound gardens to dance, swimming and fishing.

**geo-engineering:** The large-scale manipulation of natural systems to counteract climate change caused by human activities. Techniques include carbon sequestration, afforestation, solar shielding and stratospheric aerosols.

**geothermal energy:** Energy deriving from the heat below the earth's crust, extracted from steam, hot water or hot rock. The energy can be used for geothermal heat pumps, water heating or electricity generation using steam turbines.

**greenhouse gases:** Gases in the earth's atmosphere that absorb and emit radiation in the thermal infrared range. The gases prevent the release of heat into space creating a 'greenhouse effect' that makes the earth habitable. However, an increase in concentration of greenhouse gases [GHGs] partially caused by human activity has caused an imbalance in heat retention. Greenhouse gases include water vapour, methane, nitrous oxide, chlorofluorocarbons and carbon dioxide. The latter is the principal anthropogenic contributor to climate change, although water vapour accounts for the largest share of atmospheric GHGs.

**greywater:** Waste water from domestic washing processes.

**groundwater:** Water that has collected beneath the earth's surface in porous layers of rock called aquifers. A source of drinking water, the majority of groundwater has accumulated over the ages and is a finite resource, although rainwater adds to the store through percolation.

**human capital:** A form of capital stock consisting of accumulated skill and knowledge that contributes to productive power and economic value.

**hydroponics:** A technique for cultivating plants using a nutrient solution as a growing medium in lieu of soil. The productivity from hydroponic cultures is high due to the plants receiving a constant feed of nutrients with minimal risk of pest infestation. Growth can be further controlled in hermetic environments with artificial lighting and carbon dioxide flooding.

**industrial ecology:** An interdisciplinary field of research based on symbiosis between industrial and ecological systems. Industrial ecology involves the establishment of cyclical material and energy flows in which wastes from traditional waste-producing industries are used as resources in other processes while minimizing the creation of harmful by-products.

**integrated food and waste management system (IFWMS):** The coordination of different types of production such that the waste output from one component feeds another, IFWMS is an agricultural permaculture system developed by environmental engineer George Chan.

**interseasonal heat transfer [IHT]:** A means of reducing space heating and cooling demands by transferring extremes of temperature between seasons through the use of thermal stores. Pioneered by ICAX, IHT integrates solar thermal collection in summer with heat storage in thermal banks to double the efficiency and coefficient of performance of ground source heat pumps in winter.

**kelp farming:** kelp, a fast-growing alga, can absorb carbon dioxide and be used as a sustainable biofuel as well as providing a habitat for marine life. A development of this carbon sequestration technique by PODenergy proposes the harvesting of kelp in large plastic 'stomachs' in which bacteria break down the kelp into carbon dioxide and methane. The former will be piped to the surface for energy generation, the latter stored in deep ocean sinks or used in ocean liming.

**landfill:** A site for the disposal of refuse through the compaction and containment of solid waste under soil to minimize its effect on the environment. As population pressures have increased, landfill sites have been redeveloped, requiring the employment of stabilization and gas capping measures.

**lawn pier:** An elevated structure surfaced in grass for recreational purposes in the Smartcity, often extending over a productive arable landscape.

**lifelines:** The transport and communication pathways of the Smartcity.

**marine turbines:** Tidal energy has the advantage over wind and solar energies in being predictable. Regions with fast-flowing tidal streams have the potential to harvest colossal amounts of power with relatively small devices given the high energy density of tides.

**monocropping:** The cultivation of a single crop on arable land without the use of crop rotation. Whilst facilitating operational efficiencies, monocropping results in the diminution of soil fertility, overuse of chemical fertilizers and pesticides and the erosion of biodiversity.

**multi-utility service company [MUSCO]:** A community-owned or private–public delivery structure that provides a variety of utility services resulting in new operational synergies and a highly efficient customer interface.

**ocean liming:** The addition of calcium carbonate into the oceans. Carbon sequestration contributes to ocean acidity and threatens marine life. Limestone introduced into the water reacts with dissolved carbon dioxide to produce lime which neutralizes the acid and increases the GHG absorption capacity of the oceans.

**orchard hub:** An urban agriculture component of the Smartcity in which fruit trees are planted to provide fresh produce, biomass, acoustic attenuation and carbon sequestration.

**photovoltaics [PVs]:** Cell arrays, usually made from silicon with other trace elements, which convert solar radiation into electricity. PVs absorb photon energy to generate charge carriers that are attracted to a conductive contact, consequently transmitting electricity. Photovoltaic energy is particularly appropriate for use in remote locations where grid access is impossible and allows local use with minimal distribution losses. When connected to the grid, however, PV energy can reduce high cost electricity at daytime peak demand, although it requires conversion from direct to alternating current.

**planned obsolescence:** The practice of artificially shortening a product's lifespan in order to increase replacement frequency and as a result, revenue. In the agricultural industry, many high-yield engineered seeds are infertile and become obsolete after each harvest, forcing farmers to purchase new seeds year on year. While switching to new strains protects from the possibility of disease-related crop failure, there is potential for the infertility gene to spread and contaminate other fertile strains.

**podcar:** Also known as personal rapid transit vehicles, podcars are small automated vehicles that travel on guide ways directly to the destinations of their individual passengers. Developments in battery technologies are enabling hybrid vehicles to travel large distances on a single charge. It is a little known fact that in the early 20th century, prior to the Ford Model T, a third of all cars were electric.

**progress paradox:** The proposition that despite great advancements in technology and improvements in key life quality indices, people are no happier than they have been in the past.

**pyrolosis:** The anaerobic decomposition of organic material to sequester carbon. The process is carbon

105

negative, capturing up to 90% of $CO_2$ that would otherwise be released through combustion into biochar, combustible gas and bio-oils. Used for centuries in the Amazon rainforests, widespread adoption of pyrolysis is considered to be a viable geoengineering solution that produces material for soil enrichment.

**renewable energy:** Energy generated from sources that can be easily replenished from natural processes or are practically infinite. Types include biomass, geothermal, solar and wind energies.

**renewable energy sources act [EEG]:** A German parliamentary act granting priority to renewable energy and establishing minimum prices for its generation over the next 20 years. The structure of the EEG ensures high investment security and low credit interest rates, accounting for a 250% increase in clean energy generation between 2000 and 2004. The scaling back of payments for installations commissioned at a later date has averted the inertia of operators waiting for the technology to become less expensive.

**shallow ecology:** A anthropocentric approach to ecology focusing on pollution and the management of natural resources in contrast with the more holistic approach of deep ecology that places equal value on human and non-human life.

**sky garden:** A recurring motif of the Smartcity ranging from rooftop kitchen gardens to vegetative walkways that line streets in the sky. The elevated nature of the gardens explores and fulfils the need for new connections and territories at multiple levels to render vertical living socially sustainable.

**slow food movement:** An initiative formulated by Carlo Petrini espousing high-quality small-scale farming and regional cuisine as a response to fast food culture. Slow food is the precursor to and part of the broader 'slow movement' that aims to resist the homogenization and globalization of towns and cities while seeking to improve the quality and enjoyment of living.

**smart grids:** The application of digital technologies within electricity distribution networks enabling improved stability and efficiencies in transmission, monitoring and demand management. Investment in smart meter devices will permit the establishment of variable tariffs in relation to the time of day, levelling out demand fluctuations. With a reduction in maximum generation capacity requirements, the load on power plants is reduced; decentralized and diversified power generation will allow clients to choose renewable energy sources and to supply as well as consume energy; improved transparency will encourage responsible energy use while online management will streamline the customer interface.

**social capital:** A concept employed in the fields of sociology and economics describing the reciprocal relationships of trust that enable the advancement and cohesion of communities. Usually regarded as a resource in the battle against societal problems, it has been acknowledged that social capital can improve the well-being of individuals at the detriment of society at large, exemplified by old boys' networks and criminal fraternities.

**solar chimney:** A tubular device used to amplify natural stack ventilation by using solar energy to heat air at the top of the chimney, causing an updraft and suction at the base of the chimney.

**sound garden:** A sunken circular structure offering aural stimulus and diversion. Sound gardens vary in scale from amphitheatres for outdoor musical performance to small contemplation gardens focusing the mind on ambient sound.

**sustainability:** Forms of progress that meet the needs of the present without compromising the ability of future generations to meet their needs. [definition from the World Commission on Environment and Development, 1987].

Sustainable development is differentiated from green development in its inclusion of cultural and economic as well as environmental factors.

**urban + peri-urban agriculture:** The production of food in, or in the case of peri-urban agriculture, around cities and its integration within urban economies and ecologies.

**urban beach:** A recreational feature of the Smartcity adjacent to natural or artificial water bodies. More than an area for aquatic play, the urban beach is a multi-use space catering to all ages and challenging the formal codes and territories of traditional urban space.

**victory garden:** A kitchen garden planted during the World Wars to relieve pressure on food production deriving from the war effort. In addition to backyards, victory or war gardens took over the rooftops, sidewalks, vacant lots and public parks of major European and American cities.

**volatile organic compound [VOC]:** An organic compound that vaporizes under normal conditions and engages in atmospheric photochemical reactions. VOCs can be carcinogenic and can contribute to the formation of ozone and smog.

**waste-to-energy (WtE):** The creation of usable heat and electrical energy from waste sources, usually through incineration. Incineration plants now incorporate material and energy-recovery programmes along with emissions monitoring. Incineration decreases the volume of compacted waste by approximately 95%, and is therefore adopted in preference to landfill in countries of high population density. However, fly ash by-product requires disposal in toxic landfill sites. Other WtE technologies include gasification, pyrolysis, fermentation and anaerobic digestion.

**wind power:** The conversion of kinetic wind energy into usable mechanical and electrical energy through the use of turbines. Wind energy derives from differential solar radiation that causes change in atmospheric pressure. Due to its intermittent and non-dispatchable nature, wind power needs to be supplemented by good inter-regional transmission lines or energy storage infrastructure.

107

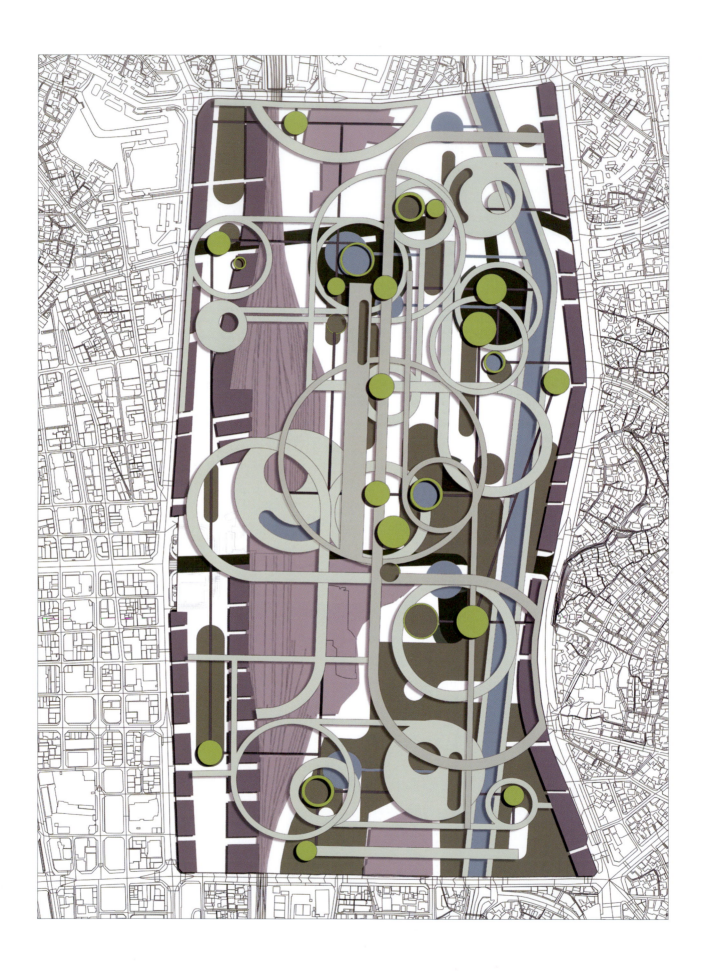

# Daejeon Urban Renaissance  South Korea

'The concept of vehicular/pedestrian segregation is now an accepted part of planning theory. But once one accepts this and the idea of multi-level single buildings, it is only logical to conceive of multi-level cities. The organisation of, say, New York, which tolerates multi-level components connected by only two horizontal levels (street and subway), and both of these at the base, is archaic.'
**- Editorial from 'Archigram 5'**

The Daejeon Urban Renaissance (DJURe) zone in South Korea, covering an area of 0.89km2, suffers from classic doughnut or inverted concentric zone complex. Daejeon Old City District, once the thriving heart of the city, has since been overtaken by surrounding towns assimilated into Daejeon by the Government in 1990. The DJURe area is currently cluttered with single-storey detached commercial, industrial and residential buildings that have fallen into disrepair and are fenced in by four and six-lane highways. Businesses and homes have migrated to newer suburbs outside the Old Town with superior infrastructure and flourishing communities.

At the same time, DJURe is the beneficiary of excellent transport links, containing a high-speed rail (KTX) and regional rail transit station linking Seoul with Busan, a subway line running across the city, and major road connections. A new scale of development is proposed for the regeneration of Daejeon's obsolescent core. Occupying a far smaller area than Guangming Smartcity, DJURe will explore vertical densities in order to free up open space for recreation and agriculture. Introducing new leisure programmes to conventional commercial, office and residential mixed-use towers will attract residents from outside the zone, preventing an island culture and stimulating wider social capital.

The height of the buildings in the DJURe Micro Smartcity will exceed that of its immediate surroundings, matching that of other major international cities, and will accommodate an increase in the district's population from 7500 to 13 000. The scale brings with it a new dynamic and intensity, and presents a bold iconic image for Daejeon. This second wave of life and development will eventually infiltrate and be adopted by the surrounding towns as a model for sustainable urban growth.

Le Corbusier imagined skyscrapers as 'streets in the sky', a compelling metaphor that has so far achieved only a one-dimensional reality. Streets are not islands; they connect to other streets, forming a lattice of complex relationships that engage in rich and unpredictable synergy. Even mixed-use high-rise buildings are connected to the rest of the city only at ground level; the disconnection from urban life increases as the storeys in a tower rise, culminating in a company boardroom or an exclusive penthouse.

facing page: Daejeon Urban Renaissance masterplan

following page: Infrastructure plans and the layered city

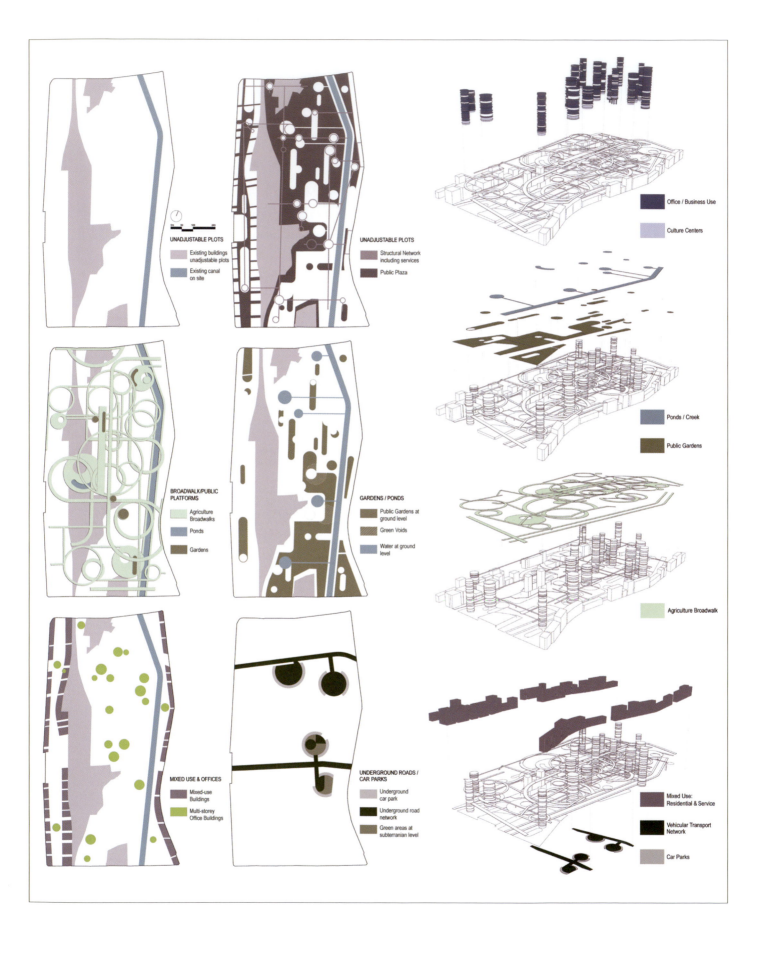

UNADJUSTABLE PLOTS
- Existing buildings unadjustable plots
- Existing canal on site

UNADJUSTABLE PLOTS
- Structural Network including services
- Public Plaza

Office / Business Use
Culture Centers

BROADWALK/PUBLIC PLATFORMS
- Agriculture Broadwalks
- Ponds
- Gardens

GARDENS / PONDS
- Public Gardens at ground level
- Green Voids
- Water at ground level

Ponds / Creek
Public Gardens

Agriculture Broadwalk

MIXED USE & OFFICES
- Mixed-use Buildings
- Multi-storey Office Buildings

UNDERGROUND ROADS / CAR PARKS
- Underground car park
- Underground road network
- Green areas at subterranian level

Mixed Use: Residential & Service
Vehicular Transport Network
Car Parks

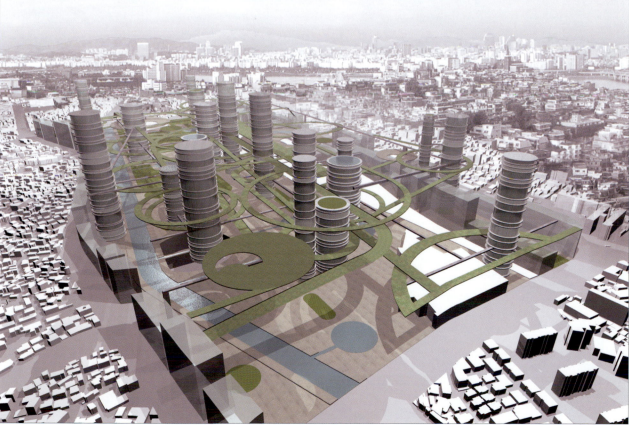

The network of elevated walkways in the Central District of Hong Kong that connects flagship commercial office space, hotels, shopping malls and the general post office has proved remarkably successful in creating a second horizontal tier of public activity. This arrangement will soon be replicated in Shanghai's Pudong district where a ring-shaped walkway will link most of the skyscrapers in the main financial and business district. The primary objective in both these installations, however, is the separation of pedestrian and vehicular traffic. Consequently, the horizontal coupling exists only a storey or two above the existing ground plane and offers little in the way of establishing new public territory in a third dimension.

At DJURe, the towers will be linked at several levels, incorporating SPIN farming and recreational activities to multiply social connections, as well as improve safety in terms of structural stability and fire evacuation. The 'streets in the sky' that Le Corbusier envisioned will be horizontal as well as vertical, giving shape to an urban landmark that is both formal and functional.

## City Framework

The boundary of Daejeon Smartcity Centre is arranged into mixed-use human-scale boulevards that are conceived as the inhabitable walls of an urban courtyard garden. The walls contain residential and commercial developments overlooking a verdant landscape punctuated by a community of towers. At the centre of the urban courtyard is a city plaza made up of hard landscaping and green open space. Deadong Creek, running along a north–south axis across the DJURe site, feeds a chain of ponds and reservoirs that store water for irrigation and maintain what precious biodiversity remains in the city. Accessed by foot through the inhabitable wall or via the underpasses, the city plaza is experienced as a secret garden, appearing as an unexpected oasis of vegetation and natural harmony within a concrete sea, while promoting vital cultural and commercial activities.

Twenty-one skyscrapers are distributed across the city centre and collectively they constitute the city's business hubs. Each tower contains a cultural facility and a sky plaza, linked at high level as well as on the ground. Associative function spaces such as the concert hall, music academy and recording studios are located next to each other to make use of beneficial adjacencies whilst ascribing individual identity to the vertical communities.

Sky gardens are located at major nodes at which more than two streets in the sky connect. The gardens are intensively planted and the elevated walkways are draped with hydroponically grown vegetation to shape a green network that provides shading for activities in the urban courtyard below.

previous page: Aerial views of an urban courtyard garden city

facing page: Exploring vertical densities for agriculture and mixed-use programmes

# Central Open Space: MAC  South Korea

The Republic of Korea is in the process of building a new Multi-functional Administrative City (MAC) to alleviate excessive concentration of the Seoul Metropolitan area by relocating the government ministries and to promote balanced national development. Located in Chungcheongnam-do Province, 150km from Seoul, MAC will cover an area of 72.19km2 and takes the form of a ring that symbolizes the government's principles of non-hierarchy and decentralization.

The MAC is intended to be a model city for sustainable growth, enhancing the quality of Korean urban environments by acting as an exemplar development. Commissioned by the Korea Land Corporation and the Multi-functional Administrative City Construction Agency, the Central Open Space (COS) is to be the green hub at the heart of the city that connects various cultural facilities and represents the government's philosophy and vision. Occupying an area of 6.982km2, the COS is a great plain that aligns with Mount Jeonweol-san and Mount Wonsu-bong, and has the Geum-gang River running through it. As befits a model city, the COS transcends traditional notions of the park as a verdant isolated island within the metropolis to become a dynamic environment that engages in dialogue with the city through regeneration, nature and culture.

The adoption of an urban agriculture programme is eminently suited to the COS, offering a true model of sustainability for a global 21st century city and re-establishes a meaningful and fluid relationship between fresh food production and the city's population. The proximity of government ministries to cultivated land sets out a clear position regarding Korea's commitment to food security. COS incorporates cultural institutions such as a performing arts complex, a history and folk museum and a design museum presenting opportunities to exploit the poetic juxtaposition of civic activities within a picturesque but functional backdrop. In contrast to Guangming Smartcity where urban fabric is integrated into farmland, fragments of the Multi-functional administrative city are inserted into the farmscape of the COS. Artists' studios, libraries and villas for eco-tourists float amongst the canopies of peach and pear trees, bringing city dwellers into unexpected contact with the verdant and scented bosom of mother nature.

The procurement of a new park of this scale is an immense undertaking and the strategy for the development of the COS is designed to minimize land movement and to keep the land in use throughout the various phases of construction. The development area is currently arable land and the existing local practice of vegetable farming will be retained along with all the local traditions of food production, although the plain will be reconfigured into striated bands of seasonal colour, bringing into being a chromatic spectacle viewed from four elevated inhabitable piers. The pier structures will house new programmatic functions and extend out over the fields.

facing page: Central Open Space masterplan

following page: Infrastructure plans of the agricultural and cultural city

New Artificial Lake
(PAT)

Geum-gang River

EXISTING WATERCOURSES

EXISTING ARABLE FIELDS
seasonal organic vegetables

1 min walk
80m

5 mins walk
400m

12 mins walk
1000m

CYCLE + PEDESTRIAN PATHS
Timber decking on existing
earth banks

CIRCULATION
Vertical (lifts + stairs) and
Inclined (ramps)

MAIN LIFELINES
Vehicle asphalt roads

PUBLIC CAR PARKS

SPORTS FACILITIES

HYDROLOGY

UNDERGROUND WATER
STORAGE
for lawn + farmlands irrigation
in dry summers

LAWN PIERS
working with boreholes to create
microclimate condition to
prevent lawn from winter frost

THERMAL BOREHOLES
to provide aquifer cooling
+ heating to all MAC buildings

PEACH ORCHARDS
PEAR ORCHARDS

LAWN PIERS
Structures with manicured grass surface floating over arable fields

LOTUS FIELDS
+ Fresh water fish farms

VEGETABLE NURSERY
ARBORETUM + TREE NURSERY
AGRICULTURE LAB + LEARNING CENTERS

SOUND GARDENS

AGRITOURISM VILLAS
with rooftop restaurants + teahouse

ANAEROBIC DIGESTERS
FARMERS MARKETS + COMMUNITY FORUMS

WETLANDS
Water/nutrients filtration treatment + wildlife sanctuary

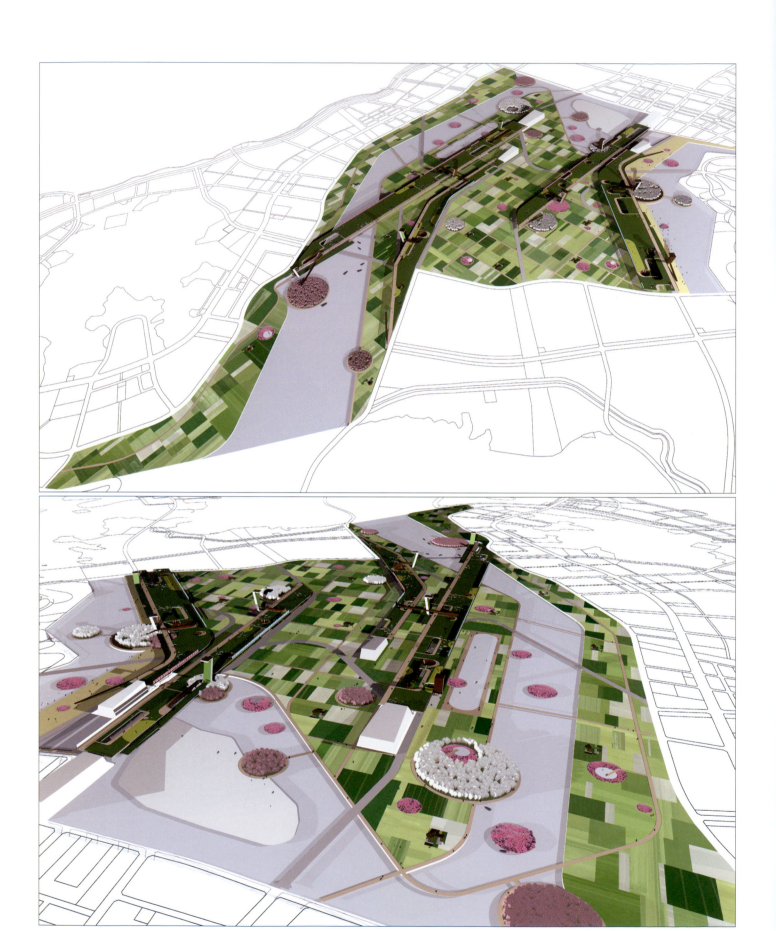

## Urban Agriculture

During the second half of the 20th century, the urban and peri-urban agriculture movement in Korea grew rapidly due to an influx of farmers to the cities who could command high prices within a large consumer market, cultivating land that was still relatively inexpensive. Rapid industrialization and spiralling land prices have resulted in a strategic shift in Korean urban agriculture, with a new focus on green tourism and nutritional benefits. In comparison to the West, Koreans have evinced greater disquiet over the sedentary lifestyle of their children and the disjunct between the city and nature, resulting in the growth of farm-stay schemes in which city dwellers holiday on farms and reconnect with their rural heritage. Due to the high population density of the country, the only viable form that urban agriculture can take is intensive horticulture, and city cooperatives concentrating on improving quality in order to compete with low-cost imports have found new markets by setting up framework agreements to supply schoolchildren with high quality produce. The urban agricultural strategy at this exemplar city follows this model, prioritizing quality and education over quantity and a disposable culture. Less can indeed be more.

The existing farming community will play a crucial role in the upkeep of the open space and be called upon to instruct and supervise other residents who take up a support role in tending the land, disseminating cultural practices and a breath of fresh air to a generation of desk-bound urbanites. The farmers, too, will need training to integrate nutrient waste recycling and energy generation systems made possible by the farms' access to the city.

Local food production and the exchange of skills between the farming community and native city-dwellers will create new social bridging capital. Encounters between these two disparate groups will no longer be a rarity and the former, so long taken for granted, will be empowered by the arrangement. Fresh produce will be sold directly to the public and commercial interests will not be permitted any control on the produce farmed that would otherwise negatively influence the colour and texture of the COS.

## Agritourism

Farm-stay programmes in Korea have demonstrated a yearning for a calmer and more rewarding lifestyle. For people who are more interested in how their food is produced, the Central Open Space is the place to go, without the inconvenience of long congested journeys into the countryside. Vegetable fields, fruit orchards and watercourses offer scenic beauty and green space. Visitors will be able to stay in villas on the farm where they can assist with farming tasks or pick their own fruit and vegetables, relax and enjoy the fresh country air. Hiking and trekking paths will be marked out on the Jeonweol-san and Wonsu-bong mountains. At the peak of each mountain, viewing posts in the forest clearings will present stunning vistas back over the COS.

The new urban beach sandwiched between the Public Adminstrative Town (PAT) Development and arable farm-scape, is a more convenient leisure destination than the northern coastline, making the COS an ideal weekend resort.

facing page: Aerial views of a sustainable food production city

following page: Views showing the relationship between lawn piers and existing agricultural carpet

## Culture

The new landscape of COS aims to be a public recreational green space, simultaneously mixing culture with ecology. A 50 000m2 Performing Arts Complex including music halls and theatres for the performance of operas and traditional Korean music, a 25 000m2 History and Folk Museum celebrating the nation's cultural heritage, a 50 000m2 Design Museum and a fourth cultural facility are planned for construction within the COS.

Interactive technologies will be introduced to increase the interface between nature and culture. Soundtracks will be composed to stimulate the senses and choreograph mood to complement the landscape. Sound gardens and gathering wells break up the plain, providing areas to sit, converse and relax. Changes in the topography, textural variation and ephemeral acoustic boundaries demarcate zones of occupation. Seated in these garden oases, rich in haptic sensation, visitors will experience the vanishing sound of wind chimes and rhythmic melodies whilst viewing some of the country's historic artefacts positioned at the focal point of the wells.

## Organizational Framework

The restructuring of the landscape starts with preserving the area's historical and cultural identity; minimal modification is made to the existing fields. A new planting schedule displaying seasonal texture and colour change will be implemented to this hybridization of kitchen garden and park. Strong horizontal spatial moves are introduced to accentuate the flatness of the site. A matrix of five interacting systems are laid onto the inhabitable vegetative canvas:

(1)    A network of paths radiating from the five principal roads surrounding the site extends into and weaves across the open space, designated as the primary lifelines. These are used for vehicular circulation and parking, and connect the cultural buildings and leisure nodes.

(2)    The existing network of mud banks and ridges are made good and covered with timber decking. These constitute the secondary lifelines, available for cycling and walking.

(3)    Four lawn piers accommodate the non-farming activity infrastructure and are distinguished by the four designated cultural museums and arts venues. Built in lightweight steel and timber construction, the piers float over the arable plain making reference to the urban roof garden as well as the ringed form of the Governmental Complex of Administrative City. The expanses of green lawn provide a multi-functional surface for picnics, sunbathing and ballgames while the elevated plane presents spectacular panoramic views. Sports facilities, farmers markets, tourist accommodation and other future urban space-forms will emerge beneath these four living earth structures.

(4)    A scattering of fruit and lotus orchard hubs provide new natural habitats and introduce a new dynamic to the arable plain. The region is celebrated for its peaches and pears, and the trees impart a dramatic seasonal colour change from emerald green to white and pink. The lotus, a versatile plant, is used in a number of cooking preparations and represents classical notions of beauty that contrast with the large-scale composition of arable striations.

(5)    A nexus of watercourses reinforces the hydrology and ecological dynamics of the site, linking a new artificial lake with the Geum-gang River and offering opportunities for fresh water fish farming, recreational fishing and boating.

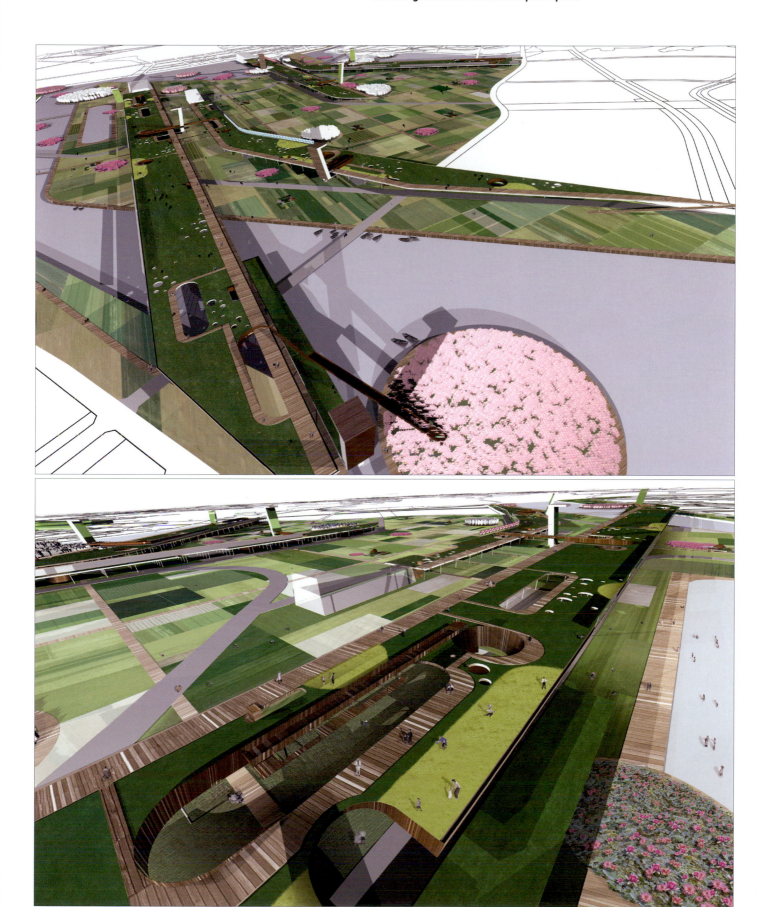

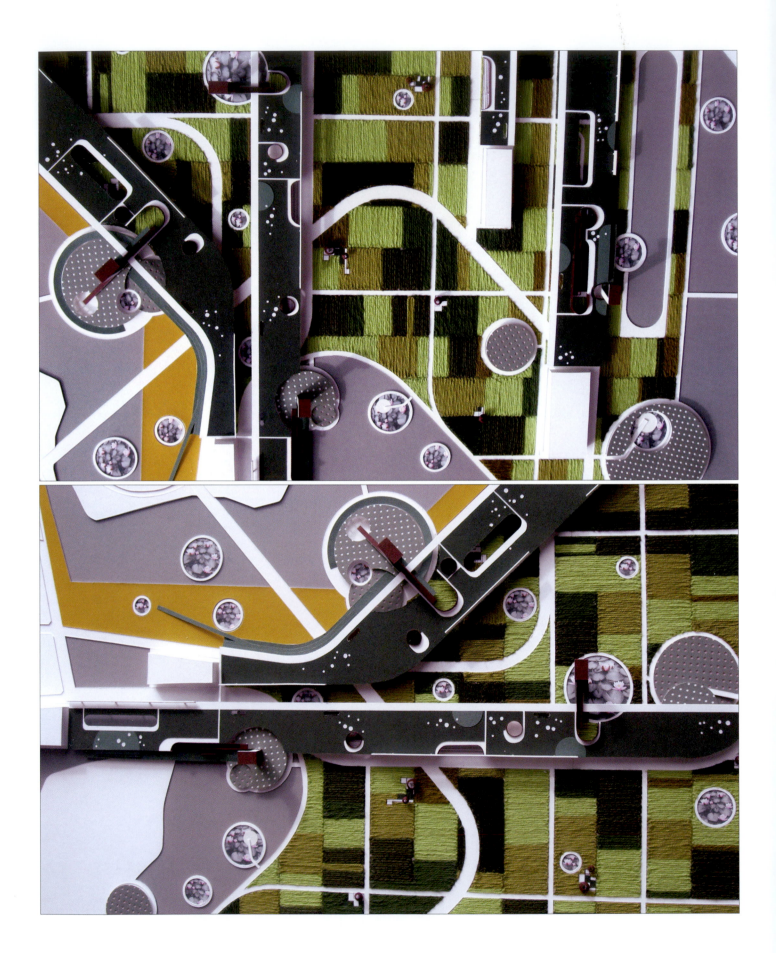

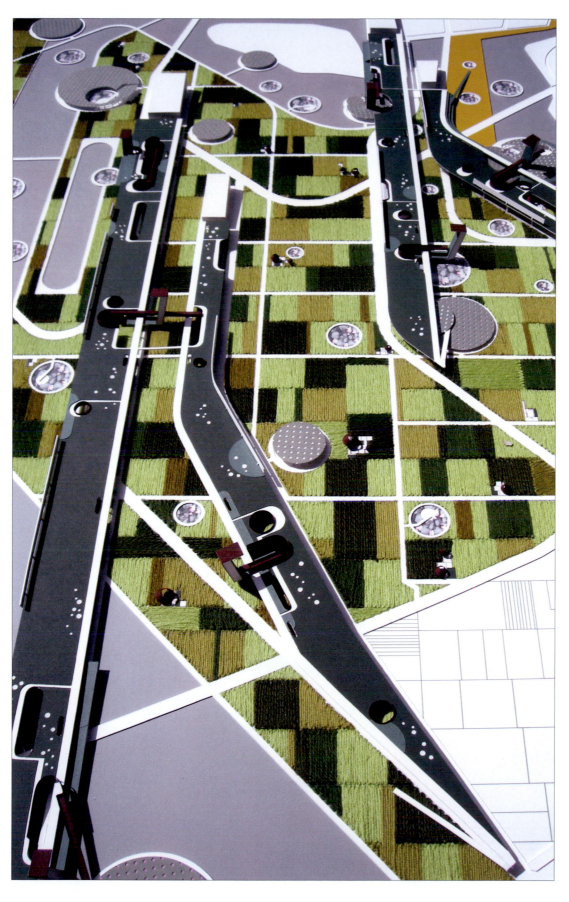

facing page + left: Model of the
COS – knitted texture of the existing
agricultural carpet

Section through typical bicycle path    Scale 1:200

Section through typical road    Scale 1:200

Section through mud bank    Scale 1:200

Pedestrian
boardwalk    Bicycle
boardwalk

Plan of typical bicycle path    Scale 1:200

Section of typical road    Scale 1:200

Section through mud bank    Scale 1:200

MUD BANK CONDITION

Street lights -
precast concrete columns
energy -saving bulbs

Timber deck battons
Span 2m
Dimensions:
50mm x 100mm deep

Precast beam grid
Span 3.6m
Beam section
300mm x 300mm

Precast pile section
Diameter 150mm
driven 4m into clay soil

Bicycle path construction

BICYCLE CONDITION

Dark tarmac acts
as a solar water
collector in summer

Water coils are
heating in summer

Boaster pump set for
distributing water

Warm water is stored
in submersible pump
in borehole

Environmental road diagram

ROAD CONDITION

Bicycles are stored in
vertical towers for space
efficiency

BUS STOP CONDITION

Bicycles lock in ground

Efficient bicycle storage

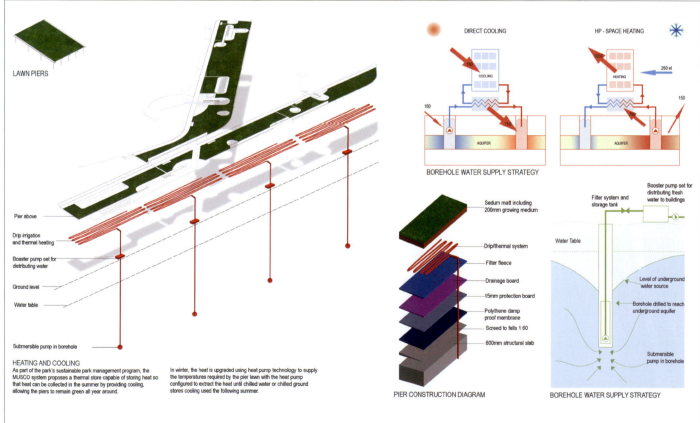

LAWN PIERS

Pier above

Drip irrigation
and thermal heating

Boaster pump set for
distributing water

Ground level

Water table

Submersible pump in borehole

HEATING AND COOLING
As part of the park's sustainable park management program, the MUSCO system proposes a thermal store capable of storing heat so that heat can be collected in the summer by providing cooling, allowing the piers to remain green all year around.

In winter, the heat is upgraded using heat pump technology to supply the temperatures required by the pier lawn with the heat pump configured to extract the heat until chilled water or chilled ground stores cooling used the following summer.

DIRECT COOLING    HP - SPACE HEATING

COOLING    HEATING

AQUIFER    AQUIFER

BOREHOLE WATER SUPPLY STRATEGY

Sedum matt including
200mm growing medium

Drip/thermal system

Filter fleece

Drainage board

15mm protection board

Polythene damp
proof membrane

Screed to falls 1:60

600mm structural slab

PIER CONSTRUCTION DIAGRAM

Booster pump set for
distributing fresh
water to buildings

Filter system and
storage tank

Water Table

Level of underground
water source

Borehole drilled to reach
underground aquifer

Submersible
pump in borehole

BOREHOLE WATER SUPPLY STRATEGY

**Sustainable Energy + Resource Management**

The opportunities to provide an exemplar open space in the middle of a new planned city include methods of providing not only sustainable energy and resource management for the park, but also commercial possibilities where the park itself can offer these facilities to the city as a whole. The Central Open Space will therefore adopt a commercial sustainable energy and resource management system in the form of a MUSCO (Multi Utility Service Company) that holds the following advantages over more traditional single supply commercial models:

125

-        A model of local governance can be applied to energy and water supplies.

-        Local high-level employment and training possibilities are presented.

-        Efficiencies in management costs and possible income from low carbon grants and tax advantages offered by the South Korean government should enable a well-designed and efficiently operated supply system to offer services which are lower carbon and cheaper tariff than those offered by single supply models, reducing fuel poverty and attracting commercial organizations to the area.

-        Forms of supply can be tailored to meet the precise needs of the customers. The Public Administrative Town will require high quality office and commercial space. Where many National Grid systems have proved unable to provide a high quality electricity supply essential for new technology businesses, the MUSCO would be able to ensure low-fluctuation electricity.

-        Electricity generation from the combustion of fossil fuels inherently produces far more waste heat than electrical energy. This heat, when produced and rejected in summer, can worsen urban heat island effects and when released in winter is wasteful when the MAC depends on winter heating for thermal comfort. The MUSCO arrangement will provide combined cooling, heat and power to enable electricity to be sold alongside waste heat, either as district heating or cooling via an absorption chiller installation. Costs and the carbon content of heat, cooling and electricity will be reduced.

-        An average annual precipitation in excess of 1500mm provides more than enough water for urban expansion. However, the irrigation necessary for the arable kitchen garden park constitutes a good business case for a separate irrigation quality. Where groundwater is available from the alluvial deposits in the area, it can be treated to drinking water quality and water can be abstracted from river water in the treatment plant on site. Wetlands adjoining the river can be made beautiful and still serve in a final cleansing process. Studies have shown that the plant and distribution network servicing the Central Open Space could be efficiently scaled up to supply the immediately surrounding city. Excess urban nutrients that would otherwise be pumped into the river and lead to eutrophication can be dealt with by tertiary filtering using the wetlands together with sustainable surface drainage features such as ˙gravel bed hydroponic networks.

facing page top: Solar collection paths

facing page bottom: Borehole Water Supply strategy

-        Nutrients produced in the arable plain and orchards will leave the COS as food consumed

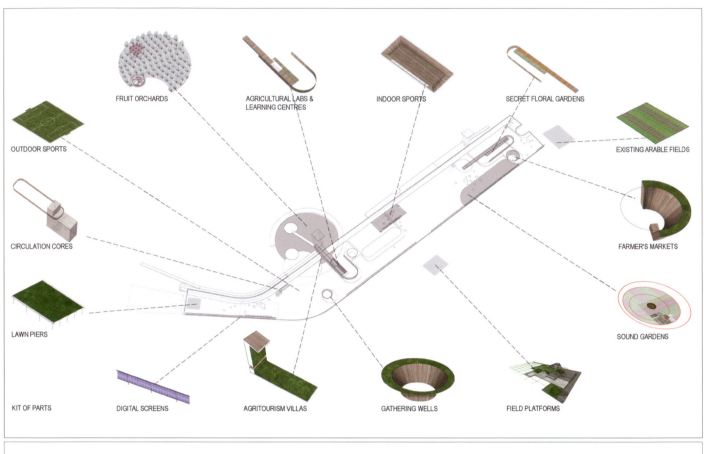

FRUIT ORCHARDS

AGRICULTURAL LABS & LEARNING CENTRES

INDOOR SPORTS

SECRET FLORAL GARDENS

OUTDOOR SPORTS

EXISTING ARABLE FIELDS

CIRCULATION CORES

FARMER'S MARKETS

LAWN PIERS

SOUND GARDENS

KIT OF PARTS

DIGITAL SCREENS

AGRITOURISM VILLAS

GATHERING WELLS

FIELD PLATFORMS

SECRET FLORAL GARDENS

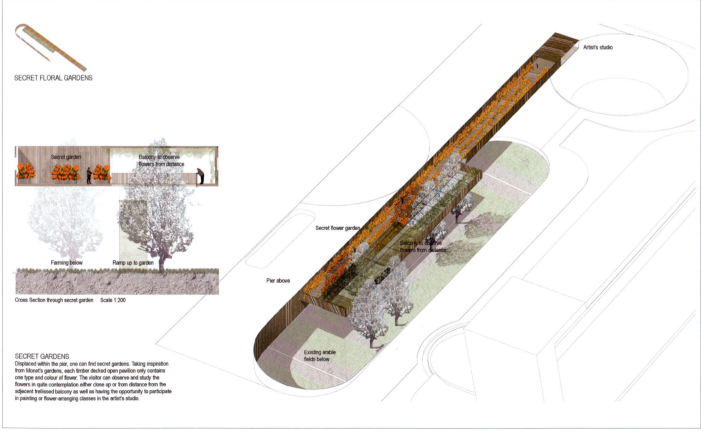

Artist's studio

Secret flower garden

Balcony to observe flowers from distance

Pier above

Existing arable fields below

Secret garden

Balcony to observe flowers from distance

Farming below

Ramp up to garden

Cross Section through secret garden    Scale 1:200

SECRET GARDENS

Displaced within the pier, one can find secret gardens. Taking inspiration from Monet's gardens, each timber decked open pavilion only contains one type and colour of flower. The visitor can observe and study the flowers in quite contemplation either close up or from distance from the adjacent trellissed balcony as well as having the opportunity to participate in painting or flower-arranging classes in the artist's studio.

by the local community. In order to establish a classic urban nutrient cycle, the COS will act as the local organic waste treatment authority, receiving an annual income for treating organic waste using anaerobic digesters to yield biogas that can be converted into saleable energy. Remaining nutrients can be returned to the soil as fertilizer.

-        The management / public interface of the MUSCO will take the form of outlets on each pier set to maximize the farming income run by the city's utilities management company, the setup similar to that established in Guangming Smartcity.

### Electricity + Biomass

Energy from photovoltaic panels will serve localized demand within the COS and illuminate streets, bus stops and bicycle stations in the neighbouring city. Integrated PV panels along the lifelines will provide shading and further increase electricity supply.

Biomass waste from landscaping and agriculture is carbon neutral and can be burnt to generate energy, processed into biogas or converted into high-quality compost. In addition to district heating and district cooling via the use of biomass CCHP installations, interseasonal thermal storage will be employed.

COS is underlain by quaternary alluvial deposits suggesting the possibility of aquifer thermal energy storage (ATES), the most advanced and lowest energy of inter-seasonal thermal storage forms. This system uses boreholes to access different sections of the aquifer to create separate warm and cool zones. A single thermal borehole into a sandstone aquifer could yield 2MW of cooling or heating. As aquifer water is merely pumped from one part to another, there is no risk of aquifer depletion.

A similar system can be utilized by turning the earth itself into separate large-scale heat and cooling stores. There will be an element of cut and fill earth movement in planning the open space, providing an opportunity to install circulating coils within the fill.

If the buildings served by these interseasonal thermal storage systems are not in equilibrium, that is if too many commercial buildings are served and too much heat begins to build up towards the end of summer or if buildings requiring heat outweigh those requiring cooling and overall, additional heat is required, there are new opportunities at the scale of landscape for the redistribution of stored temperature. New pathways, roads and hard surfaced areas will incorporate circulating plastic pipework taking heat from close to the surface during the summer (asphalt is approximately 60% to 70% efficient as a solar collector) to 'top up' heat in the warm thermal store. Similarly the same surfaces can be used to reject heat in the winter ensuring that they remain ice and snow-free.

Operating on a similar principle, thermal coils fixed to the underside of the piers above multi-use games areas will emit radiant heat, extending the time available for sporting activities.

facing page top: The lawn pier accommodates non-farming infrastructure

facing page bottom: Secret gardens hover over the fruit orchards

LAWN PIERS

300mm growing medium

2.5m wide precast elements
2.5m long, 600 deep
Prestressed plank

In situ cast post-tensioned
beam 1.8m deep, span 50m
with 600mm prestressing ducts

In situ cast column with in-built
drainage and water supply
1000mm diameter

Piers one and two construction starting from culture centre

Piers one and two construction

Piers three and four construction

All piers constructed
CONSTRUCTION PHASING

50 m
20 m
25 m

CONSTRUCTION DIAGRAM
Easy construction using Jean Mueller's
bridge construction technique.

Cantilever "jetting" frame

50 m
20 m

Construction disruption

Un-disturbed farming

Piles installed from high level
with no ground disturbance

Un-disturbed farming

Un-disturbed farming

CONSTRUCTION SEQUENCE OF PIER

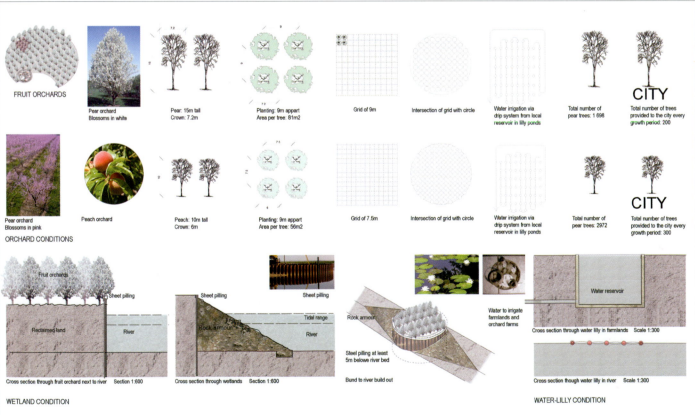

FRUIT ORCHARDS

Pear orchard
Blossoms in white

Pear: 15m tall
Crown: 7.2m

Planting: 9m appart
Area per tree: 81m2

Grid of 9m

Intersection of grid with circle

Water irrigation via
drip system from local
reservoir in lilly ponds

Total number of
pear trees: 1 698

Total number of trees
provided to the city every
growth period: 200

CITY

Pear orchard
Blossoms in pink

ORCHARD CONDITIONS

Peach orchard

Peach: 10m tall
Crown: 6m

Planting: 9m appart
Area per tree: 56m2

Grid of 7.5m

Intersection of grid with circle

Water irrigation via
drip system from local
reservoir in lilly ponds

Total number of
pear trees: 2972

Total number of trees
provided to the city every
growth period: 300

CITY

Fruit orchards

Sheet pilling

Reclaimed land

River

Cross section through fruit orchard next to river    Section 1:600

Sheet pilling

Sheet pilling

Tidal range

Rock armour

River

Cross section through wetlands    Section 1:600

Rock armour

Steel pilling at least
5m belowe river bed

Bund to river build out

Water to irrigate
farmlands and
orchard farms

Water reservoir

Cross section through water lilly in farmlands    Scale 1:300

Cross section though water lilly in river    Scale 1:300

WETLAND CONDITION

WATER-LILLY CONDITION

### Data and communications

Relatively basic web-based software is used to collect data from digital meters and to manage the MUSCO accounts online, resulting in reduced management costs. The MUSCO will also serve as the local data network provider, making the upgrade of data cabling to energy meters cost efficient.

A community intranet offering free access between residents and the MUSCO will create new community connections by offering information on local training and employment opportunities, become part of the local education system and provide all civic data. It will also manage a car-sharing scheme, provide real time public transport information and the delivery of guaranteed locally produced food to the doorstep of subscribers. A similar intranet arrangement will allow the COS and other local farmers to offer their produce to the community directly, reducing costs and improving local competitive advantage over larger national or multi-national scale retail suppliers.

### Structural Sequencing

The construction of the very large elevated decks, freestanding pavilions and auditoria are designed for longevity, low maintenance and minimal disruption to the existing landscape. The decks are economic concrete structures with lateral stability of the structural tables provided by the columns acting as sway frames in bending. Additional elements, adjacent pavilions and suspended structures within the deck are framed in steel to reduce weight and to accelerate construction times. Thermal movement is allowed for with movement joints every third bay.

Work commences with the levelling and paving of access roads. From these primary routes, pre-cast concrete frames are assembled on short driven piles to provide support for timber boardwalks. The principal deck beams are formed in place with sliding shutters. Pre-cast deck elements are then added sequentially. The assembly will be completed with grouted joints to ensure robustness.

An innovative adaptation of the French engineer Jean Muller's bridge construction methodology is adopted to avoid disrupting the ground plane. A temporary steel 'jetting frame' is erected at deck level and cantilevered forward as work proceeds so that new foundation bases, columns and cross-beams can all be placed from above without direct access to the support points.

facing page top: Construction sequence of a lawn pier

facing page bottom: Planting strategy for the orchards; construction of the water's edges

following page left (top): Contemplation in the sound gardens

following page left (bottom): Gathering on the lawn piers

following page right (top): Demarcation of the fruit orchards through colour and smell

following page right (bottom): Nurseries forming the facades of agritourism villas

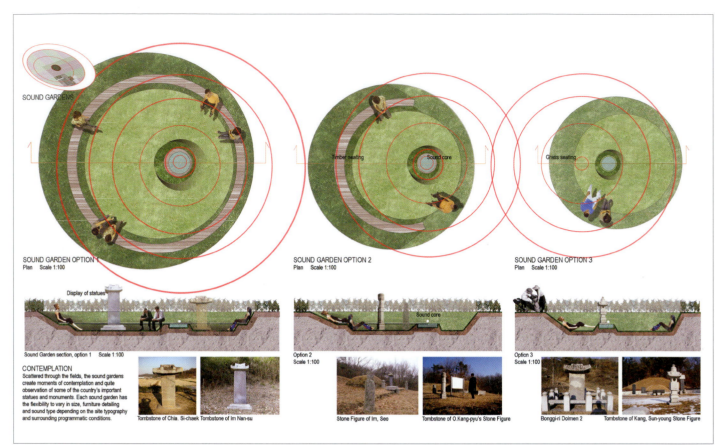

SOUND GARDENS

SOUND GARDEN OPTION 1
Plan    Scale 1:100

SOUND GARDEN OPTION 2
Plan    Scale 1:100

Timber seating            Sound core

SOUND GARDEN OPTION 3
Plan    Scale 1:100

Grass seating

Display of statues

Sound Garden section, option 1    Scale 1:100

Option 2
Scale 1:100

Sound core

Option 3
Scale 1:100

## CONTEMPLATION
Scattered through the fields, the sound gardens create moments of contemplation and quite observation of some of the country's important statues and monuments. Each sound garden has the flexibility to vary in size, furniture detailing and sound type depending on the site typography and surrounding programmatic conditions.

Tombstone of Chia. Si-chaek    Tombstone of Im Nan-su

Stone Figure of Im, Seo    Tombstone of O.Kang-pyu's Stone Figure

Bonggi-ri Dolmen 2    Tombstone of Kang, Sun-young Stone Figure

GATHERING WELLS

Clusters of gathering wells on the piers

INHABITABLE
GRASS WELL
Plan    Scale 1:100

Football pitch below

FLAT GLASS WELL
Plan    Scale 1:100

Football pitch below

INHABITABLE
TIMBER WELL
Plan    Scale 1:100

INHABITABLE GLASS WELL
Plan    Scale 1:100

Light fitting underneath

Section    Scale 1:100

Section    Scale 1:100

Section    Scale 1:100

## GATHERING MOMENTS
The piers are introduced with punctures of different textures and sizes, ranging from grass, glass, timber and water surface. Strategically positioned in clusters on top of the pier, they are a valuable element of the piers, not just by bringing valuable natural sunlight to the farmlands underneath the pier, but also encouraging public gathering moments for pic-nic areas, watching the sport games below, public festivities and cinema viewing during the night.

Stepped entrance to inhabitable gathering wells    Contemplation zones    Green wall    Watching the football game below

SOUND GARDENS

Pear orchard

Pear tree

Extent of sound represented with peach tree plantations

Peach tree

Pear orchard

Extend of sound demarcates division of trees

**PHYSICAL DEMARCATION OF THE EPHEMERAL**
The ephemeral sound zone from the sound garden is physically demarcated and suggested within the orchard farms through changes in height of surrounding trees.

Pier above

Farmlands below

Creeping Bent - Agrostis stolonifera

Pier above

Sound garden below

Extent of sound raised to pier level

Perennial Ryegrass - Lolium perenne

**PHYSICAL DEMARCATION OF THE EPHEMERAL**
The ephemeral sound zone from the sound garden is physically demarcated within the pier through changes of grass texture and colour. This further allows for a more fluid interface between the piers above and the fields below.

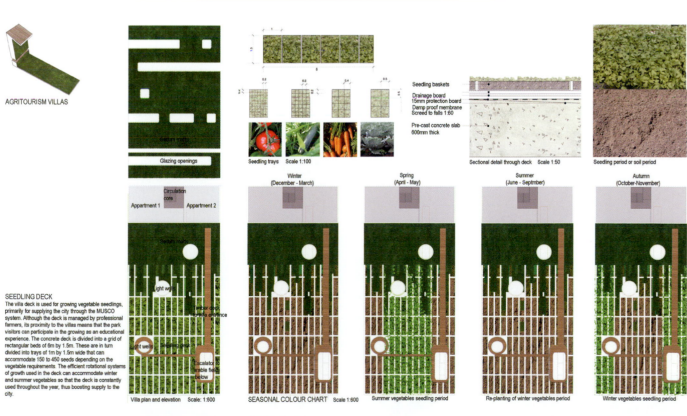

AGRITOURISM VILLAS

Sedum mats

Glazing openings

Seedling baskets
Drainage board
15mm protection board
Damp proof membrane
Screed to falls 1:60
Pre-cast concrete slab 600mm thick

Seedling trays     Scale 1:100

Sectional detail through deck     Scale 1:50

Seedling period or soil period

Circulation core

Appartment 1     Appartment 2

Sedum mats

Light well

Arbor deck to villa entrance

**SEEDLING DECK**
The villa deck is used for growing vegetable seedlings, primarily for supplying the city through the MUSCO system. Although the deck is managed by professional farmers, its proximity to the villas means that the park visitors can participate in the growing as an educational experience. The concrete deck is divided into a grid of rectangular beds of 6m by 1.5m. These are in turn divided into trays of 1m by 1.5m wide that can accommodate 150 to 450 seeds depending on the vegetable requirements. The efficient rotational systems of growth used in the deck can accommodate winter and summer vegetables so that the deck is constantly used throughout the year, thus boosting supply to the city.

Light wells     Seedling deck

Escalator to arable field below

Villa plan and elevation     Scale: 1:600

Winter (December - March)

Spring (April - May)

Summer (June - September)

Autumn (October-November)

SEASONAL COLOUR CHART     Scale 1:600

Summer vegetables seeding period

Re-planting of winter vegetables period

Winter vegetables seeding period

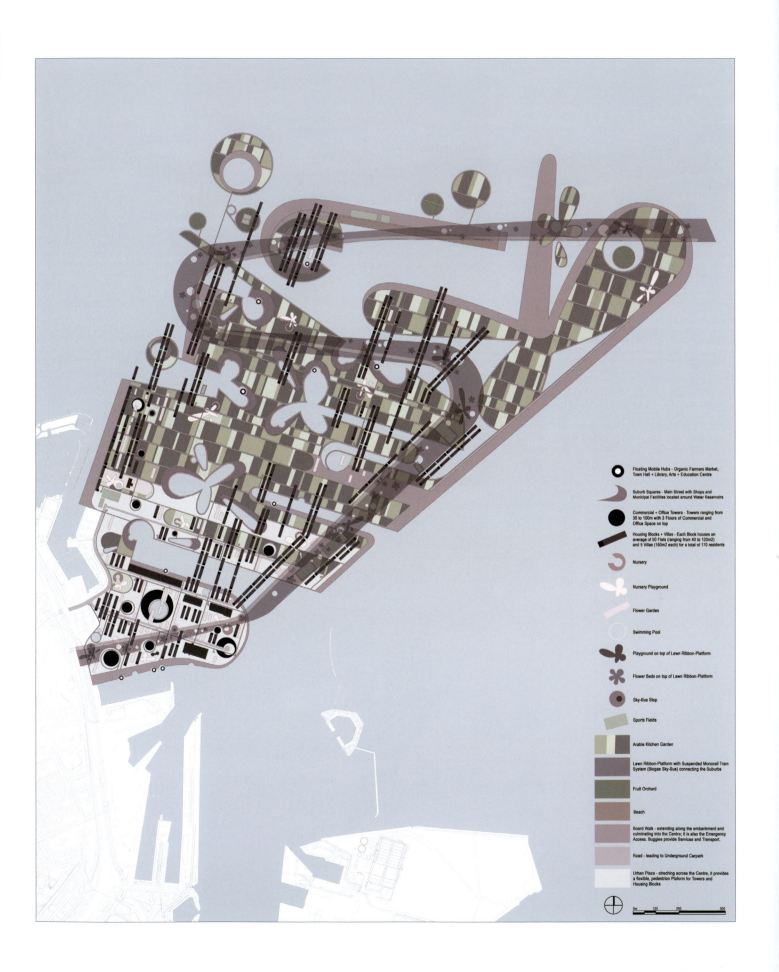

Floating Mobile Hubs - Organic Farmers Market, Town Hall + Library, Arts + Education Centre

Suburb Squares - Main Street with Shops and Municipal Facilities located around Water Reservoirs

Commercial + Office Towers - Towers ranging from 30 to 100m with 3 Floors of Commercial and Office Space on top

Housing Blocks + Villas - Each Block houses an average of 50 Flats (ranging from 40 to 120m2) and 5 Villas (160m2 each) for a total of 170 residents

Nursery

Nursery Playground

Flower Garden

Swimming Pool

Playground on top of Lawn Ribbon-Platform

Flower Beds on top of Lawn Ribbon-Platform

Sky-Bus Stop

Sports Fields

Arable Kitchen Garden

Lawn Ribbon-Platform with Suspended Monorail Tram System (Biogas Sky-Bus) connecting the Suburbs

Fruit Orchard

Beach

Board Walk - extending along the embankment and culminating into the Centre; it is also the Emergency Access. Buggies provide Services and Transport.

Road - leading to Underground Carpark

Urban Plaza - streching across the Centre, it provides a flexible, pedestrian Platform for Towers and Housing Blocks

0m    125    250    500

# Nordhavnen Smartcity Denmark

**'There is more to life than increasing its speed.'**
**- Mahatma Gandhi**

Nordhavnen, a harbour area on the coast of the Øresund in Copenhagen, represents Scandinavia's largest metropolitan development project. Covering 200 hectares of land reclaimed in the late 19th century, Nordhavnen is surrounded by water on three sides and is the potential site for Northern Europe's first Smartcity.

Nordhavnen Smartcity takes the same philosophies and infrastructural elements from Guangming but situates them within a Western context on a site defined by water. In contrast with Shenzhen, Copenhagen is already a world leader in sustainable living, and hosted the 2009 UN climate change summit. The National Technical and Environment Administration has recently formulated a strategy aimed at making Copenhagen the world's leading environmental capital by 2015, and Nordhavnen is seen as a key development in this ambition.

The population of the city is expected to increase by 45 000 by 2025 and will require new housing, workplaces and community facilities to counter the undesirable trend of increased commuting in the region and to reduce car traffic congestion. Nordhavnen Smartcity will provide housing and workplaces for 40 000 people and herald a new breed of individual, the citizen farmer.

Denmark is a net exporter of food and has a tradition of allotment or colony gardens stretching back to the 18th Century. Legislation in 2001 secured the future of communal gardens by designating them with 'permanent' status, protecting them from urban development. The implementation of urban agriculture at a truly urban scale, however, would introduce a new dimension and further environmental synergies to programmes in low-energy transport, waste recycling and wind-based facilities that are already world-leading. The Smartcity will not be suburban in character; it will overlay a rural blanket onto the form of a city, benefitting both from the vitality and social bonds of dense diverse communities and the recreational well-being that comes from large tracts of open space.

The increased local sufficiency engendered will also lead to a modification of attitude towards nature and communities, and make use of immigrants' expertise in non-indigenous cuisine and cultivating new food types. Differences in age, race, wealth and class can be celebrated instead of being the cause of friction and hostility.

facing page: Nordhavnen Smartcity masterplan

following page: Aerial views of the Smartcity on the Øresund coast

Suburb Squares - Main Street with Shops
Municipal Facilities around Reservoirs

● Floating Mobile Hubs - Farmers Market,
Town Hall + Library, + Education Centre

Dock for Mobile Hubs - 2 per District

Residential Strips

Flower Garden

Residential Strips

Roads leading to Underground
Carpark

Underground Carpark

● Anaerobic Digestor

Reedbed Filtration System

Housing Blocks + Villas

Villas - 4 to 6 per Block
(160m2 each)
Housing Blocks

Housing Blocks - Each Block has
50 Flats (ranging from 40 to 120m2)

Boardwalk

Suburb Sq- Municipal Facilities

Suburb Sq- Local High Street

Phase 1 (Development Plan)

Phase 2a (Development Plan)

Phase 2b (Development Plan)

Phase 3 (Strategic Plan)

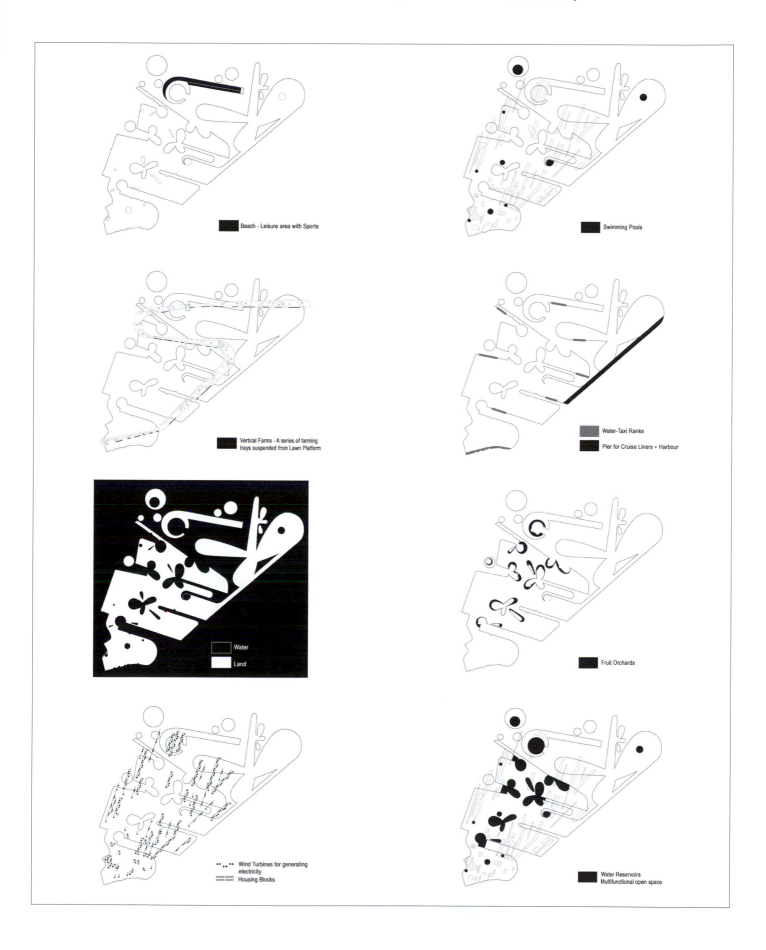

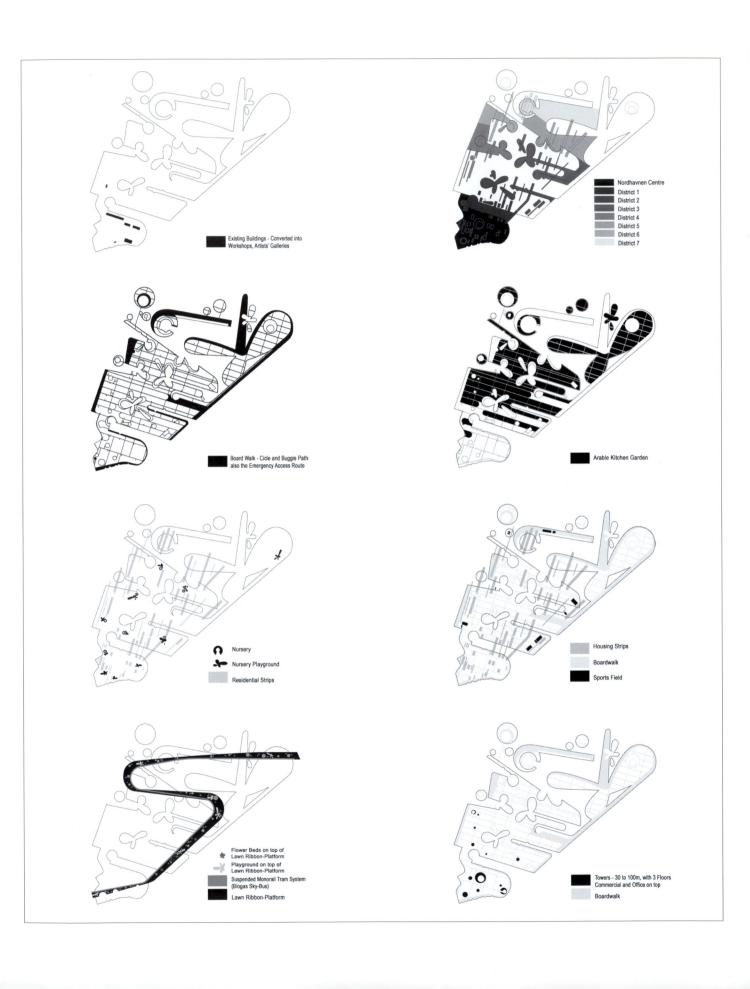

Existing Buildings - Converted into
Workshops, Artists' Galleries

Nordhavnen Centre
District 1
District 2
District 3
District 4
District 5
District 6
District 7

Board Walk - Cicle and Buggie Path
also the Emergency Access Route

Arable Kitchen Garden

Nursery
Nursery Playground
Residential Strips

Housing Strips
Boardwalk
Sports Field

Flower Beds on top of
Lawn Ribbon-Platform
Playground on top of
Lawn Ribbon-Platform
Suspended Monorail Tram System
(Biogas Sky-Bus)
Lawn Ribbon-Platform

Towers - 30 to 100m, with 3 Floors
Commercial and Office on top
Boardwalk

## City Framework

The water landscape of Nordhavnen has striking qualities that have the potential for conversion into unique recreational facilities. In outer Nordhavnen, Copenhagen meets the Øresund, offering views of the sea, Sweden, the historical fortifications of Copenhagen and a beautiful northern coastline characterized by beaches and forests. Currently, the site is used for harbour-based activities that will be retained and complemented by specialized infrastructure:

**Arable Kitchen Garden Park:** The new landscaped carpet of arable fields is carefully ordered both to provide a variety of environments and to take advantage of symbiotic sustainable polycultures. Over 70% of the ground is dedicated to vegetable farming with occasional zones assigned to livestock grazing. The presence of generous scattered water bodies allows the establishment of a cyclical farming system similar to the mulberry dyke fishpond model used in China's Pearl River Delta.

The biomass of fast-growing shrubs will provide nutrients for arable crops with manure retrieved from fishponds where carp, perch and pike are farmed. Mild winters in Copenhagen, together with nutrient rich water will combine to produce healthy yields of fish that receive their nutrients from the leaves of the cultivated plants. The integration of urban waste streams from the city's buildings will take this continuous culture a step further by permitting a real world application of the Integrated Food and Waste Management System (IFWMS) theorized by George Chan.

Irrigation of the arable land will require large quantities of water. Despite its omnipresence, water from the Øresund cannot be used to grow conventional crops and desalination is exceedingly energy inefficient. The kitchen garden park will therefore specialize in halophtic crops such as samphire and edible seaweed species including sea lettuce, carrageen moss, dulse and kelp. Such marine algae are a natural food, rich in gastronomic and nutritional qualities that are a key component of Asian cuisine and have also formed part of the European diet in the past. Samphire, which can be eaten raw or cooked, is rich in unsaturated oils and protein, making it additionally suitable for animal feed and biofuel. Effluent from the carp and perch will accelerate crop yields.

**Live-Work Clusters:** Residential and office developments are arranged into clusters overlaid above the newly cultivated landscape. The housing forms, inspired by the existing docks, are arranged as three-dimensional streets that are mixed tenure and encourage communal interaction. Each cluster is equipped with an energy station that controls a bank of PV arrays, wind turbines, and a combined heat and power plant that services and is fuelled by the adjoining farming zone. The tower components of the housing units contain villas for short- and long-term visitor accommodation.

**Municipal Facilities:** The communities of each cluster are served by a suburb square located along the canal that provides basic high street facilities, a reservoir and an event space that hosts a farmers' market. This urban arrangement encourages interaction within and between community clusters.

**Ribbon-Platform:** The live-work clusters are physically stitched together by a ribbon-platform elevated

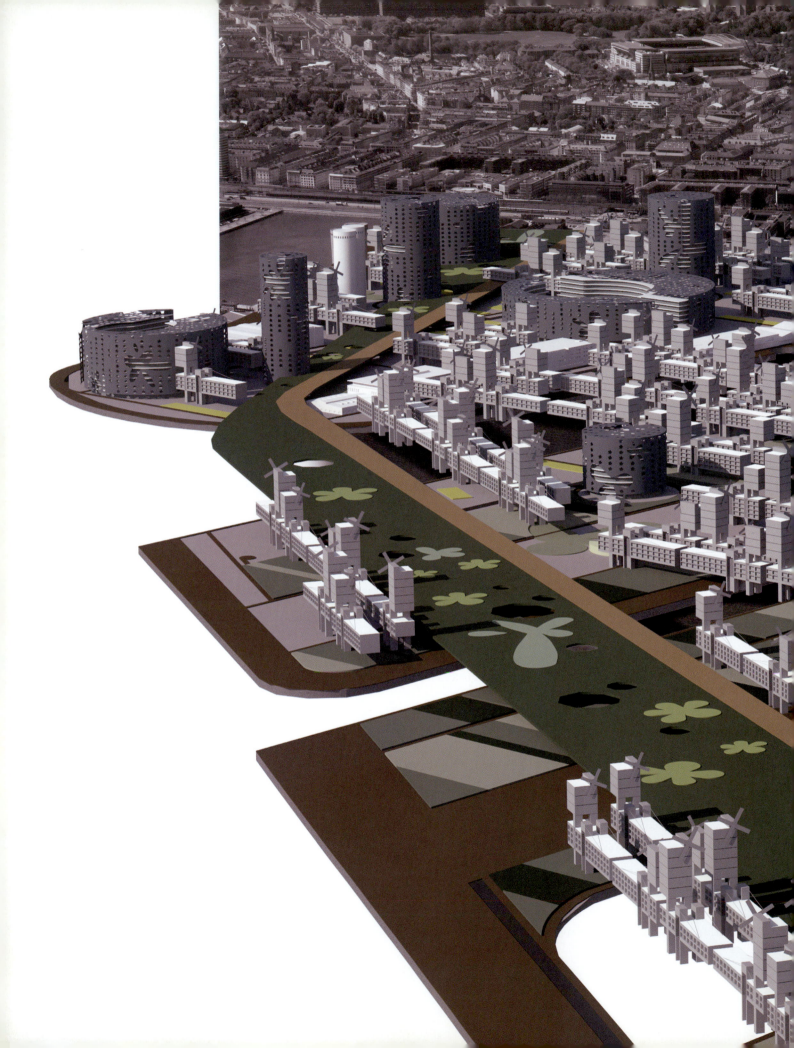

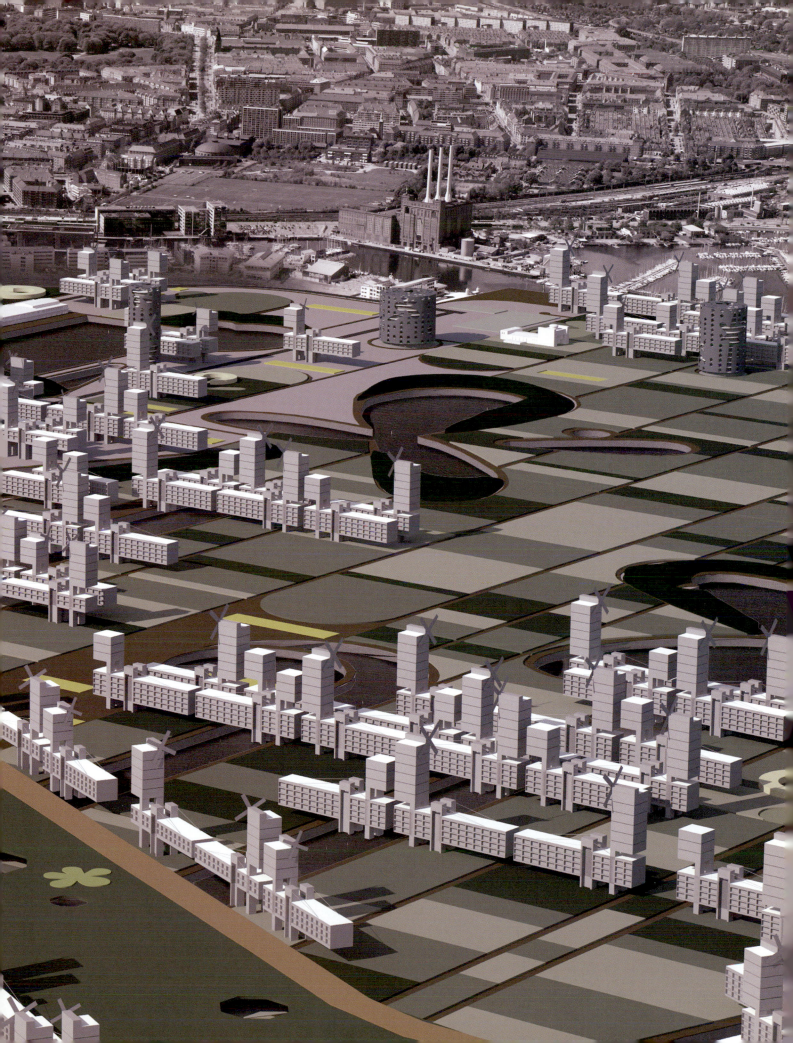

12m above ground which is accessed by vertical circulation cores. Uninterrupted stretches of recreational green space on the platform provide surfaces for picnics, sunbathing and sport. An ideal vantage point to watch the shifting canvas of sea and sky, the raised manicured grass plane presents spectacular panoramic views over the productive landscape and the Øresund. Gymnasia, cultural facilities, agritourist accommodation and the biogas-driven Skybus are suspended from the ribbon. Hydroponic curtains drape the sides of the platform, yielding a further farming site.

**Lifelines:** The Nordhavnen development is virtually car-free. The main intra-regional transport system is the Skybus monorail that connects live-work clusters while defining new civic territories in the sky. The network of surrounding roads extends into the Smartcity via the commercial gateway district and rapidly softens into decked pathways that weave across the site. These are the primary lifelines providing circulation for both vehicles and pedestrians. A boardwalk next to the natural beach stretches along the coastline creating a threshold between the land and water that culminates at the heart of the Smartcity.

**The Gateway:** Phase I of the development, containing the creative and business district, is located at the southwest edge of the site towards the centre of Copenhagen. Refurbished warehouses accommodate craft workshops and artists' studios that retain an industrial character and present a transitional threshold to the cultivated city.

**Water Interfaces:** The harbour and adjoining sand beaches along the northern edge of Nordhavnen will be a regional tourist attraction offering marine based recreation including sailing and deep-sea fishing. The Øresund flows into the site via a series of water avenues traversed by water taxi. These are complemented by trefoil-shaped lagoons, whose convoluted form increase the length of the land–water interface and divide up the water bodies into discrete activities. Residents will be in contact with water immediately outside their doors; recreation in the Smartcity will be where people live rather than a destination. Visitors will have a different relationship with the water, jogging, walking, cycling or sunbathing alongside it, or swimming, rowing or paddling in it.

**Mobile Hubs:** Three mobile floating hubs containing an organic farmers' market, town hall and library, and an arts and education centre navigate around the canals providing services to each town cluster on a shared basis. These floating hubs double as mobile public plazas for events and periodically perform outreach visits to other parts of Denmark, spreading the ideals of the Smartcity.

## Activities Framework

**Organic Food + Ecogastronomy:** Nordhavnen would benefit from a twin town relationship with Guangming Smartcity, making it a North European capital for Food and Agriculture. Its location in Copenhagen has a number of inherent advantages where the ratio of organic food consumed is the highest in the world. Where every other European city has submitted to the monopoly of supermarket chains, Nordhavnen will offer an alternative by re-establishing traditional markets as a part of Danish culture and social communication.

previous page: An armada of housing units on a sea of cultivated landscape

facing page: Housing, inspired by the existing docks, are arranged as three-dimensional streets encourage communal interaction

following page: Each housing cluster is equipped with an energy station fuelled by the adjoining farming zone

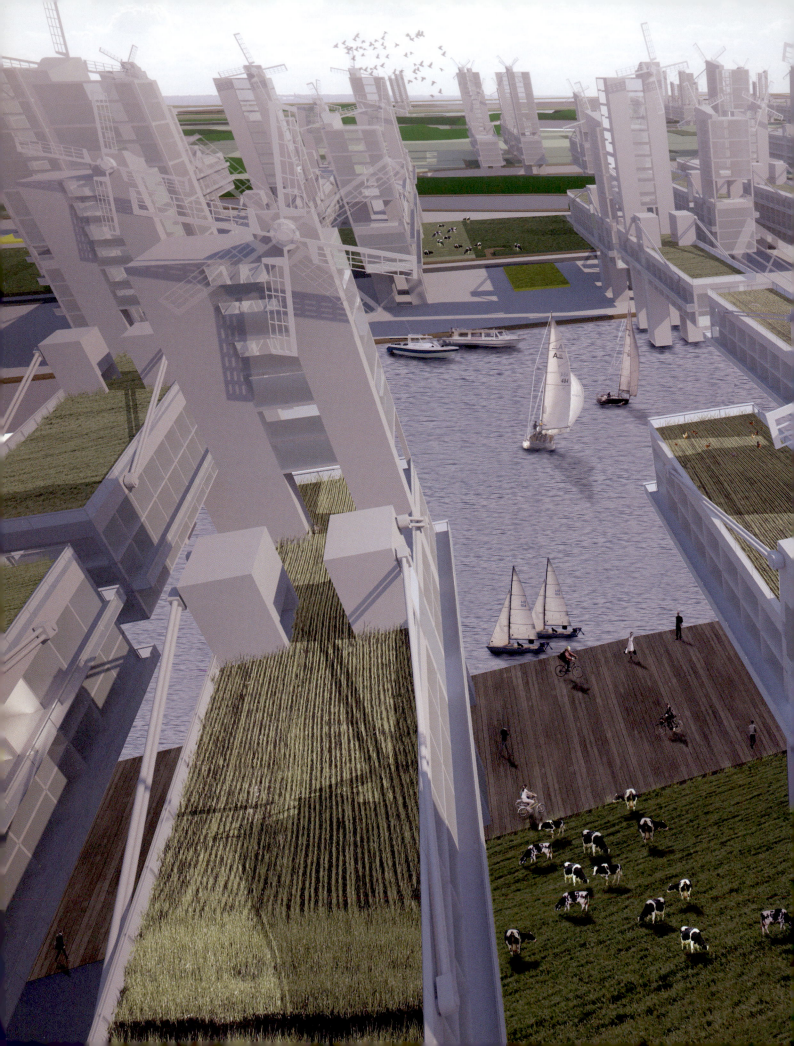

The city is also increasingly being recognized internationally as a gourmet destination and hosts Copenhagen Cooking, a food festival that takes place every August in various urban locations. Copenhagen's proximity to global cities and an international airport would make Nordhavnen Smartcity an ideal international conference location.

**Water-based Activities:** The Smartcity offers harbour bathing that supplements the baths at Islands Brygge, South harbour and Svanemølle Bay, to take advantage of the Øresund's clean water. Deep-sea fishing excursions for pike and garfish that pass through the waters on their spring spawning migration will be a further attraction.

## Transport

The ring road at the Smartcity's southwest boundary provides the main regional road traffic connection with Central Copenhagen. Secondary roads branch off the expressway into the site below ground level, connecting into public car parks. The Smartcity is also connected at this point with the main railway line between Copenhagen and Elsinore. Harbour buses and a new pedestrian bridge connect areas on both sides of the main harbour basin. The CityCirkel electric bus fleet will also extend its route into the commercial gateway area.

Inter-local scale travel will be provided in the form of the Skybus monorail and a shared cycle network. Whenever a resident leaves their home or an employee leaves their workplace, he or she will pass a bicycle station before encountering a bus stop, followed by a metro station and lastly a car park. Copenhagen is already one of the most bicycle-friendly cities in the world and municipal policies are aiming for 50% of all commutes to work, school or university being by bicycle by 2015. A fine mesh network of pathways surrounded by canals, basins and the coastline will be conducive to both cycling and walking while water taxis ferry groups along the aquatic avenues.

## Environmental sustainability

The Danish Environmental Protection Agency (EPA) has reported that approximately 99% of waste from the food industry is recycled into animal feed or fertilizer. Treatment of solid organic waste from domestic households, however, has focused more on hygiene and protection of aquatic ecosystems than energy efficiency. Organic human waste constitutes just 1% of household waste by volume, but contains approximately 85% of the nutrients. In usual urban environments, conversion of this waste into energy and fertilizer is unviable due to the distance between urban and agricultural locales. At Nordhavnen, human waste can be conveniently combined with organic farm waste and be broken down in anaerobic digesters to produce digestate to fertilize the adjoining farmland as well as biogas and biomass. The latter will be added to municipal solid waste to fuel combined heat and power plants local to each cluster community. Copenhagen already possesses one of the world's most efficient waste handling systems, recycling 90% of construction waste and incinerating 75% of domestic waste to generate electricity and district heating. The Smartcity will sustain and improve these efficiencies using local expertise.

Precipitation averages between 40mm and 70mm a month and will be captured and stored in freshwater zones of the trefoil lagoons. Greywater and blackwater will also be recycled for crop irrigation and should be sufficient in quantity, given that marine plants are also farmed and do not require fresh water.

Further renewable energy is generated through wind and solar collection. Smartcity residents will be eligible for tax exemptions by investing in local energy production. The prevailing winds at Nordhavnen are westerly or southwesterly, although from February to May and from October to November, there may be easterly and southeasterly wind. High energy potentials can be expected as the site is bordered by water on three sides. The construction of the cluster buildings is sufficiently robust to mount significantly sized turbines without causing adverse vibration effects.

The cluster buildings will also be equipped with photovoltaic arrays. The annual solar energy available per square metre of open surface areas facing south is a little more than 900kWh, ranging from 30–100kWh in certain months.

149

left: The biogas-powered Skybus suspended from the ribbon-platform weaves over grazing fields

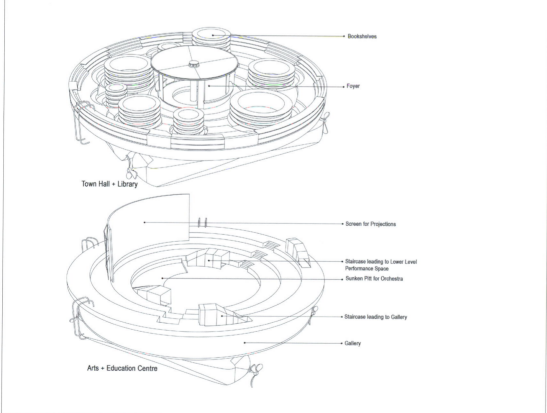

Bookshelves

Foyer

Town Hall + Library

Screen for Projections

Staircase leading to Lower Level
Performance Space

Sunken Pitt for Orchestra

Staircase leading to Gallery

Gallery

Arts + Education Centre

facing page: A landscape of cultivated
streets between the living units

left: Mobile hubs navigate around
the canal, docking at public plazas
to engage with different residential
communities

following page: View of Scandinavia's
largest metropolitan development

'A technological revolution, centered around information technologies, began to reshape, at accelerated pace, the material basis of society. Economies throughout the world have become globally interdependent, introducing a new form of relationship between economy, state, and society, in a system of variable geometry.'

**- 'The Rise of the Network Society', Manuel Castells, 1996**

Manuel Castells, widely regarded as the authority on communications research and information societies, has argued that the global city is not a single city – not London, New York, Tokyo or Johannesburg – but the fragment of each that is connected to its analogous counterparts in other world cities. Where suburban and rural areas have well-developed community infrastructures, the community of a metropolis tends towards a network of telematic relationships.

Community centres in the modern metropolis are a rarity. Conceived in the early 20th century in America, community centres were established to provide facilities for gatherings, group activities, social support and public information, premised on the idea that local communities are the permanent homes of most of their residents. The mobility and peripatetic nature of modern society has led to dispersion and diversity, challenging the relevance of the traditional community centre. Cities such as London celebrate their cosmopolitan spirit through events and processions through the calendar year, but these festivities tend towards the monocultural, and there is no permanent forum for intercultural exchange celebrating the ethnic diversity of world cities.

The Tomato Exchange is a 21st century community centre for the Smartcity that redresses this oversight in the form of 16 gleaming glass bell-like structures hovering over London's Trafalgar Square. The under-croft of these concave tubular towers provides shelter for preparing and sharing tomato-based delicacies and recipes specific to a variety of non-indigenous cuisines. Surrounded by circular tiers of sprawling solanum vines peppered with colourful fruit, scent and visual lushness pervade each campana structure.

Ranging in size from 5mm diameter tomberries to 5-inch 'big boys' and encompassing a colour spectrum of yellows, oranges, pinks, purples, greens, blacks and whites, tomatoes become the raw materials for intercultural exchange. Urban agriculture has a rich history in London, providing precious food in the world war victory gardens that took over public spaces such as Hyde Park and the moat around the Tower of London. In addition to providing food towards the war effort, the gardens demonstrated the

facing page: Plan of a 21st century global community centre – the Tomato Exchange

following page: London's Tomato Exchange in Trafalgar Square

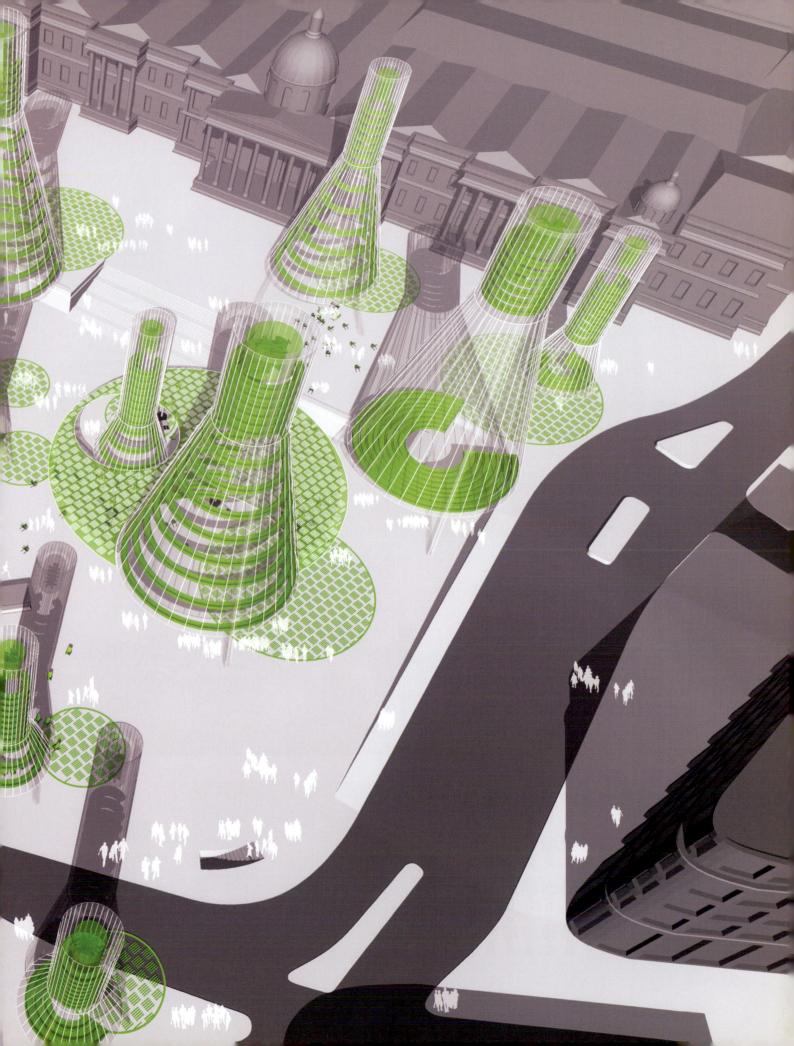

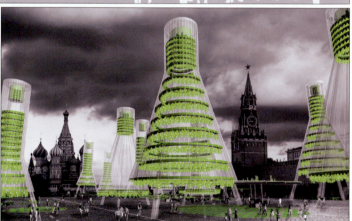

| TIANANMEN SQUARE BEIJING | SAFRA SQUARE JERUSALEM | RED SQUARE MOSCOW | OLD TOWN SQUARE PRAGUE |
|---|---|---|---|
| DONEGALL SQUARE BELFAST | MARKET SQUARE KRAKÓW | RADHUSPLASSEN OSLO | AZADI SQUARE TEHRAN |
| PLAZA DE MAYO BUENOS AIRES | TRAFALGAR SQUARE LONDON | PLACE de la CONCORDE PARIS | NATHAN P. SQUARE TORONTO |
| TAKSIM SQUARE ISTANBUL | CITY SQUARE MELBOURNE | CHURCH SQUARE PRETORIA | MCPHERSON SQUARE WASHINGTON DC |

worth of growing and sharing meals as a catalyst for social cohesion.

A tinted glass lift car, doubling as the quarters of the bell's custodian, is a beacon at the top of each structure and doubles as a seed bank. Raised high above the ground, the custodians are brought toe-to-toe with Vice Admiral Nelson on his column – eco-warriors for the 21st century.

The semi-enclosed glass skin of the towers traps the sun's energies to create an ideal microclimate and provides protection from winds and pests. High plant density is achieved through a hydroponic nutrient system, facilitating the growth of over seven thousand heirloom tomato species and ensuring the survival of rare and threatened strains. Improved crop yields are achieved by inverting the plants, which has the added benefit of enhancing the visual spectacle from below, and facilitating the harvesting process.

At periodic intervals, the concentric planting trays, suspended in a concertina arrangement, are lowered to ground level in a piece of dramatic spatial theatre. The fruits are then harvested by the capital's community of able and disable-bodied, young and old, local and migrant, slowly transforming into salsa, gazpacho, ketchup, ragu, borscht, chutney, relish, marmalade, bloody mary, chow chow and jumabalaya under the supervision of the preparation's cultural originators adopted by the city. Responsible for tending the square's edible produce, the custodians of the bells also disperse seeds from the nursery to visitors and the suburban populace who in turn propagate and share the plants, fruit, recipes, knowledge and stories to their own communities thereby creating a secondary network for the exchange.

Dissemination extends at a global scale through replication in other metropolitan squares round the world including Tiananmen in Beijing, Paris' Place de la Concorde, and Moscow's Red Square. Collectively, the exchanges become nodes of an international network that simultaneously encourage social integration and celebrate ethnic diversity.

Castells believes that the physical infrastructure which we 'collectively consume', such as public transport, social housing and city squares, are symbiotic with rather than in competition against global virtual networks. The Tomato Exchange trades in both social commodities, employing transient and permanent populations as an exchange medium and transforming physical monuments into meaningful social spaces.

159

facing top: The semi-enclosed glass skin traps the sun's energies to create an ideal microclimate

facing middle: The Tomato Exchange in Tiananmen Square, Beijing; and in Red Square, Moscow

facing bottom (left to right): Global citizens and local communities; Global networks for social integration and ethnic diversity; Inverted tomato plant culture

left: Sixteen glass bell-like structures hover over London's principal square

following page: Night views of the Tomato Exchange

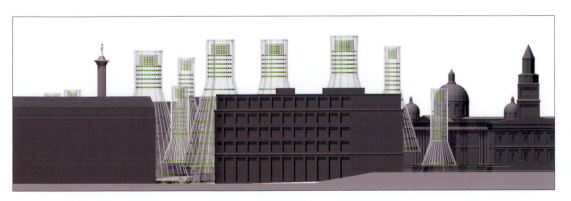

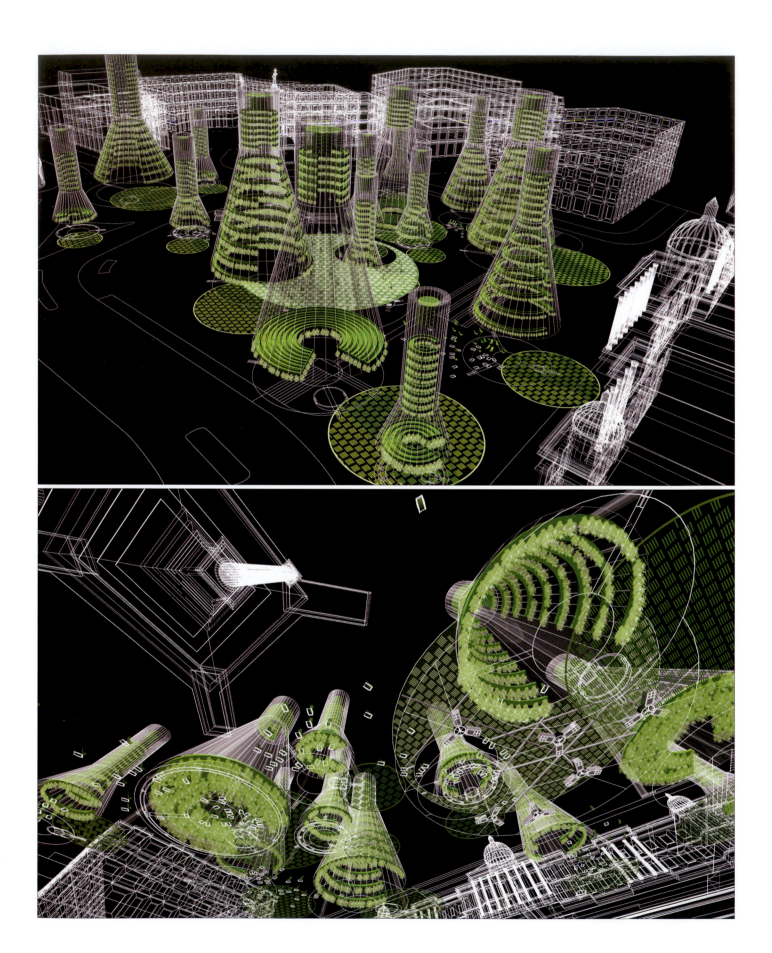

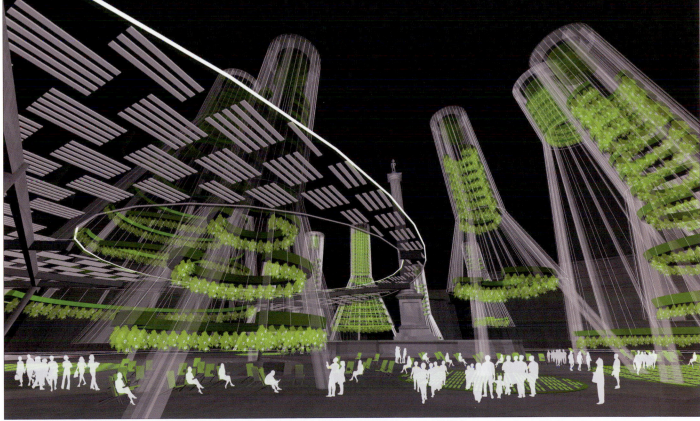

Car Park

Concrete Pavings

Existing Sand Fields

Timber Decking

Tree Gardens

Grass Lawn

Agriculture

Agriculture

Agriculture

Rock Field (Medium Polished Rocks)

Timber Decking

Sand Beach with Trees

Marina Clubhouse

Shallow pools

Swimming Pools

Marina

0m    50    100         200         300

# Dongyi Wan East Waterfront China

The waterfront development at Dongyi Wan East in the Ronggui sub district of Shunde in Southern China is an amphibious landscape bordering the DeSheng River, providing recreational and urban agriculture resources to a new residential quarter that occupies a green field site of approximately five square kilometres.

Following China's era of 'opening up' to the outside world that began in 1978, Shunde has taken advantage of its cultural position and geographical proximity to Hong Kong, Macau and Taiwan to develop into a major manufacturing centre from traditional agricultural origins and was designated as a pilot city for the comprehensive reform of Guangdong in the 1990s.

Located in the centre of the Pearl River Delta, the area is characterized by intersecting rivers that flow around and through the new residential and school district, resulting in a special relationship between the water and its residents. The waterfront site, which occupies approximately half a square kilometre, lies three metres below the perimeter road that separates the main development from the DeSheng River and is subject to annual flooding. Although the floods are relatively predictable, arriving during the summer monsoon period, the waterfront is unsuitable for conventional development. This condition, however, frees up welcome opportunities for creating an innovative hybrid landscape of marina, artificial beach, cultivated land and wetland wildlife reserve.

163

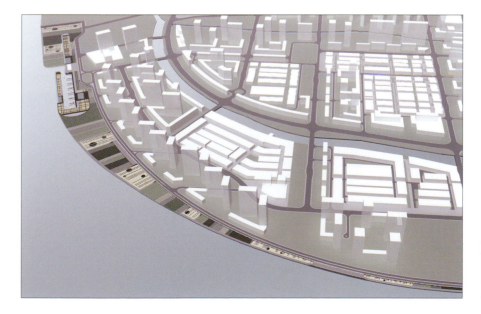

facing page: Dongyi Wan East Waterfront masterplan

left: Aerial view of the cultivated amphibious landscape

The Pearl River Delta is a vast alluvial plain containing possibly the highest density of intersecting rivers in the world, and is one of the most fertile regions in China. The climate is moderate and rainfall plentiful, providing ideal conditions for growing crops such as pak choi and choi sum. By establishing the majority of the low-lying plain as agricultural land, the floods are transformed from a nuisance and potential catastrophe into a benefit by using the soil recharged with nutrients from alluvial deposits. Additionally, the floodplains support rich biodiversity – the river water supplies an instant rush of nutrients in the form of decomposing organic matter on which microorganisms flourish. The microorganisms in turn attract a sequence of predators on the food chain ruled by migratory waterfowl such as winter swans and cranes that reward human study.

The wetland wildlife reserves and agricultural land are just two of the textures that make up an amphibious community landscape. A variety of hydrophilic ornamental grasses, concrete walkways, riparian tree gardens, sand fields, grass lawns and hard standing for seasonal parking combine to form a heterogeneous and unstructured recreational ground made of flood resistant or sacrificial organic material where traditional pursuits of calligraphy, painting and wildlife watching are encouraged.

More formal and flood-sensitive community spaces are accommodated around the marina to the southeast of the site where the activity plane is raised level with the adjacent developments and unaffected by the floods. Heavy river traffic and the unknown quality of the water in the DuSheng River prevent swimming activities and the water can be too cool in the winter months. To ensure year-round occupation, heated outdoor pools, steam baths, jacuzzis and diving facilities are arranged around the marina and clubhouse. The pools vary in depth and temperature and are contained by an infinity edge, extending the pools visually into the aquatic landscape. The remainder of the raised plain is landscaped with lawn grass, artificial beaches, trees, timber decking and semi-polished pebble fields.

facing page + left: Amphibious community landscape mixed with wildlife reserves and farmland

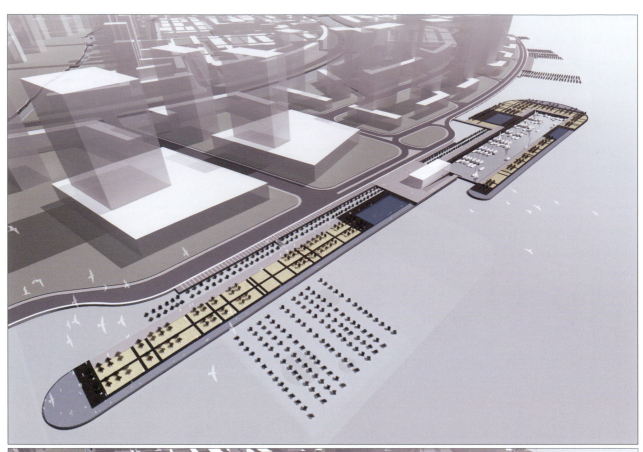

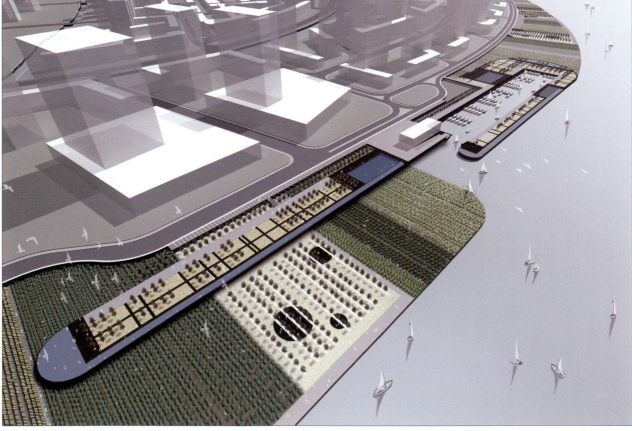

The character and occupation of the waterfront change dramatically through the year. During the flood period, the majority of the site is submerged and the ambience contemplative with only the marina area animated. The fields and hard landscaping are barely visible beneath the surface of the water. After the waters recede, there is a clean-up operation with the timber and concrete decks swept, washed and rubbish removed. The farming community emerges, sowing seeds and planting crops in the revitalized ground as wildlife begins to proliferate, attracting visitors and school study groups. During the spring and summer, the waterfront will become particularly busy with visitors arriving from further inland before the farmers harvest their crops and the cycle begins anew.

Dongyi Wan East is an archetypal yet unusual Smartcity trope in its application of a new functional hybridized landscape on land previously considered unoccupiable. The development is sustainable, taking advantage of natural flood cycles to grow produce for the local populace. Spatially, the architecture is created through human occupation and a plethora of recreational spaces encourages social interaction. The landscape is flexible and inclusive, with the allocation of multiple functions on the same space depending on the season. Industrial growth in the region has in the past eroded and damaged vital wetlands in pursuit of economic expansion, a process that needs urgent reversal to renew and clean the country's watercourses and to preserve natural wildlife habitats. Dongyi Wan East belatedly provides a model for coexistence with natural systems that will benefit the community as well as the environment.

facing page top: A contemplative ambience during the flood period

facing page bottom: Sowing, planting and cleaning after the waters recede

left: Pools extending visually into the aquatic landscape

following page: An innovative hybrid landscape that supports biodiversity

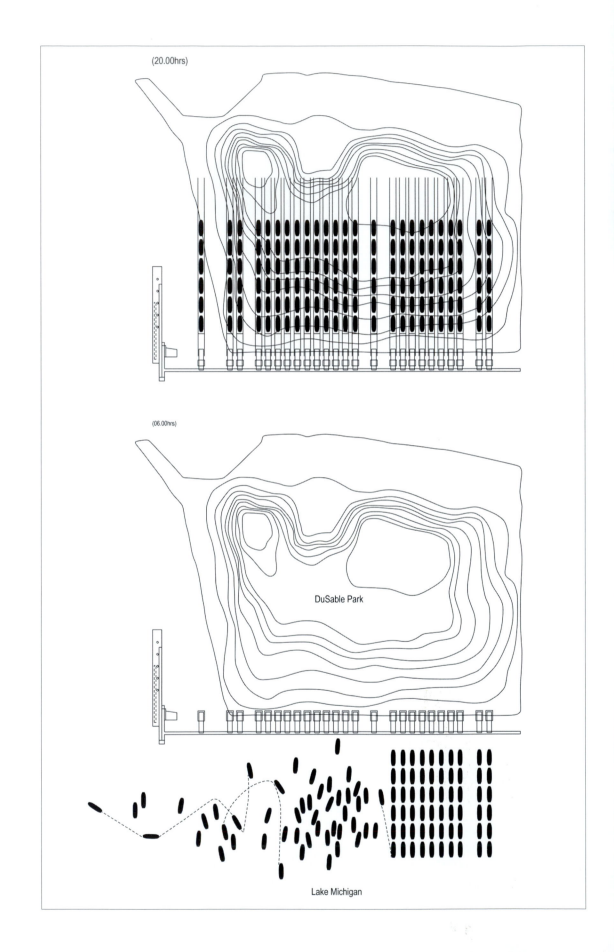

(20.00hrs)

(06.00hrs)

DuSable Park

Lake Michigan

DuSable Park is a park in waiting. Located on a peninsula accessible only by trespassing on private land, three acres on the shore of Lake Michigan in downtown Chicago were designated as parkland in 1987 under the administration of Mayor Harold Washington. These three acres represent a chronological, geographic and social anomaly. Abandoned for over two decades, the site is an overgrown meadow, surrounded by exclusive privatized urban space and colonized by opportunistic weed flowers, butterflies, songbirds and intrepid humans. The site attracted the attention of artist Laurie Palmer in 2001 who decided to invite artists and architects to conjure up multiple and co-existing manifestations of DuSable Park to provoke debate and lobby for action on the part of the Chicago Park District.

DuSable Park derives its name from Jean Baptiste Pointe DuSable, a Haitian-French pioneer who became the first permanent non-indigenous settler of Chicago in 1772, and is popularly known as the 'Father of Chicago'. Representing a key black historical figure, a park commemorating DuSable would go some distance to redressing long-standing inequities of privilege between the African American and Latino communities west of the lake, and the predominantly Caucasian population who have monopolized the waterfront following government policy that encouraged high-income development over public space.

In July 2000, a proposal to lease the land to a development agency as a 'temporary' parking lot was blocked by vociferous local opposition and later that year, radioactive thorium, with a half-life of 14 billion years, was purportedly found to contaminate the site, put forward as the reason for the Park Authority's failure to deliver on its promise of developing the land as a public recreational space. Two

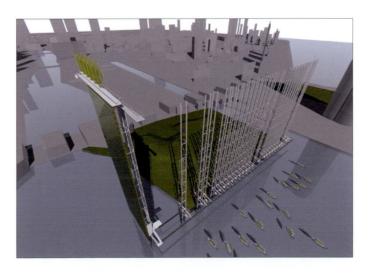

facing page: The cyclical reconfiguration of DuSable Park

left : Daytime view of the park with floating boat-gardens deployed onto Lake Michigan

following page top: The skyscraper nursery defines the boundary of the meadow

following page bottom: At night the boat-gardens are secured on an array of lightweight pier structures years later, three cubic metres of soil and the contamination problem were putatively removed, a claim which has since been repudiated.

Palmer notes that 'public space is ostensibly available to everyone, but someone is always excluded: the person who wants to sleep on the bench a little too long, set up camp for a few weeks, have sex in the tall grass, make loud noises, plant vegetables, roast a pig, roar her dirt bike in circles around the toxic hill, or have the whole place to himself for an ecological experiment.' Any single proposition for the development cannot be wholly inclusive, but the proposal for the DuSable Park preserves the overgrown meadow and its rich human and non-human biodiversity by elevating a piece of community landscape over the existing ground plane, concurrently serving as a stark reminder of the environmental damage caused by human industrial activity.

This community landscape is composed of an armada of hovering boats decked out in flora and edible produce, a skyscraper-plant-nursery and a drawbridge linking the meadow with Grant Park. The skiffs that make up the floating garden symbolically celebrate the arrival of DuSable and other subsequent immigrants who have contributed to the city's cosmopolitan but segregated make-up.

Each floating boat-garden can be leased to individual members of the local community, opening up the waterfront to other ethnic and deprived groups. Equipped with planting trays, clear frost-protection covers and lighting, the roving skiffs result in an endlessly expanding and contracting park, displaying a tapestry of non-indigenous vegetation and a multitude of colour change. The park gradually develops an ecological cycle of migrated plants, fostering the growth of new wildlife habitats. The individual boat-gardens are secured on an array of lightweight pier structures pinned to the water's edge. By day, the floating gardens are deployed onto the lake by remote controlled cranes, releasing the pier structures into a vertical configuration to expose the meadow, mirroring the performance of drawbridges around the city. Operating on a diurnal cycle, the structures return to their horizontal positions at dusk, collecting the skiffs and rolling them back into place for the night. The boats are either navigated remotely or sailed by local residents into the lake. The choreography and arrangement of the park on the lake is infinitely variable.

The skyscraper nursery is an inhabitable south-facing glass structure, borrowing from the windy city's idiom of glass facades. The nursery cultivates non-indigenous flowers, vegetables and rare seedlings and supplies plants for the boat-gardens and outlying neighbourhoods. Individual glass seedling boxes are accessed via a vertical farming device similar to that of window-cleaning cradles on surrounding skyscrapers. The structure is capped by a sky garden of hydroponically grown trees and offers dramatic views over Lake Michigan and the city. Open to the entire community, the tower presents a spatial experience usually accessible only to the privileged few.

The skyscraper nursery not only serves as the entrance to the floating gardens of DuSable Park but also defines the boundary of Grant Park. The base of the vertical structure accommodates public washing facilities, gardening tool and material stores, a retractable open-deck market and a small kitchen. On Sundays at the end of each month, fresh produce from the floating gardens is sold at the market and the kitchen can prepare picnic hampers to be enjoyed in the park. With sufficient public pressure, the tableau of dining amongst the floating gardens of Lake Michigan on a clear midsummer's evening with Chicago city as the backdrop could well become reality.

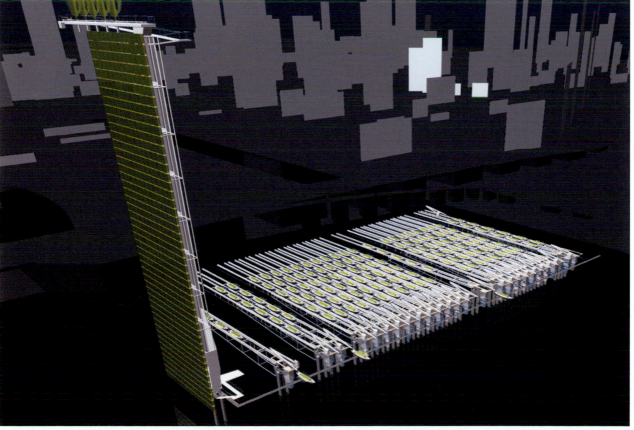

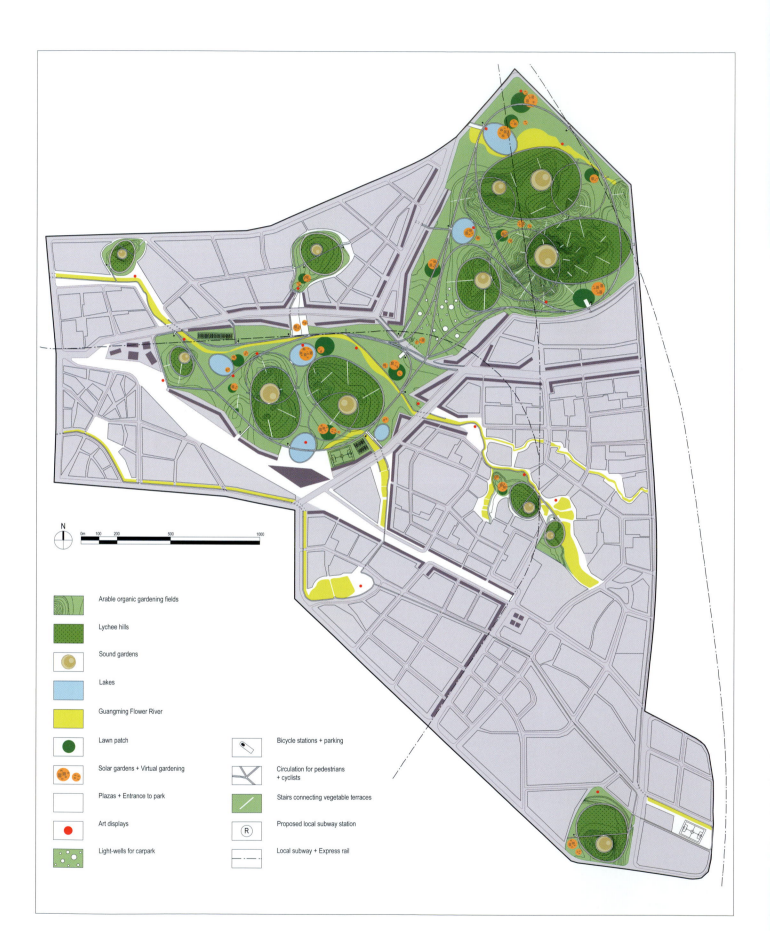

N
0m 100 200    500                    1000

Arable organic gardening fields

Lychee hills

Sound gardens

Lakes

Guangming Flower River

Lawn patch

Solar gardens + Virtual gardening

Plazas + Entrance to park

Art displays

Light-wells for carpark

Bicycle stations + parking

Circulation for pedestrians
+ cyclists

Stairs connecting vegetable terraces

(R)    Proposed local subway station

Local subway + Express rail

# Guangming Energy Park  China

Hunger, or fear of hunger, remains a powerful driving force of the Chinese mentality. Many of China's inhabitants still remember the 'Three Years of Natural Disasters', the world's largest famine causing an estimated 30 million 'excess' deaths between 1958 and 1961. China's cities were not left unaffected, leading to the government issuing food coupons in urban areas and a subsequent insistence on food self-sufficiency. Farming continues to be at the forefront of national policy with Wen Jiabao, the Chinese premier, declaring, not unjustifiably, that feeding 1.3 billion people would be China's biggest contribution to the world.

Guangming Energy + Art Park stretches from the centre to the north of New Guangming Radiant City, Shenzhen, and covers 2.37km2 of agricultural land. The government brief called for an exploration of 'new relationships between (a) city and green belt, (b) urban life and park life and, (c) city development and ecological effects under rapid urbanisation.'

The park is a site for energy creation of many types, one of which is the production of human fuel, food. The agricultural heritage of the site, along with the local farming skills and livelihoods of the populace, are therefore preserved whilst providing neighbourhood sustenance for Guangming's residents. Seventy

facing page: Guangming Energy Park masterplan

left: The park maintains a synergistic relationship with the city through its food and renewable energy production

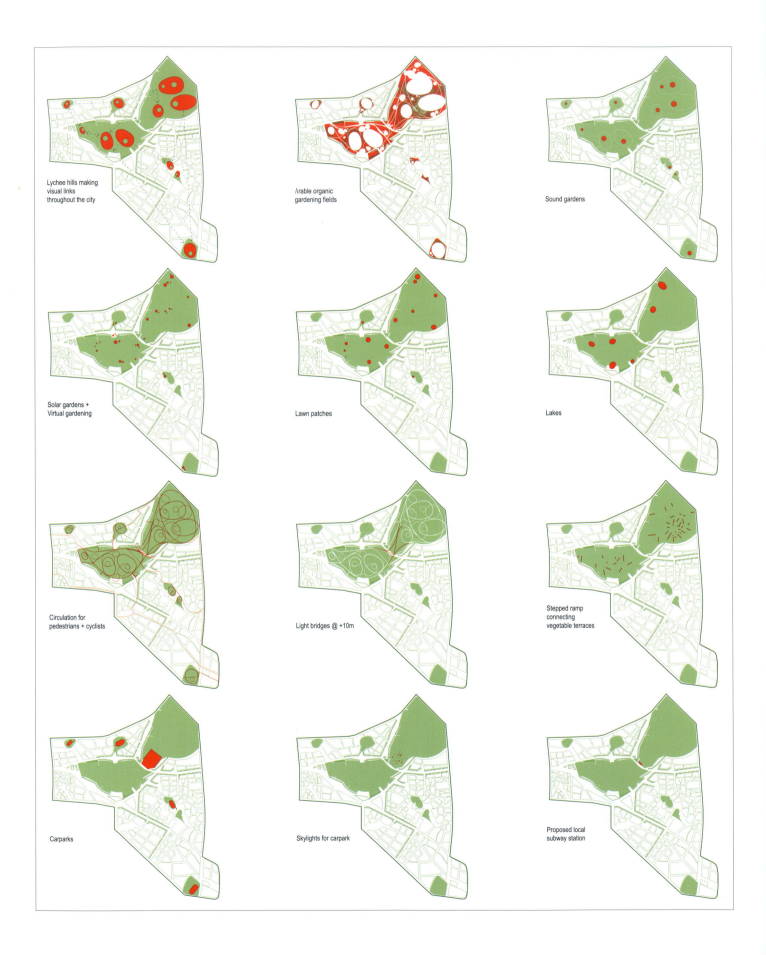

Lychee hills making
visual links
throughout the city

Arable organic
gardening fields

Sound gardens

Solar gardens +
Virtual gardening

Lawn patches

Lakes

Circulation for
pedestrians + cyclists

Light bridges @ +10m

Stepped ramp
connecting
vegetable terraces

Carparks

Skylights for carpark

Proposed local
subway station

per cent of the park is covered by an 'arable carpet' similar to that found in Nordhavnen, but without the marine-based vegetation. The remainder of the site is taken up by hills of lychees, plazas, lawns, sound gardens and paths for cyclists and pedestrians. Existing elements of the green zone are preserved, adopting a 'do-more-by-building-less' approach. Natural resources are enhanced by redistributing and reorganizing the park into landscaped clusters of flexible programme, and making the land more accessible, welcoming and ecologically sound.

Occupying all of the green space within the Radiant City, the main park is linked to five satellite gardens at higher altitude. The existing topography is amplified by mounded non-biodegradable landfill forming a farming and leisure network that spreads through the city to propagate the park's environmental and landscape strategies, and contributing to the character and iconography of the new city. These 'green-passive-ripples' seed new civic, recreational, agricultural, cultural and tourist facilities into the wider region. The park also maintains a diverse ecosystem and a synergistic relationship with the city through its food and solar power production.

The Radiant City is not car-free but discourages car use. Located beneath the central and most constricted part of the site are a subway station and the city's principal car park. Commuters emerge directly into the park from the subterranean areas past a cycle station and pass through the park to the north or south either on foot or by bicycle, decelerating the frenetic pace of the Chinese city.

The brief from the Shenzhen Municipal Planning Bureau called for innovative administration strategies for the park, suggesting a possible public–private partnership renting green space to individuals or companies to construct and maintain. Such partnerships are all the more essential in a productive landscape, with the arable carpet divided into 300 plots and tenured by the town's resident farmers. Every two years, the Energy + Art Park hosts an Arable Garden Festival to mark the start of a new gardening calendar. A lottery is drawn to select new gardeners for plots, with the ten winners from the previous year's competition given the option to extend their occupancy, mirroring the land reform of the 1980s during which rural plots were leased to individual households for 15-year periods; farmers were permitted to sell excess produce once they had fulfilled an agreed quota.

177

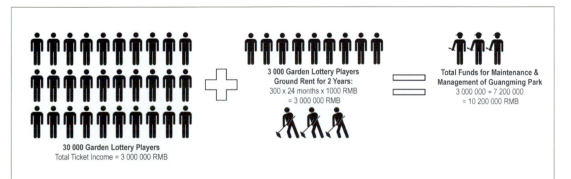

30 000 Garden Lottery Players
Total Ticket Income = 3 000 000 RMB

3 000 Garden Lottery Players
Ground Rent for 2 Years:
300 x 24 months x 1000 RMB
= 3 000 000 RMB

Total Funds for Maintenance &
Management of Guangming Park
3 000 000 + 7 200 000
= 10 200 000 RMB

facing page: Infrastructure plans of Guangming Energy Park

left: Administration strategy for the park

following page left: Sections – a journey of texture, colour, sound and scent through the park

following page right: Lychee orchard hills and sound gardens punctuate the arable carpet

## Economic, Social + Cultural Viability

The construction of Guangming Energy + Art Park is to be phased in conjunction with the development of the city. The topography is sculpted into contoured zones using inert recycled landfill and excavated soil from the city's construction. The existing farming community will be employed to construct the new landscape and will play an important role in the long-term park gardening workforce.

The existing farming strip within the valley is conserved and extended by employing terraces on inclined ground, reclaiming more land for agricultural production. Fresh produce will be sold directly to the community and the gardeners' markets will become vital social spaces where produce and news can be exchanged. The park will also organize an annual lychee-picking festival, drawing in tourists from neighbouring cities and beyond.

As one of the world's first large-scale urban agriculture initiatives, the Energy + Art Park will generate income and inter-city exchange through agritourism, offering visitors the opportunity to pick their own produce and have it prepared for them in the on-site kitchens or local restaurants. The Park is also the city's cultural centre, running a year-round programme of art and music. Urban topiaries, giant sculptures and digital art sit alongside fields of local produce, equating the importance of, and connection between, culture and agriculture. A series of public flora sound gardens and manicured lawns punctuate the vegetable and lychee landscape for relaxation and contemplation.

## Landscape Infrastructure

Topographical adjustments are managed to minimize disturbance to the existing wildlife and natural habitats by employing non-invasive construction methods and intelligent manipulation of the ground. The revitalized lakes and new topography, sculpted from inert landfill and retained by gabions and adobe walls, provide controlled natural spaces and choreograph the naturally prevailing winds over the water to passively cool the Energy Park. The lower lying areas that constitute the organic farming carpet is a 'Centre of Excellence' for education and research, simultaneously offering leisure facilities and preserving tradition. Educational activities such as natural habitat exploration, bird watching, art exhibitions and nature walks work in conjunction with the local training, schools and tourism board. These activities encourage inhabitants to engage with and learn from their inner-city park, and help preserve the natural ecosystems financially.

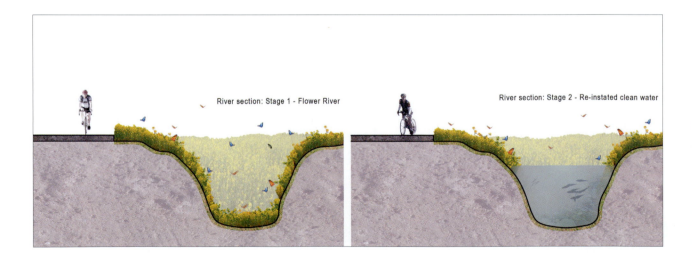

River section: Stage 1 - Flower River

River section: Stage 2 - Re-instated clean water

Existing watercourses on the site are enlarged to form lakes and reservoirs, and the canal is retained to reinforce the hydrology and water-based ecosystems present. The increased expanse of water encourages displacement cooling of the surrounding areas and fresh water fish farming using the mulberry dyke fishpond system.

The municipal authorities have determined that cleaning the entire Maozhou River that flows through and terminates within the park is unfeasible. The smaller arteries of the watercourse are therefore to be locked off and planted with flowers. A floral river will flow through the Energy Park to spread colour and biodiversity throughout the New Town. Once the Maozhou River has been cleaned, the locks will be deactivated to allow nature to run its established course.

Public art in China has in the past been highly politicized, whether in the form of official works under the sponsorship of the Communist Party, or guerilla art in reaction to an autocratic regime. Guangming Park will provide a forum for new forms of art free of political affiliations, and will be curated to play off the surrounding landscape. Thematically, the installations will experiment with scale in the manner of Claes Oldenburg and Jeff Koons, and involve the community in their creation. Urban-scale topiaries will be scattered through the park and change throughout the calendar year, reflecting the farming culture and heritage of Guangming.

181

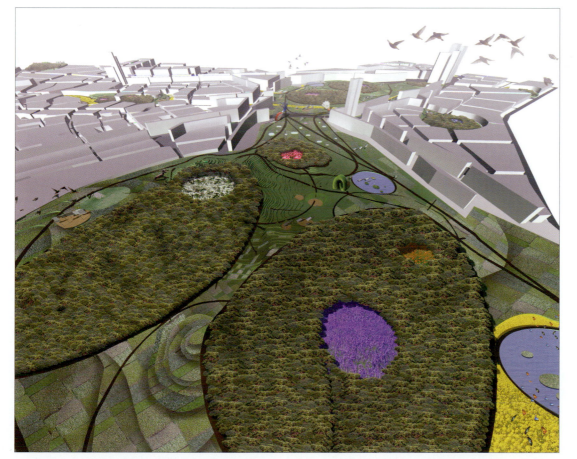

facing page: Guangming Flower River – mustard flowers are planted in drained polluted canals to encourage biodiversity

left: Sound gardens and the visual linkage between the city's satellite parks

following page: Urban topiary amongst the cultivated fields

184

SCREEN ONE
Flower: Common Lily
Votes this week: 36,205

SCREEN TWO
Flower: Poppy
Votes this week: 31,067

SCREEN THREE
Flower: Gazania
Votes this week: 28,983

SCREEN FOUR
Flower: Water Lily
Votes this week: 26,741

SCREEN FOUR
Flower: Common Daisy
Votes this week: 25,978

scroll down for next 5

1 Click = 1 Virtual Watering

3,000 votes    10,000 votes    20,000 votes    30,000 votes

Virtual gardens will contrast with their real-world counterparts. As part of the new dynamic cultural landscape, the inhabitants of Guangming Radiant City are encouraged to select floral arrangements online which are abstracted and displayed on large-scale digital screens. During the day, the screens fold into a horizontal aspect to become shading devices and to collect solar energy from an array of photovoltaic cells. When dusk falls, the screens rotate into a vertical position to screen a luminescent floral spectacle that lights the boardwalk and discourages crime. Once voting is complete, the public can 'virtually water' their flowers to watch them grow. After two weeks, the images are reset and voting recommences.

The addition of sound gardens dispersed through the park creates a multi-sensory environment; accessed off the boardwalk, the sound gardens provide moments of contemplation and quiet observation of some of the park's more distinguished flora. Each sound garden has its own identity defined by the colour and smell of its unique plants. The gardens vary in size and music genre depending on the site typography and surrounding conditions. Sound is generated from both organic and mechanical sources.

## Access

Plazas are located at entrance points on the perimeter of the park. They serve as meeting hubs, information points and spaces to inhabit with creative and recreational activities. The stone floor is an important theme for these spaces, providing a stage for traditional pastimes that occupy urban space such as the practice of tai chi, water calligraphy, public poetry and chess.

The city's car parks are housed beneath the green landscape of the Energy + Art Park and its satellites. Visitors and residents are encouraged to leave their car and utilize the extensive network of cycle paths to promote an environmentally greener city. Glazed towers are stationed at key locations from which bicycles can be rented with a refundable deposit. The towers operate on a rotary mechanism to take up a small footprint and appear as illuminated beacons at night.

## Park Management

Photovoltaic panels take advantage of the region's abundant sunlight to harvest energy during the day to power a low energy lighting system in the park. There are four lighting environments: (1) bollards and floor-recessed fittings in the plazas and entrance, (2) uplighters for the lychee orchards, (3) LED strips in the pedestrian and cyclist boardwalk and (4) fluorescent lighting for the cycle towers and underground parking.

Maintenance of park's grounds is minimized by the disposition of agricultural land that is tended by the farmers. Additionally, there is a park keeper's lodge located in the centre of the park next to the subway station. Upkeep of the park is paid for through lottery money and ground rent, used for dredging and lake maintenance, hedge and topiary pruning, mowing, leaf collection, electronic maintenance and general cleaning.

facing page top: Virtual Gardening

facing page bottom: Digital screens attached to the solar structures are used for outdoor screenings as well as virtual gardening

following page: 'Green-passive-ripples' seed civic, cultural and agricultural facilities into the wider region

# Nanyui Urban Living Room China

The Nanyui Urban Living Room is a 0.5km2 mixed-use development for the city of Shenzhen, China. A joint venture between the Shenzhen Municipal Planning Bureau and the Jin Long and Fu An Na Development Agencies, the project is a public–private partnership project that aims to integrate public green space with residential and commercial activities.

The conceptual motif for the Nanyui Urban Living Room is a golden bowl, an auspicious symbol of health and prosperity in the ancient art of Chinese Feng Shui.

Originally designated as a public park, the site is a patchwork of poorly maintained scrub, hard standing and dilapidated cabins surrounded by high-rise buildings. In order to breathe new life into the area, the local authorities sold the land to two private agencies while retaining a minority shareholding, allowing them to develop a shopping complex, offices, residential apartments and a hotel in exchange for the creation and maintenance of green amenity space. Additional planning gains include a cultural ring including a community arts centre, sports strip and the renovation of an existing school.

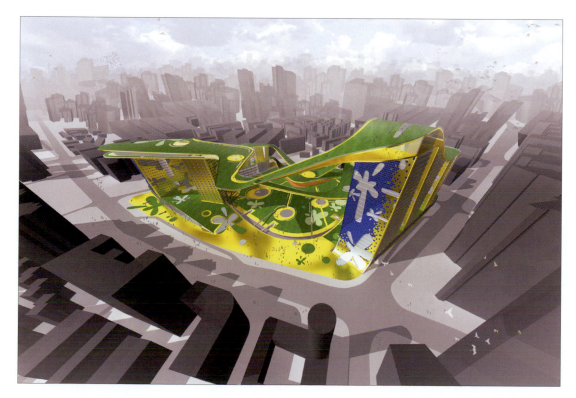

facing page: Nanyui Urban Living
Room masterplan

left: A public–private partnership
project integrates public green space
with mixed-use activities

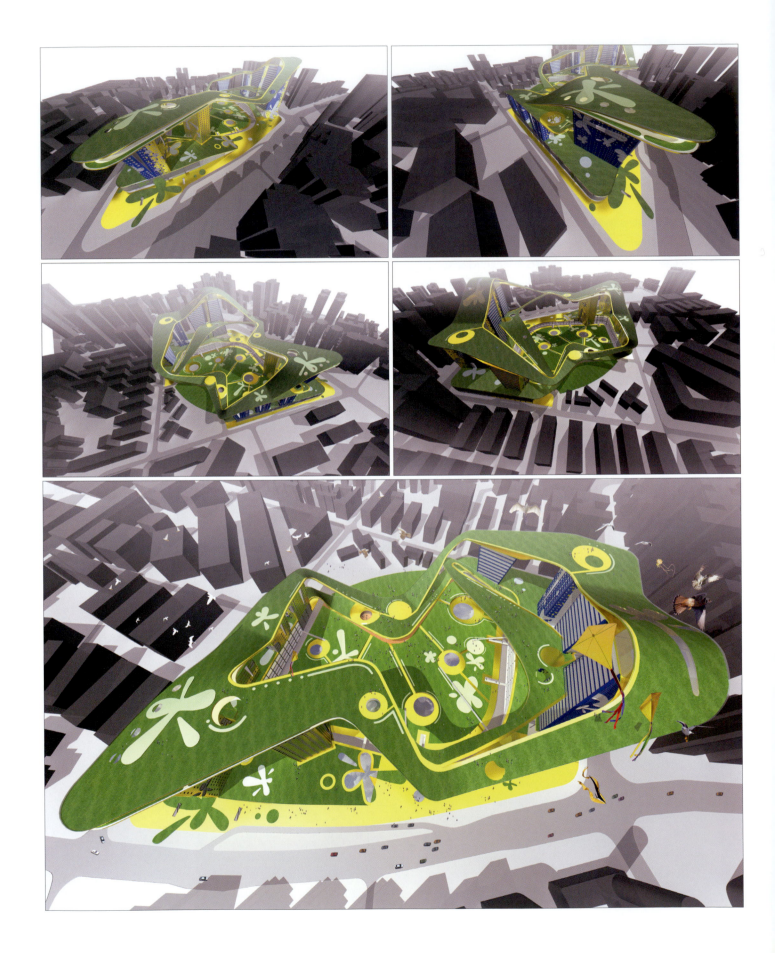

Incorporating all the staples of an urban settlement, the development may be regarded as a modern-day radiant city (Cité Radieuse) operating on similar principles of communal living as Le Corbusier's first Unité d'Habitation in Marseilles, but one birthed from economic pressures rather than utopian ideals. Although the form as village landscape is experimental, dense stratified living, treated with suspicion in the West, is relatively conventional in the Far East, with the problems of vandalism and anti-social behaviour largely absent.

Physically, the village landscape is a green urban living room for the city, ramping from street level at the north entrance plaza on Nanhai Road and folding into a floating podium. Instead of competing with the high-rise towers of the surrounding Nan Shan district, the 'Golden Bowl' eschews vertical dominance for a fluid horizontal continuity that uses landscape to link the individual buildings that make up the complex.

The public landscape, including the central public park, expands into designated building areas and otherwise private spaces. The atypical relationship between landscape and building changes the politics of circulation and spatial programming – a series of bridges and ramps link the park directly into the shops, apartments and offices. The eastern edge of the sloped podium and park contains vehicular parking, department stores and shopping arcades. The western under-croft of the courtyard is a flexible and changeable culture/sports strip with a mobile art gallery and sports facilities. The new landscape also visually draws the existing school into the development. Within the park, trees and floral patches form shaded and cooler sound gardens for public relaxation and recreation. Five public pools, water gardens and plazas provide further microclimatic pockets for cooling and play.

Nine mid-rise towers of varying height housing offices, apartments and a hotel rise up from the podium, connected by a green ribbon of private garden. Appearing to float over the entire development, the ribbon is a private park exclusively for residential, office and hotel use. Whether jogging, performing tai chi or just relaxing, the views presented from this skyscape are spectacular. In sections requiring additional depth for structural reasons, the ribbon incorporates penthouses, long-stay hotel apartments, a club-house and a panoramic conference facility.

191

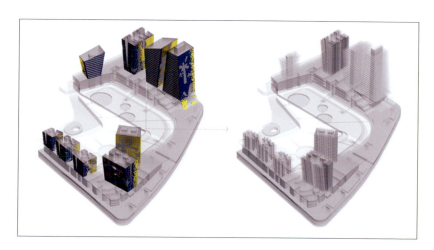

facing page top: Aerial views around the Urban Living Room

facing page bottom: A ribbon of private gardens hovers above the public central park

left: Nine mid-rise towers sit above the commercial podium (left); the dressed buildings

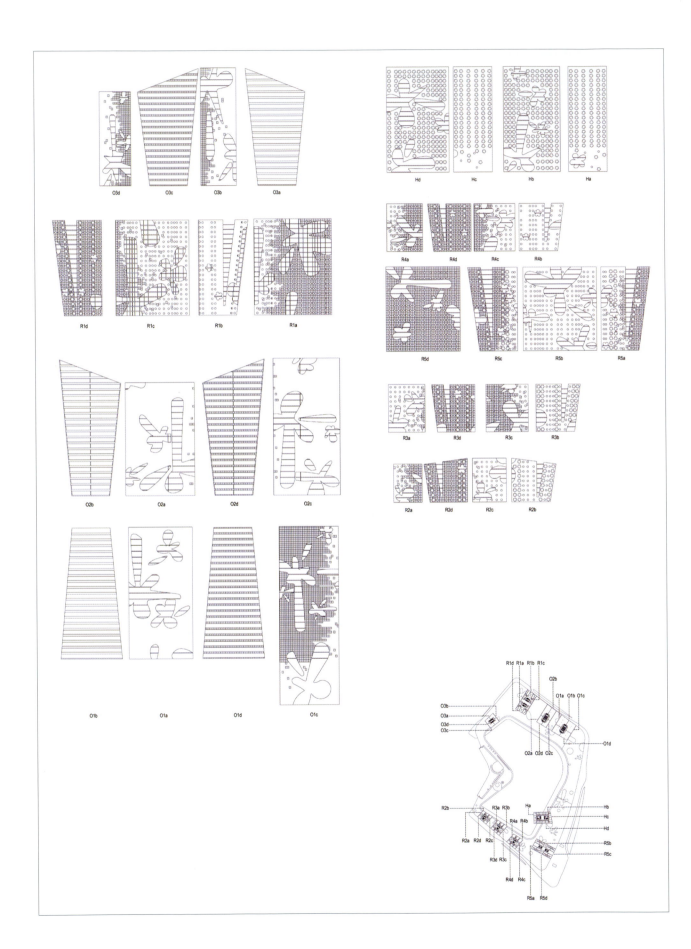

## Planning considerations

- Flexible Ownership: The key strategy of the development is to allow maximum flexibility for private sector clients, permitting changes of ownership and use. 'Plot' ownership can easily be divided into four sectors or broken down further, with the park and entrance plaza retained by the Shenzhen Government.

- Economical Spatial Planning: The internal layouts of all buildings are efficiently designed with simple floor plates to provide maximum floor area and also allow easy change of use. Strategically positioned voids cut through the towers for ventilation, natural light and views. The residential layout introduces double-height garden decks that bring the green landscape into the buildings and encourage communal activities.

- Dressing the Building: The building facades are designed in direct response to the environmental strategy. On the south, east and west elevations, solar mosaics are applied to harvest solar energy and engage in a dynamic aesthetic dialogue with the powder-coated gold aluminium panels. South-facing openings have external louvres to minimize solar heat gain and glare. By structuring the building floor plates around the service cores, however, the clients and future owners retain the flexibility of dressing the individual buildings with different facades. The suggested urban-scale blossom motif abstractly expresses the vision of inhabitating a gargantuan landscaped courtyard.

## Traffic Engineering

- Permeability of Space: At ground level, the linear commercial arcades in the podium and the mobile gallery allow a high degree of permeability from around the edges of the site into the central public park. This will maximize the flow of people through the building and the park.

- The Grand Entrance: A 200m-wide opening on Nanhai Road, as stipulated by the planning authorities, is emphasized as the grand entrance plaza into the Golden Bowl by the continuous green sky ribbon that forms a monumental portal. Acting as the key orientation element of the development, the golden surface of the entrance plaza folds up as a continuous facade for the main office building; on the south side of the podium, the gold-anodized aluminium surface morphs into a green public landscape.

- Vehicular Circulation: On each edge of the site, there are four drop-off bays that provide easy access by car and taxi. Two levels of cark parking provide over 4000 parking spaces for public and private use. There are a number of access points to the public car park on the less busy western edge, thereby reducing traffic congestion on the two main roads – Nanhai Road and Chuangye Road.

- Pedestrian Circulation: The landscaped surfaces at podium and sky level are inviting and highly accessible, combining pathways with defined relaxation and social meeting areas. At ground level, the Grand Entrance and numerous arcades around the perimeter present multiple entry points to the development and the central park. Internal and external circulation cores are arrayed to provide easy and direct access to shops, apartments and offices.

193

facing page: Dressing the building – a key design strategy responding to environmental performance

following page: The width of the Grand Entrance stipulated by the planning authorities allows maximum permeability into the central park

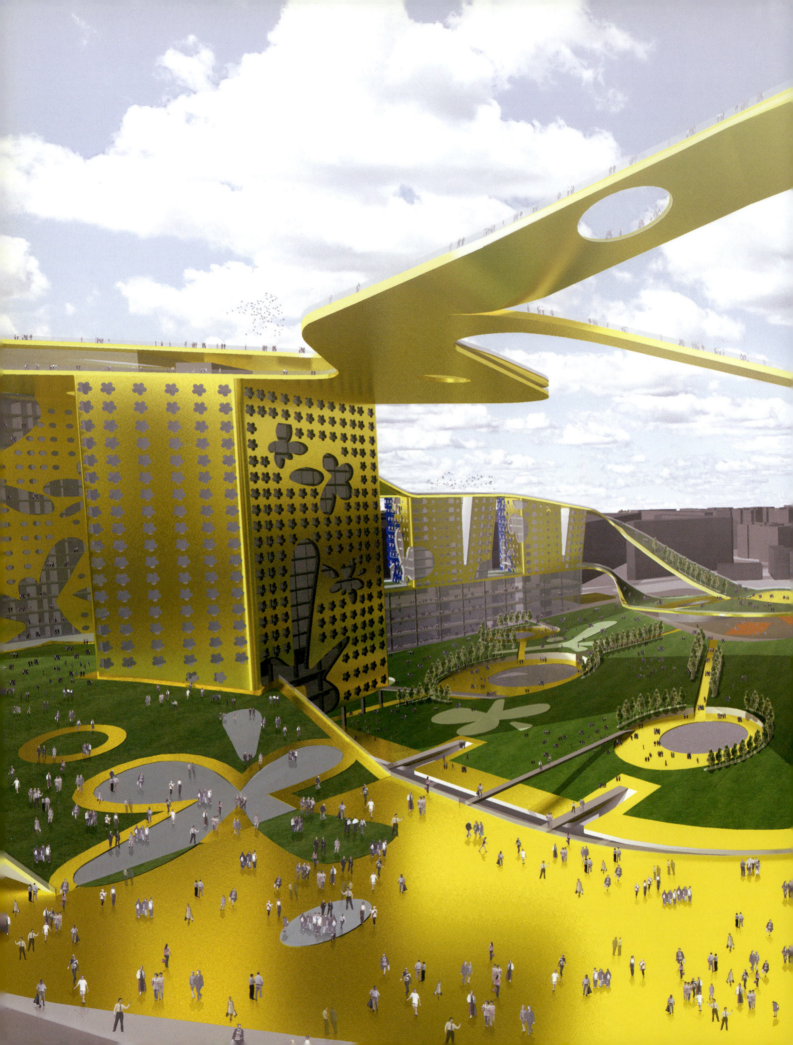

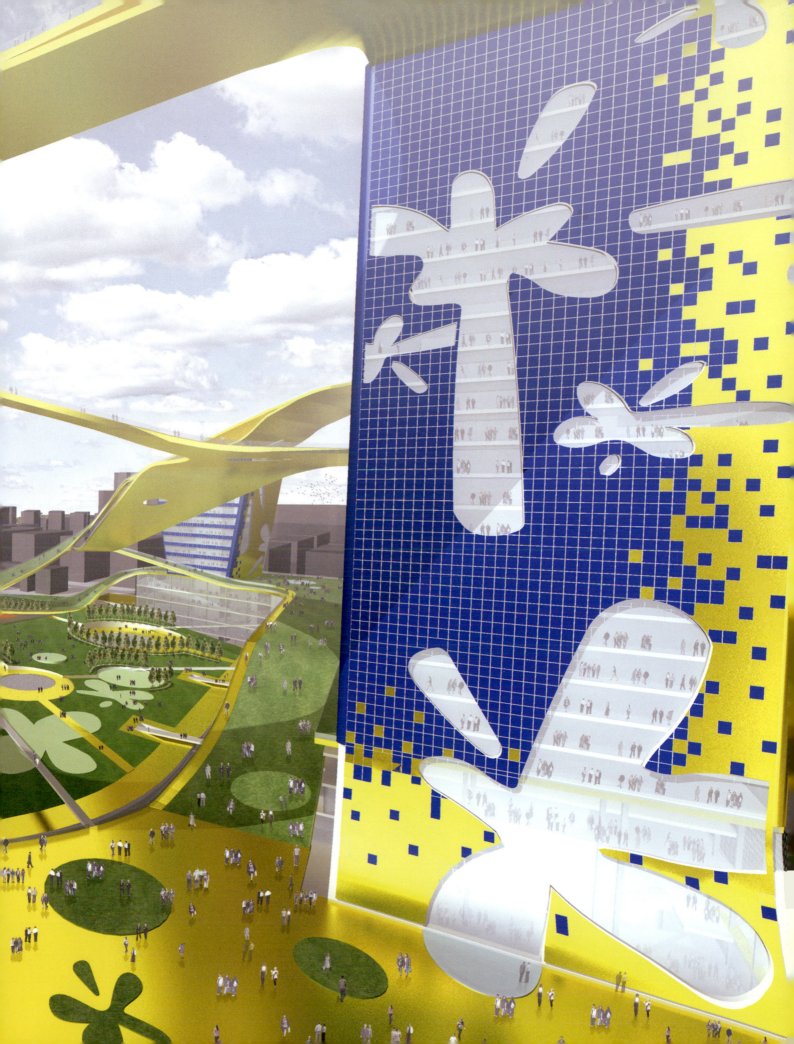

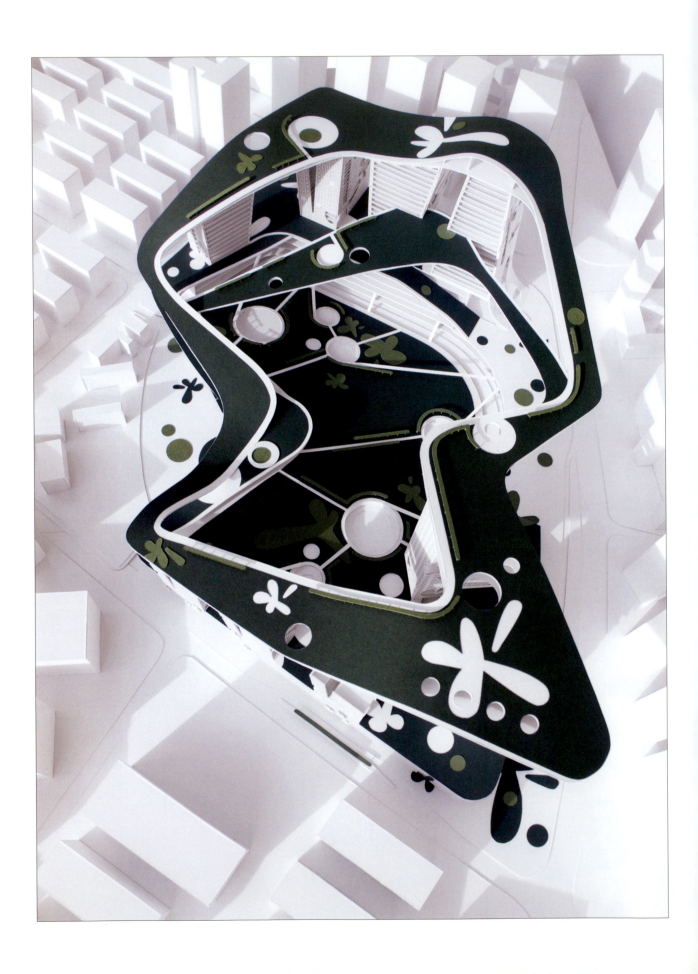

## Structure

The structure comprises three main components – plinth, accommodation units and roof terraces. The lower levels of the building, car parks, ground floor and first two storeys are formed in conventional in-situ cast reinforced concrete construction. Simple flat slabs are supported on circular columns sized to sustain all superstructure loads. Lateral forces are resisted by cross walls, stairs and lift cores. Excavated areas have retaining walls formed as contiguous bored pile walls. The overall plan is divided into six areas by full separation joints in the structure. Foundations will be a combination of piled bases and raft elements to suit the superimposed loads.

Above the podium, the nine vertical buildings are arranged in reinforced concrete structures with pre-stressed wide span flat slabs supported on simple columns. Sidewalls and cores of reinforced concrete provide lateral stability. External walls facing outwards and towards the centre of the development are formed in lightweight curtain-wall cladding.

The hotel block is made with cellular construction, reinforced concrete slabs, walls and cores. Similarly, residential units are made with a combination of flat slabs, columns and solid walls.

The upper storeys, roof and roof terraces are all framed in steel with composite steel and lightweight concrete decking. Storey height truss frames are set within the top two storeys to span between tower tops. Ramps act as strutting to support the terrace decks and arch between the concrete blocks.

## Construction Sequence

Work will commence with site clearance and the erection of contractor's facilities and compounds. Piling works will include the contiguous bored pile walls installed from ground level. Excavations will be made and waterproof reinforced concrete basement areas formed. Standard steel table forms will be used to make the car-park area quickly and economically. The main floors will be formed in in-situ reinforced concrete and fitting out will follow on.

The main towers of the building will commence with the slip-forming of the vertical cores and side walls. Floors will follow and wider spans will be post-tensioned when curing is complete. All towers will be taken up simultaneously as separate constructions.

The upper storeys are framed in steel. These elements will be constructed as 'balanced cantilevers' proceeding outwards from each tower. Once the entire roof frame is joined together, floors will be added and the envelope completed.

facing page: The vertical multi-layering of green space fosters social interaction

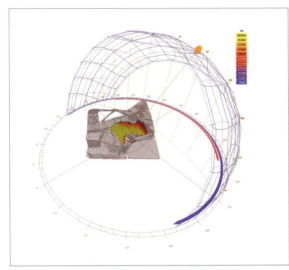 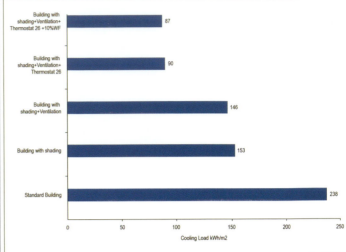

### Environmental Strategy

The environmental strategy is designed to maximize energy efficiency of the development utilizing a combination of robust proven technologies and a holistic approach for the masterplan. This includes methods to minimize the ongoing running costs and to maximize the energy benefits for future tenants.

The annual adaptive comfort range for Shenzhen varies from 20°C to 28°C. Internally, thermal comfort can be achieved for most of the year without the intervention of mechanical systems, and passive strategies have been adopted to minimize the use of air conditioning. Passive design strategies applicable for the region encourage resistance to heat gain and the dissipation of excess heat through the building fabric and reducing the cooling demand. This is achieved by employing the following complementary strategies:

(1) Solar Control: Heat gain is controlled by the distinctive aperture geometry, provision of shading elements at a monolithic and local scale, and careful specification of the solar-optical properties of transparent and opaque surfaces.

(2) Natural Ventilation / Air Permeability: Non-compact layouts provide effective cross ventilation; optimally sized windows are calculated and orientated to wind direction and internal environments coupled with external spaces in the form of sky courts and transitional spaces. Natural ventilation is enhanced by wind assisted ventilation and the stack effect. Balanced wind-stack ventilation is applied in vertically continuous atria or core spaces in the vertical buildings.

(3) Heat Sinks: Natural air, water, ground and built mass heat sinks are all employed. Vegetation in the form of green roofs, gardens and a ventilated double facade and roof encourage heat dissipation. Indirect cooling is achieved through roof ponds and landscaped water bodies.

(4) Thermal Inertia: Lower thermal inertia is acceptable for walls and other vertical surfaces enclosing spaces that rely on natural ventilation for cooling. This allows rapid heat loss, the air acting as a natural heat sink during favourable periods of the year.

Considerable reduction in energy demand is achievable by adopting a mixed-mode approach to cooling. In the shopping malls, mechanical cooling is confined to shops and offices that are buffered by naturally ventilated circulation areas. In the residential areas, mechanical fans running on solar power improve air movement, alleviating humidity by improving the sensation of comfort even at higher air temperatures.

The controlled use of daylighting minimizes the need for artificial lighting that contributes heavily to electricity consumption, $CO_2$ emissions associated with electricity generation, and the development's cooling loads. Considering the luminance available in Shenzhen, a daylight factor of 1.7 to 2.9% of the outdoor luminance would be sufficient for illumination levels in the 300–500 lx range required for typical indoor activities; excess luminance would lead to overheating and visual discomfort. The size, geometry and location of openings and the reflectance of room surfaces are therefore the main controllable design parameters. Good daylighting strategies for Shenzhen include the use of apertures with cleverly designed shading elements, shaded rooflights for deep plans, and appropriate coatings for glazed elements.

## Site-wide Energy Consideration

Underground thermal mass-based technologies will be used to deliver the project's cooling demands in the form of underground voids, Aquifer Thermal Energy Storage (ATES) or Borehole Thermal Energy Storage (BTES), resulting in extremely low energy and environmental costs. Where aquifers do not exist, underground heat exchangers will be constructed using boreholes and closed-loop pipe circuits.

In addition to reducing energy demand, low carbon and renewable energy technologies are employed including solar water heating and photovoltaics. The considerable hot water demand from mixed-use facilities such as apartments and hotels combined with abundant solar radiation make the former particularly appropriate. Similarly, the abundant solar resource in this region, height and orientation of the buildings and sloping roof profiles are ideal for use of photovoltaics. The yearly average total incident solar radiation is 2000kWh/m2/year, amongst the highest in the world; a panel of 1m2 supplies approximately 200kWh/year. The economics of photovoltaics need to be considered for cost evaluation and the payback period would be long, probably approaching 40 years. However, when doubling up as cladding and shading elements on the building facades, the panels become more economically attractive, simultaneously providing a visible demonstration of the building's commitment to low environmental impact.

## Space Specific Energy Considerations

The commercial areas have two distinct cooling strategies. Shop units are cooled to tight control levels, with limited variations over the day and year. The naturally ventilated circulation areas are controlled to higher temperatures, and receive free cooling from the shop units and the void space under the car park. With this control strategy, the circulation areas have extremely low cooling energy requirements and running costs. They also provide an adequate thermal transition space between the outside environment and the shop units. Low energy lighting in the circulation areas is provided to adequate levels, but with spatial variations. This minimizes energy requirements, and the cooling loads created by the lighting systems.

199

facing page left: Insolation analysis

facing page right: Annual cooling load for the various building types

The apartments operate most of the time under natural ventilation mode, with the exception of periods with extreme ambient temperatures when they are air conditioned. The cooling strategy reduces energy demands to a third of conventional building design requirements. Low energy, low cost cooling energy is provided from the ATES or BTES system. The ATES or BTES system will reduce energy consumption figures even further due to their high COP. Sufficient low energy lighting is provided to all the spaces, but not in excess to prevent overheating. The hotel has a more strictly controlled cooling infrastructure than the apartment buildings, but will still benefit from shading and ventilation.

Since the offices are occupied during the day and also generate considerable internal heat gains from occupants, equipment and lighting, they require more cooling than the apartments. However, the saving in comparison to a conventional building design is in the order of 40%, excluding savings though the ATES or BTES systems.

Tight humidity and air temperature control systems in the art gallery ensure that there are no significant temperature changes. Lighting will be balanced to adequate levels. This addresses glare problems, which are often recorded in buildings where the facade is not optimized under environmental considerations.

Due to the high internal heat gains from exercising occupants, the rooftop gym and clubhouse will have higher cooling energy requirements, but are reduced through fan assisted cooling of the occupants and cooling provision from the ATES/ BTES systems. Lighting levels are adequate with medium level of natural lighting.

Circulation areas are generally seen in the design as transition areas from the outside to the longer occupied areas of the building (which have a tighter cooling control strategy). With this approach in mind, a thermal 'adaptation space' is provided for people entering the building from outside, in contrast to the 'thermal shock' experienced in many other local buildings. Whenever possible, naturally driven ambient air is flushed through the spaces. Variations in light level create interesting spatial hierarchy and reduced energy requirements for artificial lighting.

The car park is ventilated by means of a low energy, low velocity passive ventilation system. Sufficient low energy lighting is provided.

Externally, trees in the park will provide shading, the primary requirement for comfort. Additionally, air channelled through concrete labyrinths below the surface pools will release cooling pockets around the seating areas.

left: Facade treatments – solar mosaics engage in a dynamic aesthetic dialogue with the gold powder-coated aluminium panels and urban-scale blossom motif

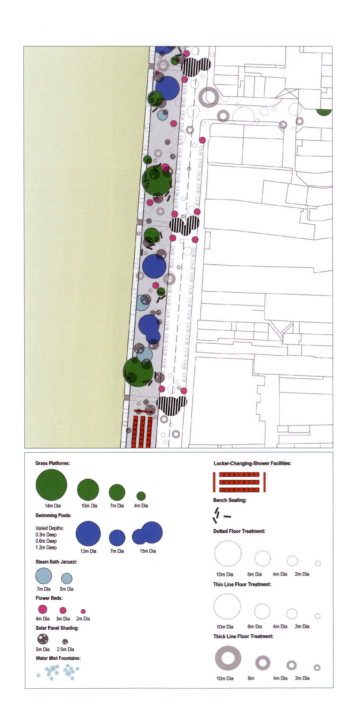

**Grass Platforms:**

14m Dia    10m Dia    7m Dia    4m Dia

**Swimming Pools:**

Varied Depths:
0.3m Deep
0.6m Deep
1.2m Deep                12m Dia    7m Dia    15m Dia

**Steam Bath Jacuzzi:**

7m Dia    5m Dia

**Flower Beds:**

4m Dia    3m Dia    2m Dia

**Solar Panel Shading:**

5m Dia    2.5m Dia

**Water Mist Fountains:**

**Locker-Changing-Shower Facilities:**

**Bench Seating:**

**Dotted Floor Treatment:**

10m Dia    6m Dia    4m Dia    2m Dia

**Thin Line Floor Treatment:**

10m Dia    6m Dia    4m Dia    2m Dia

**Thick Line Floor Treatment:**

10m Dia    6m    4m Dia    2m Dia

# Redcar Seafront Development UK

**Have you watched waves spilling onto shore**

**In a swash of foamy white?**

**Have you felt them swirl around your toes**

**And laughed in sheer delight.**

**Have you heard the gentle swishing sound,**

**As waves wash stone and shingle?**

**Have you listened to the music that they make,**

**As among the seashells they mingle?**

**- 'Waves', Pam Ramage, 2003**

Redcar is a seaside town in the Tees Valley region of Northeast England with a population of around 40 000. Lying 12km east northeast of Middlesbrough, Redcar originated as a fishing community in the 14th century and became a popular Victorian tourist resort following improved rail links to Middlesbrough in the mid 19th century. Redcar still attracts 1.2 million visitors per year, mainly from North England and Lowland Scotland, but has suffered from a decline of the local industry and changing holiday patterns. During the winter months, the coast draws few holidaymakers, and the urban fabric suffers from continued deterioration, deprivation in the surrounding areas and low levels of private sector investment.

In 2008, Redcar and Cleveland Borough Council, working in partnership with the Environment Agency, commissioned proposals for the regeneration of Redcar's Seafront Zone by landscaping over a kilometre of seawall that forms part of the coastal defence scheme, and to revitalize the area as a tourist destination by suggesting new and relevant enterprises.

As a stage for ever-changing light and weather conditions reflecting the mood of the sea and sky over miles of beach, Redcar's past and future lie in its special relationship with the coast. It is often forgotten that the seaside resort originated in Britain and spread across the British Empire, conceiving sun and sea bathing as health and leisure activities. Once the wellspring of extraordinary urban growth in the first half of the 19th century, Britain's coastal resorts fell victim to the warmer climes of exotic foreign shores and became enveloped in fug of anachronistic kitsch. Paradoxically, it is this temporal otherworldliness that may yet be the saviour of Redcar. Nostalgia for childhood holidays and a rekindling of appreciation

facing page: Redcar Seafront
Development masterplan and
close-up

for an unpredictable, if not always idyllic, coastline is growing, and the regeneration of the seafront must tap into its Victorian heritage as well as embracing change.

The redevelopment of Redcar addresses seasonal change and year-round recreation to benefit the local community and generate investment. British weather limits the swimming season in the sea, and the water can be bracing even in the summer months. Here, environmental sustainability has a role to play. In the same way that eating homegrown food and supporting local farmers has been successfully promoted, we must establish a movement that celebrates local holidaymaking and minimizes air travel. In order to extend the season for water-based activities and to maintain a steady influx of visitors, solar collection and thermal storage will be used to warm artificial pools and changing areas along the esplanade. Bathing will be supplemented by a host of traditional and non-traditional activities such as dance and music.

The physical intervention along the promenade is an overlay of inhabitable circular forms that facilitate outdoor activities catering for all, young and old. These circular elements form a flexible kit-of-parts that include pools, steam baths, Jacuzzis, bars and changing facilities as well as solar canopies, seating and gardens of lawn, flowers and music.

During the summer, these public ground inserts that come alive through visitor occupation complement the sea, beach and other traditional activities; for the rest of the year, they become the main attraction, extending the summer outdoor ambiance to the benefit of local businesses and the spirit of the town. The distribution of the circular elements varies and is implemented incrementally over time as funding allows and demands increase. The kit-of-parts system includes the following:

- Pools, Steam Baths and Jacuzzis: These facilities can be operational 24 hours a day and render the delights of a mid-winter dip in a steaming outdoor pool possible. The pools vary in depth and temperature, suitable for all ages, and are constructed from high quality reinforced concrete. Synthetic fibre reinforcement is used to counter deterioration through carbonation. Surface finishes will be dewatered, steam cured and polished to further improve the weathering properties of the concrete. The smooth surface and alkali environment of the material discourages organic growth.

- Dancing Pools and Skating Rinks: Once a month on weekends, when the pools are drained for cleaning purposes, the empty volumes are occupied as sunken dance arenas. Open-air discos and ballroom dancing can both be accommodated inviting cross-generational interaction. During the winter, some of the concrete rings are converted into skating rinks, creating a striking juxtaposition against the steam pools.

- Locker-changing-shower Facilities: Structures of aluminium alloy and fabric housing support infrastructure are distributed along the promenade, each sandwiched between two bars. All superstructure elements are prefabricated and easily dismantled, leaving a landscape of recessed surfaces and ground markings. The bar staff double as security personnel.

facing page top: A flexible kit-of-parts for the seafront includes steam baths, jacuzzis, bars and solar canopies

facing page bottom: Wandering steam clouds blur the threshold between town and beach

-        Music Gardens: Ring-shaped gardens hover over the promenade providing a forum for the public to congregate and enjoy eclectic music performed by professionals and amateurs.

-        Glass Wind Breakers: Toughened glass screens mounted above the seawall protect the public from wind and spray without any visual interruption to the sea and horizon. The promenade effectively becomes a new outdoor shelter.

-        Lighting: Low level mood lighting floods the pools and ground plane below the hovering gardens whilst photovoltaic canopies provide direct lighting from above. More dramatic feature lighting comes in the form of fluorescent 'fingers' that define the physical presence of the new seawall and pulsate to the rhythm of the waves.

Much of the proposal relies on bold graphic treatments that demarcate the boat storage areas and street parking. The hard standing comprises of interlocking compressed autoclaved concrete block paviors laid out in patterns and figures representing future installations. As night falls, surface patterns and floor treatments that have been treated in ultra-violet paint glow to enliven the tempo of the strip, with surface graphics spreading into the commercial centre of Redcar.

Heating of the pools is achieved by using the surface of the esplanade and canopies as solar collectors and thermal banks. Along the promenade, an insulating layer is laid beneath the paving covering a network of underfloor heating pipework; the changing facilities, canopies and filtration / water treatment plants are clad with evacuated tube solar energy collectors that operate well at low external temperatures. For each pool in winter, 200m2 of collection surface is required to maintain the ideal heat level of 30°C for hot pools and 25°C for others, equating to 20kW per pool. In spring and summer, heat will be plentiful as the solar energy received per square metre of ground is approximately five times that received during the winter. If the pools are not in use at night, insulating covers are used to retain warmth.

Roaring sea waves sprinkled with childhood laughter. Music drifting through clouds of steam wandering from pools of bubbling water. Donkey rides, ice creams, candy floss and Redcar rock. Memory and expectation. Heritage and growth. The redevelopment represents the revival of a culture as well as a town, using sustainable technology to reinvent a nostalgic tradition to be shared with future generations.

**Have you watched wild waves come storming in**
**Like monsters, dark and grey?**
**With a booming sound, they crash and pound**
**The rocks, with flying spray.**

**Have you seen the sparkle of sunbeams,**
**As they dance on waves of blue?**
**Close your eyes and just imagine,**
**That you're there, dancing too.**

facing page top: The redevelopment addresses seasonal change and year-round recreation to generate investment

facing page bottom: Emptied pools are occupied as sunken dance arenas

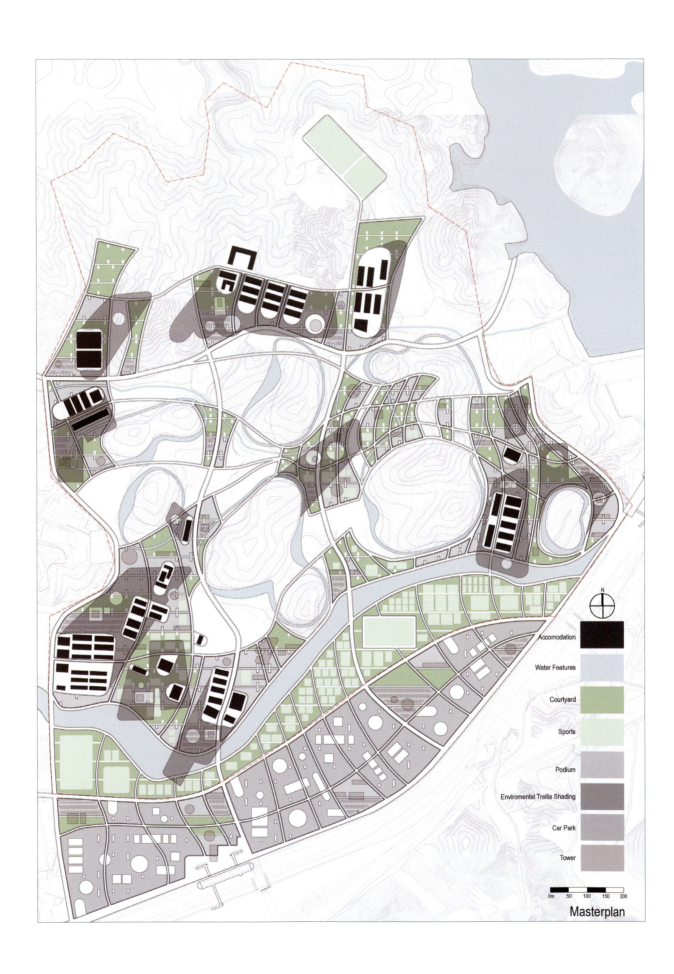

Accomodation

Water Features

Courtyard

Sports

Podium

Enviromental Trellis Shading

Car Park

Tower

0m  50  100  150  200

Masterplan

# Southern Science + Technology University China

The site for the Southern China University of Science and Technology lies in the Shenzhen special economic zone that has seen massive development and expansion since its establishment 29 years ago. The local government had identified a need for further high level education facilities in 2007, and earmarked the newly coined Xili University Town in Anshan District as a high level research scientific and technical university campus with a student scale of 15 000.

Bounded by the Yangtai Mountain Massif to the north and Chang Lingpi Reservoir Water Protectorate to the east, the 200-hectare site is characterized by a variegated landscape that required a sensitive planning approach that respected the existing ecosystem. The planning brief called for an open academic community where campus life and the urban community would meet and mix, resulting in improved land-use efficiency and reducing the need for new construction.

The land use comprises mainly of industrial, service and municipal facilities, although many of the factory buildings have fallen into disuse and been vacated by industries that have outgrown them. A significant number of the factory houses and old village buildings are in good structural condition, although of little architectural value. The decision was taken to introduce a new organizational structure whilst retaining elements with remaining life within them. The approach adopted was effectively the renovation of a property scaled up to the size of a town, a novel concept to masterplanning in China.

The retained buildings are made over with distinctive and environmentally responsive facades, and, together with new construction, conform to an organizational grid based on the Periodic Table that topographically deforms with the natural landscape. Overlaid on the grid is an ordering system of environmental trellises that cluster individual buildings into faculties whilst providing shade and social gathering areas. The existing community is relocated to a linear zone south of the site with a higher plot ratio.

The lack of identity often associated with planned communities, where construction is of necessity condensed into an abbreviated timeframe, is partly surmounted by the nature of the university campus. The programme will inherently confer a sense of place distinctive to towns centred around academia. Instead of adopting the collegiate cloister and quadrangle model of university towns such as Oxbridge and Harvard, the Southern Science and Technology Campus centres its life on the shaded transitional spaces between buildings and faculties that integrate green space, landscaped seating, cycle paths and sporting facilities. The consequential inclusiveness and shared space with the region's non-academic community is seen as beneficial, desirable and non-elitist.

facing page: Southern Science +
Technology University masterplan

210

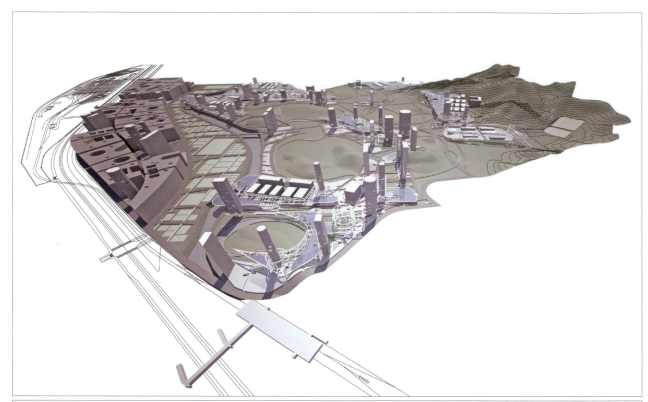

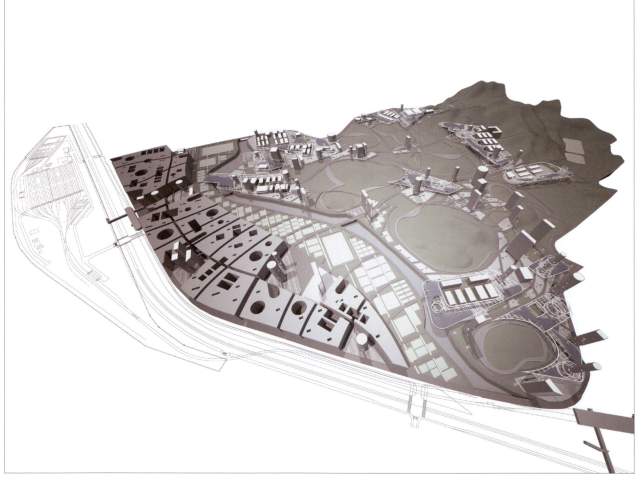

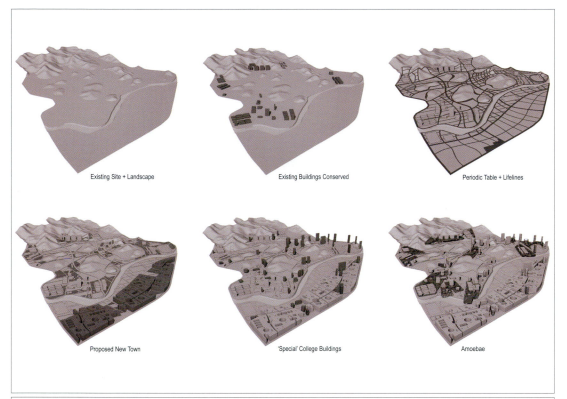

Existing Site + Landscape

Existing Buildings Conserved

Periodic Table + Lifelines

Proposed New Town

'Special' College Buildings

Amoebae

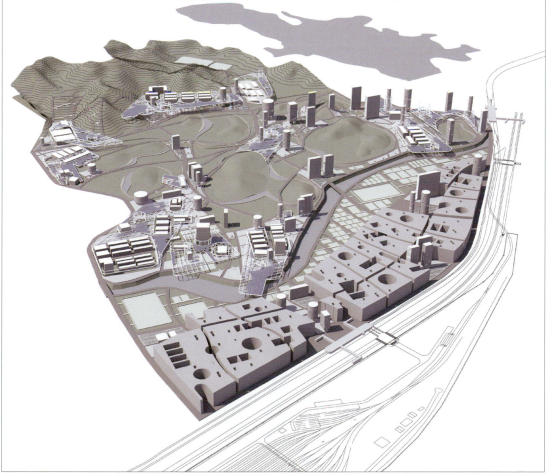

facing page: View from the southeast
(top); View from the west

left top: Tectonic and programmatic
framework of the campus

left bottom: View from the southwest

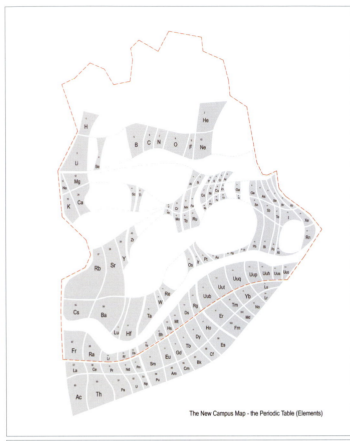

The New Campus Map - the Periodic Table (Elements)

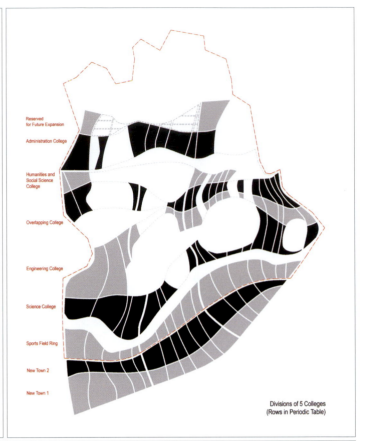

Reserved for Future Expansion

Administration College

Humanities and Social Science College

Overlapping College

Engineering College

Science College

Sports Field Ring

New Town 2

New Town 1

Divisions of 5 Colleges
(Rows in Periodic Table)

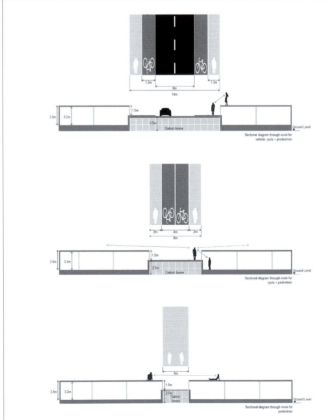

Sectional diagram through route for vehicle, cycle + pedestrian

Sectional diagram through route for cycle + pedestrian

Sectional diagram through route for pedestrian

20 Floors

18

16

15

12

10

8

5

3 Floors

Total gross floor area obtained by new buildings (within the site boundary) = 248212 m²

New Buildings Proposed with floor area

Buildings Heights for Newly Proposed Building
(Columns of Periodic Table)

**City Framework**

The organizational matrix provides a visual identity and coherence to the campus and comprises three interacting elements that incorporate the existing landscape and buildings: (1) The Periodic Table sets out the urban scale and plots of the campus and new town; (2) the amoebae (environmental trellises) support the ecological dynamics of the site, including the recycling of existing buildings; and (3) lifelines provide circulation and connections within and beyond the campus.

**Periodic Table**

Conceptually superimposed over the site, the Periodic Table establishes a planning dialogue between the existing landscape and buildings and the new activities of the campus and town. The outcome is a matrix of fluid plots that allow maximum flexibility for new forms and an amalgamation of life and nature to emerge. The buildings have been designed with efficient internal layouts and uncomplicated floor plates to maximize floor area and to accommodate easy change of use.

The horizontal rows of the Periodic Table translate into clusters of planning zones: the campus occupies the main block of rows 1–7, and the new town the remaining two rows at the base of the Table. The rows within the campus are further divided horizontally into five college groups.

The horizontal sports zone acts as the threshold between the campus and the new town. A number of the sports facilities are shared to encourage interaction between the two communities. The horizontal zoning of the Table further reinforces the physical presence of the river, the expressway and the railway.

The individual plots are projected into podia 4m above ground level to accommodate administration, libraries, education services and large lecture facilities. Over the three construction phases, the inhabitable podia may accrete 'special' buildings above or be landscaped with meadows, playing fields and gardens.

The atomic numbering of the Table lists the plot numbers, and assists in the allocation of college programmatic function. The plots are either coloured or landscaped within groups to reflect the characteristics of the Elements.

The heights of the 'special' buildings on the plots are determined by the nine vertical groups of the Table, ranging from 3 to18 floors, west to east. These structures accommodate the laboratories, seminar, study and teaching rooms, and act as orientation markers for each faculty.

The buildings of the new town are homogeneous in height. Carved into the six-storey blocks are a series of courtyards that provide natural light, ventilation and open space. The lower three floors are for commercial use, the remaining floors residential.

facing page (clockwise from top left):
Infrastructure plans showing the
'Periodic Table' – Land division of the
plots; Allocation of the five colleges;
Building heights for new buildings;
Planning guidelines in section

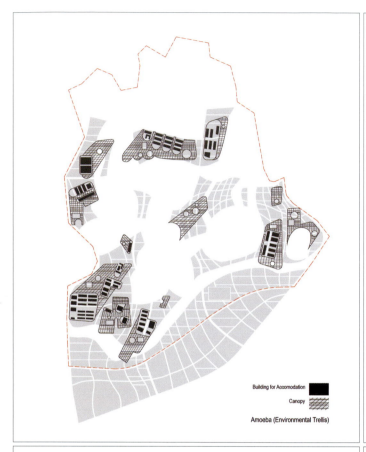

Building for Accomodation ■

Canopy ▨

Amoeba (Environmental Trellis)

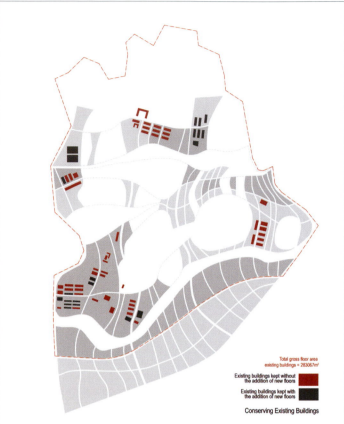

Total gross floor area
existing buildings = 283067m²

Existing buildings kept without
the addition of new floors ■

Existing buildings kept with
the addition of new floors ■

Conserving Existing Buildings

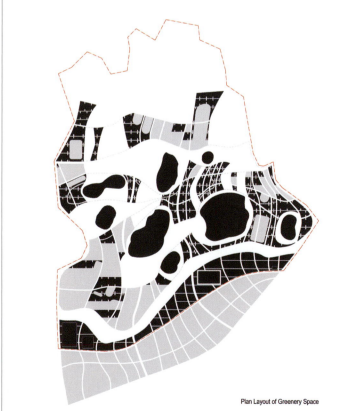

Plan Layout of Greenery Space

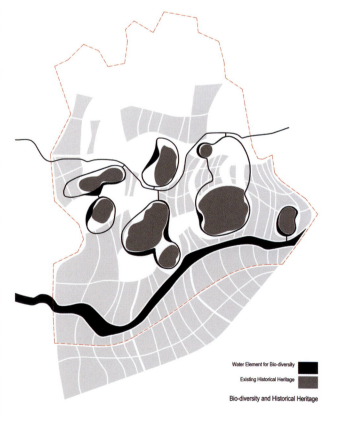

Water Element for Bio-diversity ■

Existing Historical Heritage ■

Bio-diversity and Historical Heritage

Amoebae

The dialogue between human activity and natural systems is mediated through the deployment of a series of organic structural and landscape forms. These amoebae, named for their fluid form, will support the emergence of self-organizing ecosystems and environmental sustainability.

Nine hills of the existing landscape are rich in historical heritage and retained with minimal physical disturbance; a diverse programme of flora will be introduced to encourage biodiversity and wildlife. Each hill is surrounded by a wetland moat.

The environmental trellises are urban-scaled devices that hover over the plots to provide large areas of shade for transitional and external gathering spaces. The structures also give vertical solar relief to buildings and courtyards. Photovoltaic petals 'blossom' over the southern aspects of the structure, while lush flowering plants are trained over the remaining lattice surface creating a series of floral cloud-gardens. This is where natural science meets technology.

Of the existing buildings, 100% of the grade one and 35% of the grade two structures are retained and refurbished for student accommodation. These buildings are stripped, retaining only the structural cores and concrete floors. The dining rooms and catering facilities are located at ground level. New glass and aluminium mesh facades bring a spatial lightness to the buildings and limit solar heat gain and glare. The pattern of building apertures and mesh, designed by different architects and artists, give individual identities to each cluster.

facing page (clockwise from top left):
Infrastructure plans showing the
'Amoebae' – environmental trellises;
Conservation of existing buildings;
Biodiversity and historical heritage;
Green space

left: The 'Amoebae' mediate between
the buildings and nature

following page: Tectonic and
programmatic dialogue creates a
dynamic environment for learning and
education

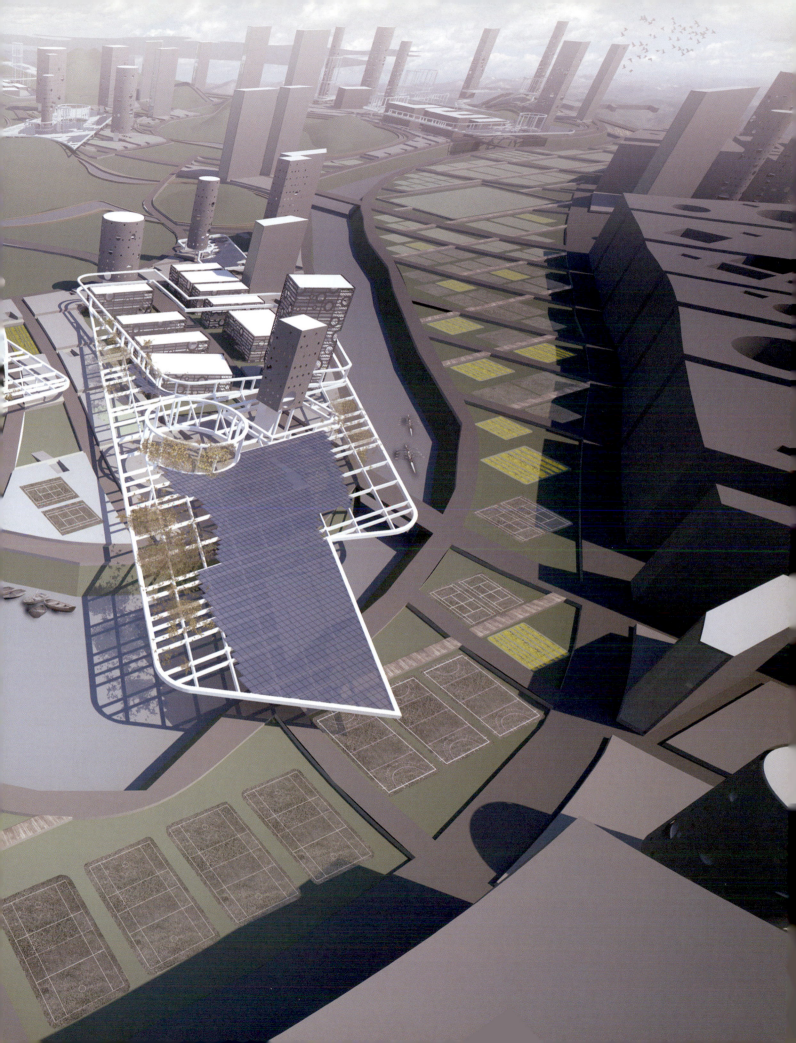

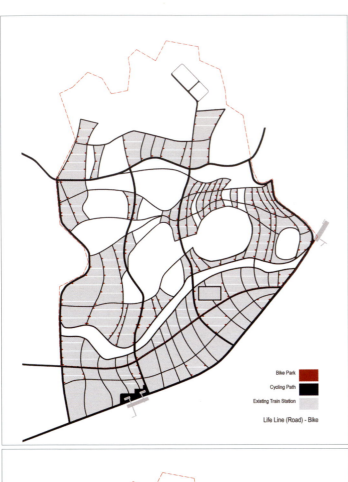

Bike Park

Cycling Path

Existing Train Station

Life Line (Road) - Bike

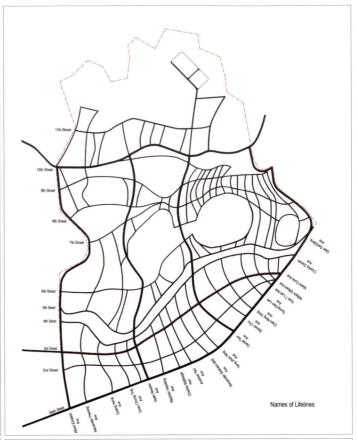

11th Street

10th Street

9th Street

8th Street

7th Street

6th Street

5th Steet

4th Street

3rd Street

2nd Street

Main Street

Names of Lifelines

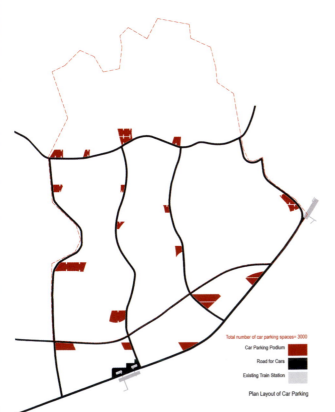

Total number of car parking spaces= 3000

Car Parking Podium

Road for Cars

Existing Train Station

Plan Layout of Car Parking

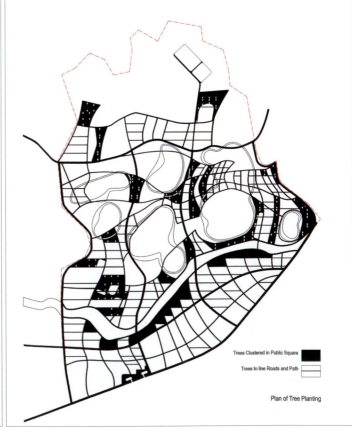

Trees Clustered in Public Square

Trees to line Roads and Path

Plan of Tree Planting

## Lifelines

Located near the railway and major expressways, the campus functions as both a point of destination and dispersal. A network of routes used by cyclists, joggers, pedestrians and vehicles complements the campus clusters. The academic community is encouraged to dispense with cars and utilize the extensive cycle system.

Seven main thoroughfares provide vehicular access linking the five colleges, the new town and the wider region; there are 17 car-parking locations, initially accommodating over 3000 vehicles, but cycling incentives will reduce these numbers by the final construction phase . The asphalt surfacing to the roads and car park plots act as a renewable-energy-carpet, harvesting solar energy for hot water heating.

Cycling paths are available on every route within the campus and new town. Pedestrian pathways are set into the podium of each plot; the act of slicing into the volumes creates the opportunity for clerestory lighting and passive ventilation to the internal spaces below.

The north–south routes are named after scientists and celebrated Nobel Laureates giving rise to Einstein, Curie and Chen Ning–Yang Avenues. The east–west routes are numbered consecutively from the station zones: 1st Main Street, 2nd Street and 3rd Street.

Waste from the demolition of existing buildings is recycled – rubble is placed into steel gabions and used throughout the campus to elevate the network of elevated pathways. The gabion zone acts as a heat-filtering membrane and also houses the service ducting and plant required for each cluster.

facing page (clockwise from top left):
Infrastructure plans showing the
'Lifelines' – Cycle collection points and
paths; Road naming; Tree planting
strategy; Roads and parking locations

left: Environmental trellis providing
urban-scale shading and transitional
gathering spaces

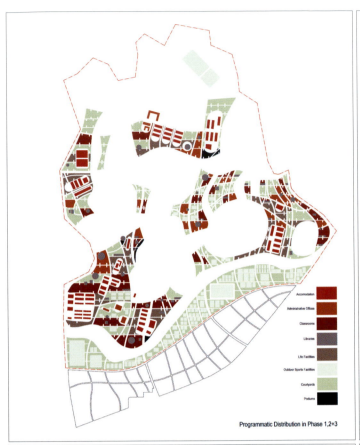

Programmatic Distribution in Phase 1,2+3

**Legend:**
- Accommodation
- Administrative Offices
- Classrooms
- Libraries
- Life Facilities
- Outdoor Sports Facilities
- Courtyards
- Podiums

Reserved for Future Expansion

Administration College

Humanities College

Overlapping College

Engineering College

Science College

Sports Field Ring

New Town 2

New Town 1

Plot to be developed

Phase 1 Development

Reserved for Future Expansion

Administration College

Humanities and Social Science College

Overlapping College

Engineering College

Science College

Sports Field Ring

New Town 2

New Town 1

Phase 4 Development/
Further Expansion

Reserved for Future Expansion

Administration College

Humanities and Social Science College

Overlapping College

Engineering College

Science College

Sports Field Ring

New Town 2

New Town 1

Plot to be developed

Phase 2+3 Development

## Construction Programme

The 15-year construction programme creatively integrates high-impact human activities with the more passive dynamics of ecosystems and native wildlife, with a flexibly engineered matrix planned to accommodate changing future scenarios. Buildings and landscape elements are implemented incrementally over time as funding allows and demands increase, gradually building up the campus's mass into a flexible patchwork of built clusters separated by open landscape. This will be staged as three long phases with a projected completion date in 2025.

## Environmental Sustainability

The Southern China University of Science and Technology is located in the same region as the development at Nanyui, and many of the same environmental strategies apply. Common elements include solar controls in the form of the environmental trellises and mesh-screen facade treatments, building apertures positioned to maximize wind-assisted ventilation, and the thermal mass of the gabion structures acting as a heat sink. Photovoltaics intersperse the floral clouds on the amoebic trellises, taking advantage of the high levels of daylight.

Given the high hot water demands of student accommodation coupled with abundant solar radiation, however, solar water heating is the most cost effective of the renewable energy solutions available; the asphalt roads and parking lots are ideal surfaces for harvesting solar energy in sub-surface heating coils.

facing page: Phasing plans

left: Photovoltaic petals and floral plants 'blossom' over the structure creating a series of floral cloud-gardens

following pages: Model of the Engineering College (southwest corner of the campus)

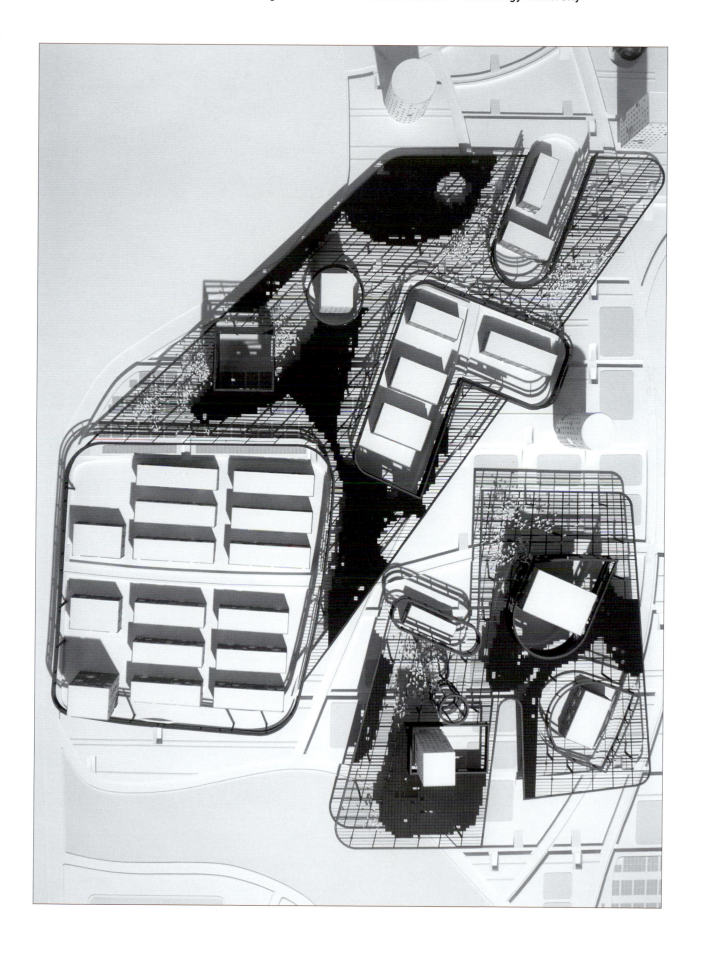

# Newark Gateway Project USA

In the field of crystallography, a small crystal is dipped in a supersaturated solution as a nucleus that accumulates material on its surfaces to grow into a large lattice structure. Compounds in solution are free to move and interact inter-molecularly, and the seed provides a pre-formed pattern for colliding molecules to follow, a process known as seeding. Similarly, cloud seeding disperses particles of silver iodide that have a similar crystal structure to ice into the air as nuclei for raindrop formation.

The new visitor's centre for Newark, located five minutes walk away from Pennsylvania Station, is a Smartcity nucleus that attracts residents interested in a sustainable lifestyle to sow seeds into the wider community. Whilst the centre is a single building, the scale of its ambit is urban. In the same way that a museum spreads culture and a football ground esprit de corps, Newark's new gateway building propagates a Smartcity lifestyle by promoting car-free commuting, fresh produce and the distribution of seeds to expand growth of the extant urban agriculture movement.

Located five miles west of Manhattan and two miles north of Staten Island, Newark is the largest city in the state of New Jersey. The make-up of its residents is diverse, with five political wards that have significant African American, Italian, Jamaican, Hispanic and Latino populations. Despite an upturn in recent years, the city has suffered heavily from problems of poverty and crime, resulting in a continual population loss since the late 1960s.

Newark Penn Station is a major transportation hub served by Newark Light Rail, New Jersey Transit commuter rail and Amtrak as well as local, regional and national bus services. Due to its close proximity, the Visitor Centre is ideally located as a gateway to the city with the potential to transform how people commute in and out of Newark by providing cycle parking, storage, shower, laundry and changing facilities. Since the 1950s, Newark has been an auto-centric environment with minimal concession to cyclists, but there is a growing lobby for the implementation of cycling infrastructure in a city once known as the nation's bike racing capital.

A less orthodox but equally transformative service provided by the gateway building is the provision of fresh locally grown produce available to commuters on their way home. The South and West Wards of Newark, along with the dense deprived neighbourhoods of cities such as Detroit and Memphis, have been subject to a phenomenon known as urban 'food desertification' – large supermarket chains, particularly in recent times of economic uncertainty, consider these neighbourhoods as high-risk ventures and have been slow to enter less affluent markets. Unless residents are prepared to travel beyond the city, the default option for the residents of Newark is fast food rather than fresh food.

facing page: Newark Gateway Project masterplan – Vacant and derelict sites (green) are transformed into community food production spaces; A new visitor's centre within the ribbon of community gardens along the Passaic Waterfront

facing page + left: The Centre is located along the Passaic Waterfront, minutes away from Penn Station; fresh local produce is made available to commuters

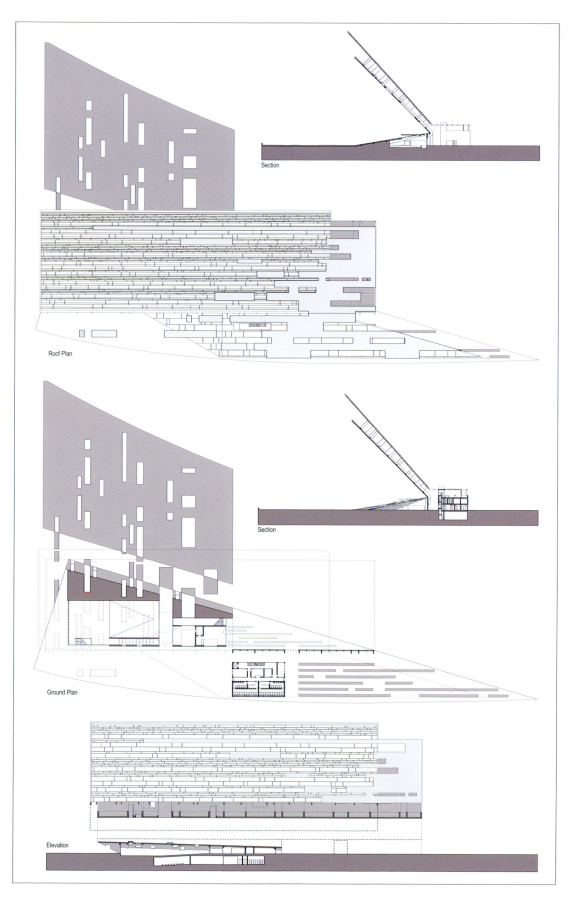

Section

Roof Plan

Section

Ground Plan

Elevation

facing page: South-facing facade
with seed nursery billboard (top); The
farmers' market and public plaza
under an inclined timber structure

left: Plans, sections and elevation of
the visitor's centre

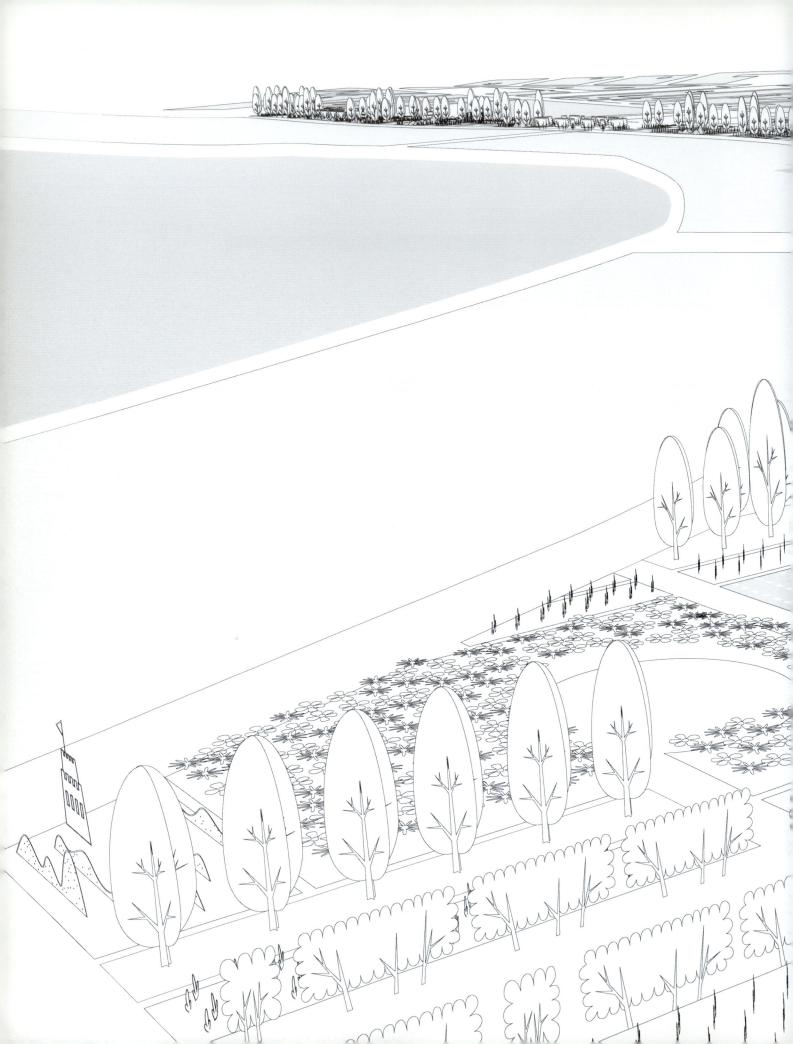

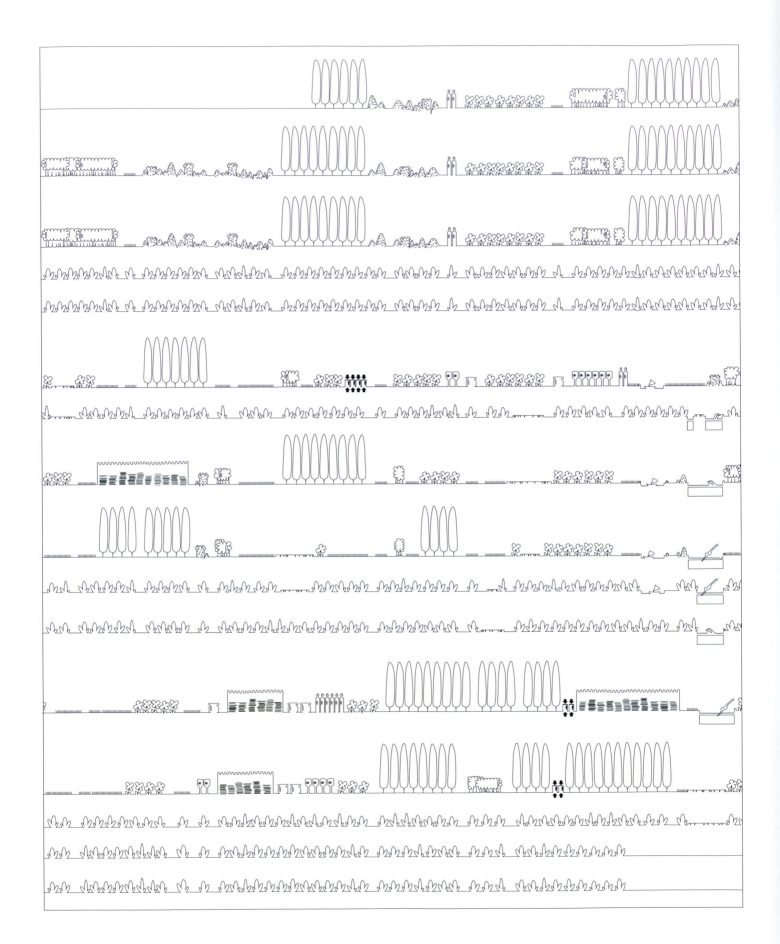

The small-plot intensive farms of the Brick City Farms initiative represent small oases in the urban food desert, employing portable earth boxes to grow fruit and vegetables on a number of unused sites. The positioning of the farms in the midst of their customer base means that the urban farmers can direct market, removing the middlemen and consequently reducing the cost of fresh nutrition paid by the general populace. Swiss chard, aubergines, peppers, cucumbers, rocket, collards, spinach, turnips and herbs have been successfully cultivated and sold to the community as well as local restaurants. The sub-irrigated planters, raised above ground contaminated by former industrial activities, are able to offer extremely high yields per square foot, and are efficient in their consumption of water and fertilizer. Encouragingly, the number of individuals willing to invest their time, funds and energy into the programme is showing little signs of abatement.

It is apparent from cursory inspection that there remain a great number of vacant lots that could be brought back into use, transforming derelict sites contributing to anti-social behaviour into community food production spaces and maximizing the spatial efficiency of precious urban real estate. To date, the Mayor has provided legislative assistance to the Brick City Farm programme, and private landowners have been sufficiently enlightened and community-minded to lease unemployed space for food production rather than as parking lots. Expansion is nonetheless necessary to significantly change the lifestyles of the Wards' residents and the appearance of the city.

The gateway building takes the form of a striking inclined fin along the riverbank that is half billboard, half greenhouse. This fin is partially covered in photovoltaic panels orientated towards the south for the collection of solar energy, and also contains a seed nursery supplying the community farms.

Within the shadow of the glass billboard, a gently inclined timber platform accommodating storage units is the venue for the farmers' market and a public plaza forming part of the planned Passaic Waterfront and Riverbank Park. Within a limited building footprint, the centre also provides exhibition spaces, a lecture theatre and an information suite for education on sustainable living.

The visitor's centre, while being the nucleus for the city's new green network of community gardens and an icon for healthy living, is just the start of the Passaic Waterfront development. Currently home to abandoned chemical factories and derelict warehouses, there are plans for a green promenade with a collection of thriving mixed-use developments to revitalize the neighbourhood by 2025. In the spirit of the temporal small-plot intensive farms, there is scope for introducing a landscape of vegetable and floral gardens, bottle and paper recycling banks, sandboxes and bathing pools in the interim that could offer a lasting legacy of social and sustainable principles for the future park.

233

previous page: The new Passaic Waterfront and Riverbank Park, and visitor's centre

facing page: Sections through the waterfront park

following page: An agricultural and recycling community landscape

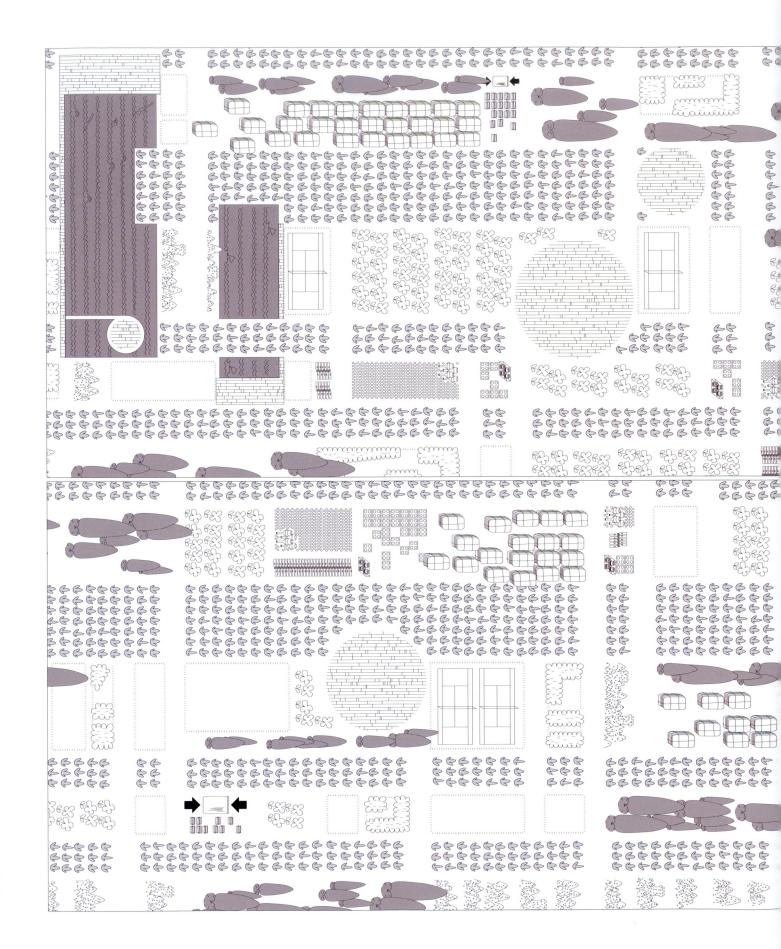

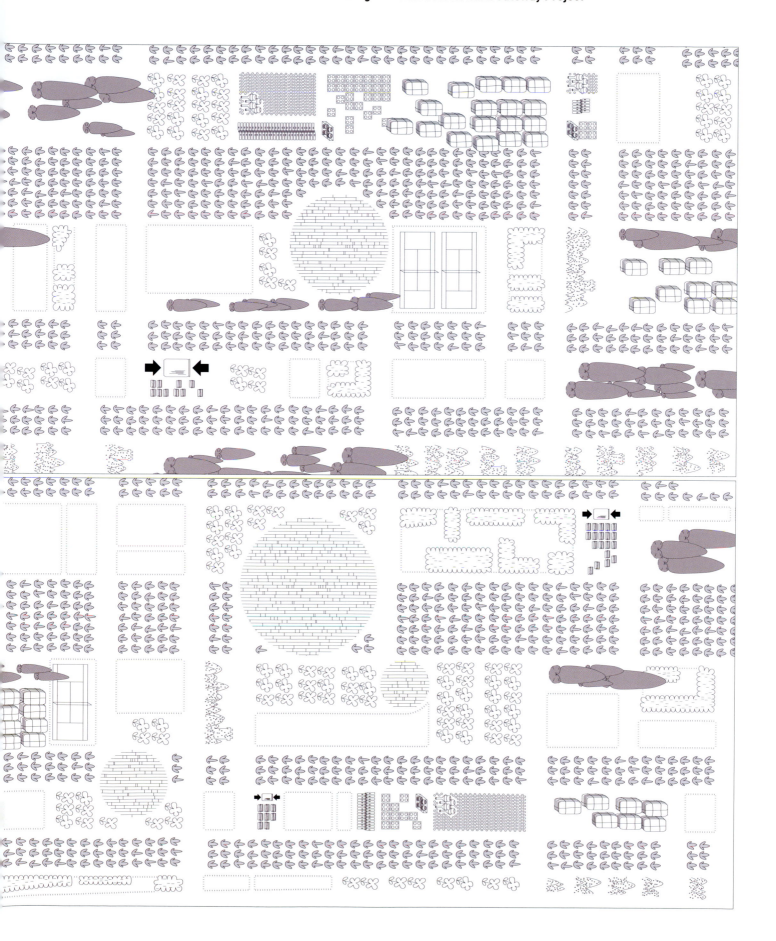

# Sitopia - The Urban Future

What might cities look like a hundred years from now? Predicting the future is never easy, yet one thing is clear: if cities in the 21st century look much as they do today, only bigger, we will have failed the greatest ecological challenge of our time. Cities are expanding faster than at any time in history, and the manner of their expansion (the ad hoc arrival every week of 1.3 million rural migrants) is altering the relationship that has for millennia underpinned civilization: that between city and country. Cities have always plundered the natural world for resources, but in the past, so few people lived in them (just three per cent in 1800) that their impact was limited. Today, with half the global population living in cities and a further three billion expected to join them by 2050, the opposite is the case. If the future is urban, we urgently need to redefine what that means.

Of all the resources needed to sustain a city, none is more important than food. In the pre-industrial world, this fact was self-evident: the sheer difficulty of feeding cities made it so. Without the benefit of farm machinery, agrichemicals, refrigeration and rapid transport (all the essentials of modern agribusiness) cities were forced to be both frugal and inventive with their food supplies. No city was ever built without first considering where were its sources of sustenance, and once established, cities kept 'food miles' to a minimum, growing perishable foods such as fruit and vegetables in the city fringes, and raising animals such as pigs and chickens within the city itself. Fresh foods, including grass-fed livestock, were consumed seasonally, with the excess preserved by salting, drying or pickling to be consumed during leaner months. The fertility of the soil was paramount, and across the centuries, various methods were employed (from blood sacrifices to crop rotation) to nurture it. No food was ever wasted: kitchen scraps were fed to pigs, human and animal waste was collected and spread as fertilizer, leftovers from kingly feasts handed to the needy.

In the post-industrial world, things are very different. We take it for granted that, if we walk into a restaurant or supermarket, food will be there, having arrived magically from somewhere else. Food is plentiful and cheap – so much so, that one could be forgiven for assuming that producing it was easy. Yet, however inexpensive food has become in supermarkets, its true cost is many times as great. Food and agriculture together account for one third of global greenhouse gas emissions. Nineteen million hectares of rainforest are lost every year to agriculture, while a similar quantity of arable land is lost to salinization and erosion. Each calorie of food we consume in the West has taken an average ten calories to produce, yet half of the food produced in the USA is thrown away. A billion people worldwide are overweight, while a further billion starve. As such statistics suggest, the global food industry is deeply flawed, yet this is the system upon which our urban life depends.

facing page: Children of the New York City Children's Aid Society work on their victory gardens at the West Side Centre

Our very concept of a city, inherited from a distant, predominantly rural past, assumes that the means of supporting urbanity can be endlessly extracted from an ever-bountiful rural hinterland. For the past two centuries, industrialization has fuelled that assumption, both by greatly accelerating the rate at which such extraction is possible, and by extending the distance (in all senses) between city and country. The result has been an unprecedented explosion of urban development, accompanied by the creation of a dangerous illusion: that cities are somehow independent, immaculate and unstoppable. Now that the illusion is wearing off, we are in urgent need of a new urban model: one that recognizes the vital role that cities play in the global ecology. But how are we to arrive at such a model?

First, we need to understand the close bond between food and cities, forged some 10 000 years ago in an area of the ancient Near East known as the Fertile Crescent. It was here that our Neolithic ancestors first began to gather wild grass seeds – experiments that were crucial to the eventual development of urban civilization, since it was the harvesting and subsequent cultivation of grain that was to provide the first source of food capable of sustaining an urban population. As the gathering of seed gradually evolved into its deliberate cultivation and harvesting, permanent farming settlements began to be built close to the fields.

The first such settlements considered complex enough by archaeologists to be described as cities were a group of Sumerian city-states, Uruk, Ur and Kish, in southern Mesopotamia (modern Iraq), dating from around 3000 BC. These early prototypes consisted of dense urban cores surrounded by intensive farmland, made fertile through irrigation from the floodwaters of the River Euphrates. The cities were dominated by large temple complexes, which held yearly cycles of festivals mirroring the agricultural seasons. These culminated in the harvest, a convulsive moment in the city's calendar involving the entire population in complex rituals of mourning, sacrifice and rebirth. Once the grain was safely gathered in, it was offered to the gods, before being carefully stored and redistributed among the people. The temples were thus the cities' spiritual centres as well as their chief means of food distribution. Physically and spiritually, they embodied the vital bond between city and country that remains (despite appearances) fundamental to all urban life.

Throughout the pre-industrial era, feeding their citizens remained every city authority's biggest priority. Apart from the physical difficulties involved, the social and political aspects of the food supply required constant management. Most cities had laws in place to prevent various malpractices including the formation of monopolies. The buying and selling of food was usually confined to open markets, where the trade could be most easily monitored. As a result, cities were fed by large numbers of small producers, selling from legally defined pitches at specific hours to regular customers. Since markets were the only places one could go to buy fresh food, they became powerful social and political spaces as well as commercial ones. From the Athenian agora and Roman forum to Les Halles and Covent Garden, markets were vital social hubs that linked cities to the countryside and expressed civic life in its fullest sense.

Food's role in shaping the pre-industrial city is easy to see, yet food is still shaping post-industrial ones, albeit in a far less obvious way. Modern food systems have emancipated cities from geography, disguising the effort of feeding them. But that doesn't mean the problem has gone away. On the contrary, in allowing the metropolitan carpet to roll out across field and forest, tundra and desert, industrial food systems have made the very thing they promised to make easier – feeding cities – infinitely more complex. Three billion of us now live, not merely remote from the sources of our sustenance, but utterly dependent on supply systems that are unsustainable.

Cities have always had their critics, but in the past, those wishing to escape them could do so if they chose. That is no longer true. The economic reach of cities is now such that few rural areas remain unaffected by them. Indeed, the steady flood of rural migrants to join the ranks of the urban poor is driven as much by the collapse of rural economies as by any allure of urban life. In many parts of the world, living in the countryside is no longer viable, precisely because the land has been transformed in order to feed cities.

Equally damaging is the mental transformation wrought on us by urbanity. The severance of man from nature – the essential achievement of modernity – has left us in danger of forgetting what, deep down, it means to be human. Ours is a world dominated by abstractions – credit crunches, bottom lines – that have little to do with the daily rhythms that once gave people's lives meaning. Divorced from the necessities of the everyday, we search instead for stimulation in the form of computer games and twitter, while all the while (like Dorian Gray's portrait in the attic) the true impact of our urban lifestyles wreaks havoc unseen. With all the efficiency and technology of modernity, we have neither succeeded in solving what E.F. Schumacher called 'the problem of production', nor made ourselves happy.[1] On the contrary, the further removed we are from our natural selves, the less capable we become of true contentment.

As a model for human dwelling, the city has outgrown itself. In its post-industrial form, it offers neither a good quality of life for most, nor a sustainable future. Yet it remains the dominant model for human development. Half of India's 700 000 small farms are expected to disappear over the next 20 years, as a centuries-old way of life finally succumbs to urbanity. Yet the question of what millions of displaced rural workers are going to do with themselves once their farms are gone remains unanswered. As China's recent experience has shown, the mass abandonment of the countryside for cities is no guarantee of a better life. On the contrary, 26 million Chinese migrant workers found themselves unemployed at the start of 2009, leaving the Chinese Government contemplating a 'social time-bomb'. If the credit crunch has taught us anything, it is that we urgently need to question the values by which we live, and the foundations upon which we build communities.

Our first step must be to acknowledge the essential paradox at the heart of all urban life: namely, that without a rural counterpart, it can't exist. Once we grasp that fact, we will be significantly closer to the essence of the problem we face. It is one of balance. In our rush to become civilized – to raise ourselves above the level of mere survival – we have forgotten that we remain animals, with animal needs. We may choose to live in shiny, glowing things called cities, but in a deeper sense, we still dwell on the land. What is needed is not so much a technological revolution as a mental one: a recognition that, once we lose our vital bond with nature, we too are lost. Our most urgent mission must be to regain a sense of that bond.

That is where food – so powerful in ancient cultures, so debased in ours – can play a vital part. Food is the sine qua non of our existence: the one thing none of us can live without. Its rituals of growing, buying, cooking, eating and sharing have, more than any others, shaped our civilization. As we face our greatest ever man-made crisis, food could hold the key to our salvation. Its central role in our lives gives

1. E F Schumacher, 'Small is Beautiful', Vintage, London, 1973, p.3

it a unique power over us – making it the perfect vehicle for interrogating, disentangling and ultimately redesigning how we dwell on earth.

My shorthand for this approach is sitopia, meaning 'food-place' (from the ancient Greek sitos, food and topos, place). It is a deliberate alternative to utopia, the theoretical ideal model that has for many centuries been the commonest method of addressing the dilemmas of human existence. Utopian themes – sociability, sustainability, equality, health, happiness – are unimpeachable; the problem is, because utopia aims at perfection, it can never be fulfilled. If we want to build a better world, we need a model that aims, not at perfection, but at something partial and attainable. That is where sitopia comes in. Because it uses food as a tool, sitopia already exists, albeit imperfectly. Food affects everything from the way we work, play and socialize, to the way we walk and talk, inhabit land, sea and sky. As soon as we learn to see how it shapes our lives, we can use food in multiple ways to shape things better. At the macro scale, that will involve finding ways to reconnect ourselves to nature, and city to country. At the micro scale, it might mean anything from changing the way we design and build houses to the sorts of foods we eat for breakfast.

If the range of sitopian opportunity seems daunting, we only have to look at existing models for inspiration. Arguably, all pre-industrial cities were sitopias of sorts: societies that recognized and celebrated the primacy of food. Although nobody would suggest a return to what was undoubtedly a tough and mephitic existence in the pre-industrial city, there is much we can learn from a time justifiably named 'the golden age of urban ecology'.[2] Limited by the constraints of geography, pre-industrial cities were forced to live within their means; something that we, in the post-industrial world, must learn to do again. With the dual benefits of technology and hindsight, we must take the ancient urban model and remould it for our times; not in order to romanticize the past, but in order to seek its wisdom. For two hundred years, we have suffered collective amnesia about our place in the organic order of things. Now we must re-embrace it.

Above all, sitopia is an approach that makes connections between apparently disparate aspects of our lives, and tries to establish a balance between them. Part of that process involves learning to frame the right questions. For instance, instead of asking how we can feed cities most 'efficiently' (a question which, by its very nature, can only yield one result), we should be asking what sort of communities we want to live in, and design our food systems accordingly.

Once you put the question that way round, what immediately becomes apparent is that industrial food systems are totally antithetical to the values to which we might aspire in an ideal society, summarized by the utopian themes listed above. Indeed, such systems are deliberately anti-social in nature, having been cleansed of any aspect of humanity that might interfere with their profit margins. Seen as diagrams, they are shaped like trees, with many roots (producers) channeled through a single trunk (supermarket) to feed many branches (customers).[3] They are thus structured so that the trunk exerts a stranglehold over the entire system, keeping producers and customers apart – the very thing that city authorities in the past struggled so hard to avoid.

Now imagine another system, in which city-dwellers forge direct relationships with those who grow their food. In such a scenario, customers would quickly become knowledgeable enough to influence the food network through their choices. They would effectively become collaborators in the supply process – what the founder of the Slow Food Movement Carlo Petrini calls 'co-producers'.[4] Such a food network would produce a very different society: one far more likely to foster the sorts of personal connections necessary for a successful community, and one far more resilient in the face of external shocks. A society, in fact, much more like those of cities in the past.

Exercises such as this remind us that food systems exert an enormous influence, and that their essential role must therefore be not merely to feed us adequately and sustainably (no mean feat in itself) but also to nourish our quality of life. If all we are concerned with is survival, then a ruthless series of calculations aimed at maximizing the ecological synergies between diet, soil, sunlight, water, energy and waste would indicate how we should arrange our lives. But if we also care about such things as joy, ethics, culture and freedom, we are faced with a far trickier – yet far more worthwhile – problem. How best to reconcile the satisfaction of our animal needs with our higher aspirations? That is the great dilemma of civilization, one that people have long struggled to answer.

241

Ultimately, the dilemma boils down to a single question: what is a good life? The answer remains elusive, but surely some part of it must involve respect for food. And if that is so, then surely a life spent nurturing others through food – so long as one is respected and rewarded for doing so – must be a good one? The reduction of food to a zero-sum commodity has done more than rob us of variety, identity, taste and smell in our lives: it has taken away the most dependable source of income and sociability we are ever likely to find.

Although food has never been used explicitly as a design tool, its presence is implicit in many utopian projects. In 1902, Ebenezer Howard published a modest pamphlet entitled 'Garden Cities of To-morrow', in which he set out his idea for a 'town-country magnet': a community that would combine the benefits of town and country life, while neutralizing the disadvantages of both.[5] The 'magnet' was effectively to be a city-state of 30 000 city-dwellers and 2000 farmers, consisting of a dense urban core surrounded by 5000 acres of farmland. Once its target population was reached, the Garden City would not expand; instead, a sister-city would be built some distance off, joined to the first by rail. In this way, the landscape would gradually be transformed into a network of connected, largely self-sufficient city-states. Howard received widespread interest in his idea, and even received the financial backing to build the first prototype, at Letchworth in Hertfordshire. But the project was ultimately a failure, since the radical nature of the proposal – incremental land reform – never took place.

Like all utopian projects, the Garden City was doomed to failure. However, in sitopian terms, it carries a powerful message. Whatever form human dwelling takes, the relationship between town and country will always be at its core, reconciling the two our greatest challenge. Because Smartcities attempt to address that challenge, they are, in my terms, sitopian. Such projects give us courage to imagine the future. But you don't have to be an architect to be sitopian. How we choose to farm, shop, eat and cook is up to us, but our choices, multiplied many times over, are what will shape our future.

2. Donald Reid, 'Paris Sewers & Sewermen: Realities and Representations', Harvard University Press, Cambridge Mass., 1993, p.10

3. For a discussion on the way such systems relate to cities (or rather, don't) see the essay by Christopher Alexander, 'A City is not a Tree', 'Architectural Forum', Vol. 122, No. 1, April 1965, (Part I) and Vol. 122, No. 2, May 1965 (Part II)

4. See Carlo Petrini, 'Slow Food Nation', Rizzoli, New York, 2007, pp.164-176

5. Identified by him as unsanitary overcrowding in towns and lack of services and opportunity in the countryside

# The Role of Cities in Climate Change[1]

Cities are often blamed for contributing disproportionately to global climate change. For instance, many sources including United Nations agencies and the Clinton Climate Initiative state that cities account for 75 to 80% of all greenhouse gases from human activities. But the actual figure seems to be around 40%. Of the 60% of emissions generated outside cities, a large part comes from agriculture and deforestation with much of the rest coming from heavy industry, fossil fuelled power stations and wealthy high-consumption people that are in rural areas or urban centres too small to be classified as cities.

In fact, many cities combine a good quality of life with relatively low levels of greenhouse gas emissions per person. There is no inherent conflict between an increasingly urbanized world and reduced global greenhouse gas emissions. Focusing on cities as 'the problem' often means that too much attention is paid to climate change mitigation (the reduction of greenhouse gas emissions), especially in low-income nations, and not enough on adaptation (minimizing climate change's damaging impacts). Certainly, the planning, management and governance of cities should have a central role in reducing greenhouse gas emissions worldwide. But this should also have a central role in protecting populations from the floods, storms, heat waves and other impacts that climate change will bring to many cities and this is an area to which far too little attention is given.

## Cities' Contribution to Global Warming

The main sources of greenhouse gas emissions in cities are from energy use – in industrial production, transport and residential, commercial and government buildings (heating or cooling, lighting and appliances). Greenhouse gas emission inventories for cities show more than a tenfold difference in average per capita emissions between cities, with Sao Paulo having 1.5 tonnes of $CO_2$ equivalent per person compared to 19.7 for Washington DC.[2] If figures were available for cities in low-income nations, the differences in per capita emissions between cities could well be more than 100-fold. In many cities in low-income nations, greenhouse gas emissions per person cannot be high because there is too little use of oil, coal and natural gas and little else to generate the other important greenhouse gases. There is little industry, very low levels of private automobile use, and limited ownership and use of electrical equipment in homes and businesses.

Transport will be an important contributor to greenhouse gas emissions in almost all cities, although its relative contribution varies a lot – for instance from around 11% in Shanghai and Beijing in 1998 (in these cities industry is much the largest generator of greenhouse gas emissions)[3] to around 20% for London, New York and Washington DC[4] to 30–35% for Rio de Janeiro, Barcelona and Toronto.[5]

243

left: Greenhouse gas emission in cities

1. David Satterthwaite, 'Cities' contribution to global warming: notes on the allocation of greenhouse gas emissions', 'Environment and Urbanization', Vol. 20, No. 2, 2008, pp. 539–549

2. David Dodman, 'Blaming cities for climate change? An analysis of urban greenhouse gas emissions inventories', 'Environment and Urbanization', Vol. 21, No. 1, 2009, pp.185–201

3. Shobhakar Dhakal, 'Urban Energy Use and Greenhouse Gas Emissions in Asian Cities: Policies for a Sustainable Future', Institute for Global Environmental Strategies (IGES), Kitakyushu, 2004, p.170

4. Mayor of London, 'Action Today to Protect Tomorrow; The Mayor's Climate Change Action Plan', Greater London Authority, London, 2007, 232 pages; Michael R Bloomberg, 'Inventory of New York Greenhouse Gas Emissions', Mayor's Office of Operations, Office of Long-term Planning and Sustainability, Washington DC, 2007, p.65

5. C Dubeux and E La Rovere, 'Local perspectives in the control of greenhouse gas emissions – the case of Rio de Janeiro', 'Cities', Vol. 24, No. 5, 2007, p.353–364; J VandeWeghe, C Kennedy, 'A Spatial Analysis of Residential Greenhouse Gas Emissions in the Toronto Census Metropolitan Area', 'Journal of Industrial Ecology', Vol. 11, No. 2, 2007, p.133–144; J Baldasano, C Soriano, L Boada, 'Emission inventory for greenhouse gases in the City of Barcelona, 1987-1996', 'Atmospheric Environment', Vol. 3, 1999, pp.3765–3775

Perhaps it is not cities in general that are the main source of greenhouse gas emissions but only cities in high-income nations. But studies of particular cities in Europe and North America show that many have much lower levels of greenhouse gas emissions compared to their national average – for instance New York and London have much lower emissions per person than the average for the USA or the UK.

### Difficulties in Allocating Emissions to Locations

Of course, it is not cities (or small urban centres or rural areas) that are responsible for human-induced greenhouse gas emissions but particular activities by particular people. An inventory of these activities can allocate them between cities, other urban centres and rural areas but this is not a simple exercise. For instance, the places with large coal-fired power stations would be very high greenhouse gas emitters although most of the electricity they generate may be used elsewhere. This is why greenhouse gas emission inventories generally assign cities the emissions generated in providing the electricity consumed within their boundaries. This helps explain why some cities have surprisingly low per capita emissions – for instance, for African, Asian or Latin American cities supplied with electricity from hydropower.

There are other difficulties in assigning greenhouse gases too. For instance, do the emissions from the fuels used by car-driving commuters get attributed to the city where they work or the suburb or rural area where they live? Which locations get assigned the carbon emissions from air travel? Total carbon emissions from any city with an international airport are much influenced by whether or not the city is assigned the fuel loaded onto the aircraft – even if most of the fuel is used in the air, outside the city.

A more fundamental question is whether greenhouse gas emissions used in producing goods or services are allocated to the producer or the consumer. If emissions are assigned to the home of the final consumer, most emissions from agriculture, deforestation and industry could be assigned to cities where the industrial goods, wood products and food are consumed. Under this, the contribution of cities to greenhouse gas emissions would increase, although most would come from the world's wealthiest cities.

Although these questions over where to assign greenhouse gas emissions might seem pedantic, they actually have enormous significance for how responsibilities for reducing emissions are assigned between and within nations. If China's manufacturing cities are assigned all the greenhouse gas emissions that go into the goods exported (including from the electricity that helped produce these goods), this implies a much larger responsibility for these Chinese cities in moderating and eventually reversing such emissions than if the emissions were allocated to the people who consume these Chinese exports (and by implication to the nations or cities where they live).

If we shift the allocation of responsibility for greenhouse gas emissions to the consumer, very large differentials become evident between the highest and the lowest consuming persons or households. The world's richest high-consumption individuals are likely to be contributing hundreds of thousands of times more to global warming than many of the poorest individuals (although this is in part because the poorest individual's contribution can be close to zero). For any individual to contribute to global warming, they have to consume goods and services that generate greenhouse gas emissions. Perhaps as many as 1.2 billion rural and urban dwellers worldwide have such low consumption levels that they contribute almost nothing to climate change. Their use of fossil fuels is very low (most use woodfuel, charcoal or dung for fuels) and they use no electricity. Most of these 1.2 billion 'very low-carbon' people will use transport that produces no carbon dioxide emissions (walking, bicycling) or low emissions (buses, mini-buses and trains, mostly used to more than full capacity).[7]

## Cities as Solutions

Seeing cities as 'the problem' draws attention away from the fact that the driver of most greenhouse gas emissions is the consumption patterns of middle- and upper-income groups in wealthier nations. Using average figures for greenhouse gas emissions per person for cities hides very large differences in emissions per person between high-income and low-income groups.[8] For low-income nations, focusing on cities as large greenhouse gas emitters ascribes too much importance to mitigation and not enough to adaptation as most such cities have very low fossil fuel use (and thus far less scope for reducing it). Seeing cities as 'the problem' also misses the extent to which well planned and governed cities can delink high living standards from high greenhouse gas emissions. This can be seen in part in the very large differentials between wealthy cities in gasoline use per person;[9] most US cities have three to five times the gasoline use per person of most European cities yet do not have a better quality of life. Cities with good public transport systems that have avoided low-density sprawl will generally have much lower levels of greenhouse gas emissions per person than cities that have not. Many of the most desirable (and expensive) residential areas in the world's wealthiest cities have high densities and building forms that can minimize the need for space heating and cooling – for instance three to five storey terraces. Energy use per dwelling can be much lower than in detached housing in suburban or rural areas. There are also examples of new residential developments that cut energy use dramatically – as in the Beddington Zero Energy Development.[10]

Most European cities have high-density centres where walking and bicycling are preferred by much of the population – especially where good provision is made for pedestrians and cyclists. High quality public transport can keep down private automobile ownership and use. Cities also concentrate so much of what contributes to a high quality of life that does not imply high material consumption levels (and thus high greenhouse gas emissions) – theatre, music, the visual arts, dance and the enjoyment of historic buildings and districts. Cities have long been places of social, economic and political innovation. This is already evident in relation to global warming; in many high-income nations, city politicians have demonstrated a greater commitment to emissions reduction than national politicians. This is also evident in Latin America, where much of the environmental and social innovation over the last 20–25 years has been driven by mayors and elected city governments. But how a city is planned, managed and governed also has important implications for how it will cope with the impacts of climate change. Many cities in Latin America, Africa and Asia may have low greenhouse gas emissions per person but they house hundreds of millions of people who are at risk from the increased frequency and/or intensity of floods, storms and heat waves and water supply constraints that climate change is likely to bring.[11] It is generally low-income groups that are most at risk as they live in informal settlements, often on sites at risk of flooding or landslides, lacking the drains and other needed protective infrastructure. Discussions of climate change priorities so often forget this. And these are risks that are not easily addressed, especially by international aid agencies that show little interest in urban areas and little capacity to support the kinds of locally driven pro-poor approaches that are needed.

6. Dodman 2009, op. cit.

7. David Satterthwaite, 'The implications of population growth and urbanization for climate change', 'Environment and Urbanization', Vol. 21, No. 2, 2009, p.545–567

8. Patricia Romero-Lankao, 'Are we missing the point? Particularities of urbanization, sustainability and carbon emissions in Latin American cities', 'Environment and Urbanization', Vol. 19, No. 1, 2007, pp.157–175

9. Peter Newman, 'The environmental impact of cities', 'Environment and Urbanization', Vol. 18, No. 2, 2006, pp.275–296

10. Tom Chance, 'Towards sustainable residential communities: The Beddington Zero Energy Development (BedZED) and beyond', 'Environment and Urbanization', Vol. 21, No. 1, 2009, pp.527–544

11. David Satterthwaite, Huq Saleemul, Mark Pelling, Hannah Reid and Patricia Romero-Lankao, 'Adapting to Climate Change in Urban Areas: The Possibilities and Constraints in Low- and Middle-income Nations', IIED, London, p.107

# Post-Sustainability

Architecture schools, the world over, are going through a pedagogical change, perhaps the most significant since the advent of Modernism. It is called Sustainability. Universities champion it, architectural firms specialize in it, politicians demand it, and corporations embrace it. But historical facts cloud the optimism associated with this development. We live in an unsustainable world, on that no one would disagree, but can 'Sustainable Development' change the course of human history? In a few decades, can we achieve the greatest civilization revolution ever? The answer is 'no'. We live in a Post-Sustainable world and should design our buildings and cities accordingly. Instead of having university departments with titles such as 'Sustainable Design' or 'Sustainability and Energy Management', we should have departments called more matter-of-factly, 'Post-Sustainable Architecture and Cities'.

One of the significant misconceptions in the new world of 'Sustainability' is that management will solve the problems and that what we need is better masterplans. But while planning – generally speaking – is certainly important, the masterplan culture, which has now fused with the emergent Sustainability culture, needs to be challenged. The masterplan culture developed in the 1960s, when, with the failures of cities looming over history, urban leaders wanted a way to restore confidence in the downtowns and to create a positive sense of destiny and purpose. Originally, the masterplan was the basis upon which the zoning ordinance and site usage regulations were defined and enforced, but in the 1980s the reach of the masterplan expanded to include questions of tourism and culture. City centers were no longer to be torn down arbitrarily, but were to be preserved as protected civic environments. In that sense, the ideals of the modernist city, as inscribed in the realities of capitalist development, came to be fused with the remnants of the so-called traditional city. Holding all this together was the image of a city that was not too new and not too old, an image based on a modern notion of block ownership in combination with a rationally controlled sentimental attachment to local contexts. In the late 1990s, masterplans began to expand their reach again by embracing ecological concerns. They came to have parks, water features and shaded, pedestrian malls. The water elements were almost always curvy and always faced onto the newly popular 'icon building.' Drawings showed people moving at a leisurely pace along a promenade, never the teaming hordes of a real city, or the shanty towns that are now such a huge percentage of urban fabric.

A masterplan is not a city. It is an illusion of a city that has been Xeroxed so many times over that one can hardly recognize its strangeness. Social and economic problems – and politics – have all been photoshopped away. It was supposed to be a transition to help cities survive in an age of urban doubt. But now, more and more people are living in cities and in increasing densities, so what we need is not new and improved masterplans, but a new understanding of the city, and in particular of a city stripped

left: From Francis Bacon's 'The New Atlantis', 1626

of the sentimental disguises relating to nature and human conduct that are embedded in the masterplan.[1] An eco-city should speak to the eco-revolution.

But what is this revolution?

'Sustainability' is, most certainly, the wrong code word for it. As water levels rise, as aquifers dry up, as grass-lands become deserts, as people move and relocate (all in the context in which democracy, viewed globally, is a marginal condition), we can expect the rise of social antagonisms at massive scales, all of which will exacerbate the tradition of exploiting natural resources in the race for supremacy or survival. Basically, Sustainability will not stop global warming and its resultant socio-political transformations. So why promise an illusion? This does not mean that we need to add new urgency to the need to find solutions to the problems, but that we need to think beyond the comfortable promise that everything will work out as long as we reduce our carbon footprint.

Instead of creating the illusion of a calm, 'Sustainable' world, we should ask: What does a city look like with a failed infrastructure? What does a city look like that has to defend its water source? What does a city look like that has its access to foreign markets cut off as retribution for a failed political alliance? What does a city look like when its local resources are being drained by a totalitarian government? What does a city look like where ten percent of its inhabitants are undocumented? What does a city look like where children get no education? These are not sociological questions, but design questions. These are also the situations of today, not the future, but we often put them into the periphery of our thinking and attribute the problems to bad planning, poverty and corruption. But these cities are also real-life glimpses into the future for all of us even in Europe and North America. This means that green roofs, eco-scaping, waste control, heritage maintenance, energy education are all only temporary fixes that, though important, represent the limits of improvementalism. Our world will never be sustainable and this means that the mission, both academically and politically, will be to develop buildings and cities suited to a Post-Sustainable world.

My criticism holds true for many of the recently designed, so-called eco-cities, including the serious-minded, Subic Bay Philippines project (Koetter, Kim and Associates) with its Euro-centric gravitas, the Siedlung-styled project of Ecolonia (Atelier Lucien Kroll), the modernist-styled Halifax EcoCity Project in Australia (Paul Francis Downtown), the shopping-mall-styled Glendale Town Center, California (Elizabeth Moule and Stephanos Polyzoides), and the 19th century-styled town, Kirchsteigfeld, Germany (Rob Krier/Christoph Kohl). All these projects demonstrate that one can take almost any approach and make it green. Has anything really changed? In all these places, as is typical, nature remains little more than a pleasant backdrop. The tendency to drip green ivy on buildings or plant grass or trees on roofs makes a parody of what needs to be done. The cumulative result has been a complete erasure - from the point of view of both architects and planners – of our capacity to more radically and more honestly think about our cities.

The much celebrated Masdar City seems to be an exception, but it is not. The official website makes not a single claim about what this city is – as a city. It is in reality a corporate enclave, 'a global center where 1500 companies will converge to address one of man's greatest challenges.'[2] Anything that has some streets, reflecting pools, public transportation nodes, and an assortment of buildings and wind turbines is now an eco-city. This is a direct consequence of decades of pretending that masterplans are cities.

There is thus a gap between a green architecture, based on a myth of Sustainability, and a green, masterplanned city, based on a pretense of urban life for the elites. Increasingly, there are architects who are capable of thinking at the scale of the city without falling back onto masterplan clichés. Take, for example, the Guangming Urban Design Competition for an eco city for half a million people in southern China that was held in 2006. Remarkably, among the final three winners, there were no urban planners! It was a message that urban planners need to heed. The most 'green' of the projects was the one proposed by CJ Lim/Studio 8 Architects. The project, entitled Smartcity, was composed of artificially constructed, residential hills that not only defined the city, but also contained aquaculture terraces and vertical farms. The hills were basically inclined, urban-economic-landscapes that maximized natural lighting, ventilation and vistas. In the water-ways between the hills, there were artificial beaches and recreation areas. The whole was interconnected by gondolas. The scheme looks 'utopian,' but in principle there is nothing about it that is beyond present day capabilities.

One could compare this project with the eco-cities of Richard Register, the noted planner and author, and the force behind the International Ecocity Conferences. Register wants to 'reshape' cities 'for long term health of human and natural systems.'[3] And while this environmentalism and its associated urban activism - usually retrofitted over existing urban conditions - is important and needs our support, it is not the same as urban design. Register's book, 'Ecocities', is filled with strange-shaped buildings, some of them quite enormous, dripping implausibly with the green goo of plant-life and exuding a fairy tale mood of summer-time, urban bliss.[4] 'Nature' is happy, friendly and green.

Studio 8 is by no means the only firm trying to work outside such predictabilities. It challenges head-on the distinction between urbs and natura by integrating farming into the urban. This is not about the need for local produce, but about the destruction of the conceptual barrier between city and farm. Unfortunately, our academic world has not made that leap. We still have 'Urban Planning Departments,' on the one hand, and 'Landscape Departments' on the other hand. How quaint. In a Post-Sustainable world these departmental identities will disappear. The very word 'urban' – from the Latin – should be abolished if only to get away from antique presumptions. The same applies to the word 'nature'. 'Nature' has been manipulated at the hands of mankind for millennia, but the Romantics in the early nineteenth century – at the very moment when the Industrial Revolution began its escalated exploitations of earthly resources – created the illusion that Nature was so big and bountiful that nothing could possibly destroy it. Today it is clear to everyone that this is not the case. In all of Europe it would be hard to find anything that one can call 'nature.' Stem to stern, it is controlled by the instruments of capital along with any number of planning and regulatory agencies. The point is not that we need to relax our controls and let nature 'be nature.' There is no 'nature' out there, even in the more remote parts of the world.

Though Smartcity forces us to abandon comfortable academic distinctions, it also does not forget the tragic ambiguity of pleasure in the Post-Sustainable. Against a backdrop of artificial beaches, it projects a Cultural Revolution where city dwellers are also farmers. Is it a civilizational fall-from-grace or a new civilization altogether? The proposition is meant to be ironic, but should we really be chuckling?

249

1. In 'Sustainable Architecture and Urbanism' we read that 'the principles of sustainable development encompass an appreciation of social and cultural roots,' which lead the 'protection of characteristic residential districts' [Dominique Gauzin-Müller, 'Sustainable Architecture and Urbanism', Bern, Birkhäuser, 2002, p.87. It is hard to know what is meant by this 'appreciation.' Its impossible to shape a city in the context of the eco-revolution, unless these historic districts are recognized as part of museo-urbanism suitable, for attracting boutiques, restaurants and residences for the elite.

2. www.masdarcity.ae/en/index.aspx (accessed August 3, 2009)

3. www.ecocitybuilders.org/

4. Richard Register, 'Ecocities, Rebuilding Cities in Balance with Nature', New Society Publishers, Gabriola Island, 2006, pp.81, 193

# Project + Reproduction Credits

## Project Credits

### Guangming Smartcity
Shenzhen, China; 2007
commissioned by: Shenzhen Municipal Planning Bureau
design team: CJ Lim/Studio 8 Architects with Pascal Bronner, Ed Liu, Daniel Wang, Lukas Wescott, Barry Cho, Nikolay Salutski, Jacqueline Chak, Anabela Chan, Dimitris Argyros, Alleen Siu, Maxwell Mutanda, Thomas Hillier, Adeline Wee, Andreas Helgesson, Tomasz Marchewka, Jonathan Hagos, Ben Masterton-Smith, Chen Chen Pang, Lei Guo, Louise Yeung
consultants: Fulcrum Consulting (environmental + sustainability engineers) Andy Ford, Brian Mark, Jules Saunderson, Shao-Nan Fan, Chani Leahon; Techniker (structural engineers) Matthew Wells; Alan Baxters + Assoc. (transport) David Taylor, Darrell Morcom, Angus Laurie; Urban Plannning + Design Institute of Shenzhen (local planners) Zhou Jin, Yang Xiaochun, Zhu Zhenlong
Total Area: 7.97km2

### Daejeon Urban Renaissance
Daejeon, Korea; 2007
commissioned by: Daejeon Metropolitan City
design team: CJ Lim/Studio 8 Architects with Pascal Bronner, Barry Cho, Maxwell Mutanda, Frank Fan
consultant: Techniker (structural engineers)
Total Area: 0.89km2

### Central Open Space: MAC
Yeongi-gun, Korea; 2007
commissioned by: Government Administrative City Agency + Korean Land Corporation
design team: CJ Lim/Studio 8 Architects with Pascal Bronner, Dimitris Argyros, Daniel Wang, Alleen Siu, Thomas Hillier, Martin Tang
consultants: Techniker (structural engineers) Matthew Wells; Fulcrum Consulting (environmental + sustainability engineers) Brian Mark; KMCS (quantity surveyors) Colin Hayward, Martin Taylor, David Finlay
Total Area: 6.982km2

### Nordhavnen Smartcity
Copenhagen, Denmark; 2008
commissioned by: CPH City + Port Development
design team: CJ Lim/Studio 8 Architects with Pascal Bronner, Kar Man Leung, Rachel Guo, Barry Cho, Thomas Hillier, Maxwell Mutanda, Yongzheng Li, Loui Lim
consultant: Fulcrum Consulting (environmental + sustainability engineers); Techniker (structural engineers)
Total Area: 2.0km2

### The Tomato Exchange
London, UK; 2009
design team: CJ Lim/Studio 8 Architects with Jen Wang, Yongzheng Li, Frank Fan, Barry Cho
consultant: Techniker (structural engineers)
Total Area: 0.008km2

### Dongyi Wan East Waterfront
Shunde, China; 2009
commissioned by: Dongseng Real Estate Development
design team: CJ Lim/Studio 8 Architects with Rachel Guo, Jen Wang, Pascal Bronner, Kar Man Leung, Julia Chen
local architect: OS Partnership China
consultant: Techniker (structural engineers); Fulcrum Consulting (environmental + sustainability engineers)
Total Area: 0.22km2

### DuSable Park
Chicago, USA; 2001
commissioned by: Laurie Palmer
supported by: Illinois Arts Council, R Driehaus Foundation Graham Foundation, USA
design team: CJ Lim/Studio 8 Architects with Michael Kong
consultant: Techniker (structural engineers)
Total Area: 0.012km2

### Guangming Energy Park
Shenzhen, China; 2008
commissioned by: Shenzhen Municipal Planning Bureau
design team: CJ Lim/Studio 8 Architects with Dimitris Argyros, Barry Cho, Kelly Chan, Louise Yeung
consultants: Fulcrum Consulting (environmental + sustainability engineers); Techniker (structural engineers)
Total Area: 2.37km2

### Nanyui Urban Living Room
Shenzhen, China; 2008
commissioned by: Shenzhen Municipal Planning Bureau, Jin Long Real Estate, Fu An Na Real Estate
design team: CJ Lim/Studio 8 Architects with Yongzheng Li, Pascal Bronner, Sarah Mui, Thomas Hillier, Maxwell Mutanda, Barry Cho, Jacqueline Chak, Martin Tang
consultants: Fulcrum Consulting (environmental + sustainability engineers) Andy Ford, Christoph Morbitzer, Annie Babu; Techniker (structural engineers) Matthew Wells
Total Area: 0.5km2

**Redcar Seafront Development**
Redcar, UK; 2009
commissioned by: Redcar + Cleveland Partnership
design team: CJ Lim/Studio 8 Architects with Thomas Hillier,
Maxwell Mutanda, Barry Cho
consultants: Techniker (structural engineers) Matthew Wells;
KMCS (quantity surveyors) Colin Hayward, David Finlay; Fulcrum
Consulting (environmental + sustainability engineers) Andy Ford
Total Area: 0.168km2

**Southern Science + Technology University**
Shenzhen, China; 2008
commissioned by: Shenzhen Municipal Planning Bureau
design team: CJ Lim/Studio 8 Architects with Pascal Bronner,
Sarah Mui, Barry Cho, Maxwell Mutanda, Thomas Hillier,
Jacqueline Chak, Martin Tang, Loui Lim, Yongzheng Li
consultants: Techniker (structural engineers); Fulcrum
Consulting (environmental + sustainability engineers)
Total Area: 2.0km2

**Newark Gateway Project**
Newark, USA; 2009
commissioned by: AIA Newark + Suburban
design team: CJ Lim/Studio 8 Architects with Jen Wang, Barry
Cho, Pascal Bronner, Daniel Wang
consultant: Techniker (structural engineers)
Total Area: 0.25km2

**Imagining Recovery**
USA; 2009
design team: CJ Lim/Studio 8 Architects with Ed Liu, Rachel Guo,
Jen Wang
Total Area: -
Note: Illustrated in the chapter 'Urban Utopias and the
Smartcity'

# Index

254